World Without Walls

Being Human, Being Tamil

Essays in Tamil Studies

EDITED BY

R Cheran

Dalbir Singh

Chelva Kanaganayakam

Sudharshan Durayappah

TSAR

We acknowledge the support of the Canada Council for the Arts for our publishing program. We also acknowledge support from the Government of Ontario through the Ontario Arts Council.

Canada Council for the Arts Conseil des Arts du Canada ONTARIO ARTS COUNCIL CONSEIL DES ARTS DE L'ONTARIO

Cover Art: Thamotharampillai Shanaathanan
Cover Design: Cynthia Griffioen

Library and Archives Canada Cataloguing in Publication

Tamil Studies Conference (3rd : 2008 : University of Toronto)
World without walls : being human, being Tamil :
research essays in Tamil studies / edited by R. Cheran . . . [et al.].

"The essays included in this volume are a selection of those presented at the Third Annual Toronto Tamil studies conference in 2008"—Introd.
Includes bibliographical references.

ISBN 978-1-894770-71-2

1. Tamil (Indic people)—Ethnic identity—Congresses.
2. Tamil literature—Congresses. I. Cheran, R. II. Title.

DS432.T3T35 2011 305.89'4811 C2011-902221-4

Printed and bound in Canada by Coach House Printing

TSAR Publications
P. O. Box 6996, Station A
Toronto, Ontario M5W 1X7
Canada

www.tsarbooks.com

Contents

Introduction

World Without Walls: Being Human, Being Tamil

CHELVA KANAGANAYAKAM AND R CHERAN

Where there is power, as Foucault reminds us, there is also resistance. Where there are attempts to enforce homogeneity, there are distinct gestures of heterogeneity. Where there is reason to celebrate, there is also the need to unpack and interrogate. Tamil studies, in recent times, have been characterized by an impulse to rethink and re-imagine traditions, conventions, and norms that have been perceived as monolithic and definitive. In the study of literature, for example, classifications that had been accepted as precise and unambiguous are being reexamined to demonstrate their fluidity and ambivalence. Such appraisals have been a cause for celebration in that they allow for new perspectives and new possibilities for change and growth. On the question of Tamil identity, multiple ways of being Tamil have entered contemporary Tamil political discourse.[1] Essentialist notions of Tamil identity that were forcefully articulated in the context of the Tamil nationalist struggle from the late 80s in Sri Lanka, the *Thamil Thamilar* movement in Tamil Nadu and the short lived "Pure Tamil" movement in Toronto spearheaded by the now defunct weekly newspaper *Muzhakkam* (Thunder) have all been challenged.

The essays included in this volume are a selection of those presented at the Third Annual Toronto Tamil studies conference in 2008 titled "Being Human; Being Tamil" (*manitharaay iruttal;Thamilaraai vaalthal*) jointly sponsored by the University of Toronto and the University of Windsor. As the title of the conference suggests, the papers and visual representations at the conference explored the multiple ways of being Tamil and the cultural, religious and poetic linkages that contributed to the emergence and articulation of Tamilness in Tamil Nadu, Sri Lanka, and in the diaspora.

Celebrated Tamil Dalit writer Bama's essay in this volume (from which part of the title is taken) is a very personal account that records the anguish of suffering experienced by Dalits and by herself. She also recounts a sense of decency and generosity among the dalits and in nature that enabled her and other dalits to remain hopeful and optimistic about the future. She ends on a note of hope that someday one would live in a world without walls. While her essay is very specific in its scope, in a curious way it connects all the essays in this collection, which, in one form or another, reflect on forms of resistance, recuperation and synthesis. The essays, taken together, range across a number of disciplines and adopt very different approaches, but they all seem to converge on the notion of multiplicity. In a sense, this is no accident. One of the key aspects of Tamil heritage is its secular nature. Over several thousand years various forms of Hinduism, Buddhism, Jainism, Islam, and Christianity have become an inseparable part of Tamil language and heritage. The essays in this volume are intellectual and creative testimonies of such multiplicity.

Frank Cody's essay on a movement called Arivoli Iyakkam in Tamil Nadu traces the genealogy and evolution of this movement against a backdrop of humanism and resistance. He traces the conceptual problems in coming to terms with Arivoli Iyakkam's attempt to offer a meaningful space to marginalized people.

Vijaya Ramaswamy's careful analysis of Neelambikai Ammaiyar looks at a canonical figure in the history of "pure" Tamil identity to demonstrate the extent to which cultural pastiche plays a role in this extremely complex figure.

Veluppillai addresses an important aspect of Tamil identity, namely the crucial role played by nature and landscape in the social and identity formation of Tamils. Continuing a key theme from our previous volumes (Cheran, Ambalavanar and Kanaganayakam, 2007; 2009), Veluppillai's essay focuses on nature and landscape from the Sangam Period to the present, in order to show how the presence of nature and the importance of landscape and *thinai* become a marker for shifting Tamil identity.

Schomburg presents an exploration of the poetic corpus of an extraordinary Tamil Muslim woman, Ilaiyaankudi Kachchippillai Ammaal. Kachchippillai Ammal's powerful poetry not only represents a confluence of Islamic and Tamil cultural traditions but an important landmark in the Tamil secular literary tradition. Kachchippillai Ammaal, as Schomburg says, "exemplifies not only extraordinary female, but extraordinary human achievement in terms of both realms. There were several female Sufis (Muslim mystics) such as Sayyida Asiya Umma of Keelakkarai, and Rasul Bivi Amma of Thenkasi in Tamil Nadu, whose contributions have strengthened the Tamil literary tradition and further scholarly work on these poets is necessary.

Buck's paper traces the development of Kuṟavar people as literary figures from their appearance in the earliest available Tamil literary works down through the ages to a famous stage drama that features them. He raises important questions about the role that literature and literary translation has played—and continues to play—in abetting or resisting the ongoing marginalization of Kuṟavar people, and other oppressed groups.

Christer Norström explores the idea of *adivasi* or indigenous that, in practice, becomes an ambivalent but politically charged term, and whose premises are often contested. As Norström argues, a paradox lies in the fact that the strong 'son-of-the-soil' theory applied by the dominant regional communities and the State governments in India fosters a strong feeling of homelands such as Tamil Nadu, meaning 'the Land of the Tamilians' excluding the indigenous or *adivasi* people.

Gil Ben-Herut's article is about an important Sanskrit text in the Nayakka Period, but one, which highlights the ongoing hybridity of Tamil culture and reiterates the extent to which Sanskrit found a home in Tamilakam and the cross-pollinations between Sanskrit and Tamil.

Janet O'Shea's essay works with the trope of dance to explore the extent to which, a strong sense of traditional identity co-existed with adaptation and development of Bharatanatyam in war-torn Jaffna, to suit the militant message of the Liberation Tigers of Tamil Eelam (LTTE). As she correctly identifies, "Bharatanatyam in Jaffna is a practice that has been maintained in situations of adversity, repression, and deprivation. However, its choreographic interpretations, unlike in India and the Indian diaspora, remain surprisingly uniform." This uniformity and continuity is interrupted when, "dancers [both LTTE cadres and civilians] depict the oppression of the Tamils. Dancers in fatigues portray invading Sri Lankan troops and the Tamil Tigers' paramilitary soldiers. Choreographers develop new *mudras* to portray the implements of modern warfare, using articulate and stylized gesture to invoke images of helicopters and machine guns."

In his incisive analysis of a monumental sixteenth century Tamil literary text *Naitatam,* Shulman connects the Tamil notions self, inner self and "innerness" to the possibilities and complexities of being human at a particular historical juncture. Shulman correctly points out that to understand the multilayered Tamil personhood we have to go beyond a single location and time. Literary productions in Kerala and Telugu are crucial since both these cultural worlds impinged on the southern Tamil country in significant ways. The discussions about Being Tamil and being Human cannot be confined to *Thamil kuurum nallulakam* (Tamil speaking world of goodness) alone but should extend to the domains of Telugu, Malayalam, Kannada, and south Indian Sanskrit. As Shulman emphasizes, all these belong to a single culture with many local variants.

A considerable number of essays in this volume address the complexities and contours of Tamil diaspora in various locations in the world. Tamil diaspora has become an important area of research for numerous scholars over the past decade. This scholarship has become deeply entrenched within contemporary Tamil studies.

Jennifer Young Yim and Ramaswami Mahalingam focus on the Tamil diaspora in the US, pointing to the convoluted and often paradoxical ways in which masculine identities are constructed among second generation Tamil immigrants.

Glynis George takes up a relatively unexplored area of inquiry as she examines the suffering and celebration of older Tamil women in Toronto. Employing an "actor-centered" approach, she explores the way older Tamils make sense of changing cultural practices and in so doing, work through the sense of suffering that marks their lives across time and space.

An earlier Tamil diaspora becomes the subject of Paul Younger's essay as he deals with various forms of discrimination experienced by "Madrasis" in Guyana and their strategies for coping with their marginality. His essay adopts a different but important lens in foregrounding notions of Tamil identity. As he states, " Tamil community [in Guyana] is not in the midst of a political crisis, and we might be able to learn from that situation what some of the more traditional issues were in the constitution of a sense of Tamil identity."

Anne Sigfrid Grønseth also deals with the diaspora, providing an insightful account of Tamil diaspora in Arctic harbour, a fishing village in Norway. She argues that the ways in which Tamils experienced aches and pains are understood by perspectives of embodiment that collapse the dichotomy of body and mind. Sigfrid Grønseth maintains, that by "such an approach it is revealed how pain can express a kind of knowledge about identity and social relations and exert a complex agency derived from the realm of intersubjectivity." In this context, as she notes, "Tamil self-identity and community can incorporate new practices and meanings that bridge between the former, indigenous aspects of social life that the asylum seeker brings as well as a cosmopolitanism." Alluding to the theme of Being Human, Being Tamil, she emphasizes that "new Tamil identities can embrace an appreciation of individuation and distinctions as part of a common humanity."

In an illuminating way, all the essays in this collection have to do with the idea of being Tamil, in all its complexity and multiplicity. It is our sincere hope that essays in this collection will contribute towards a new and rigorous approach to Tamil studies.

NOTES

1. For example, the Final Report on the Formation of a provisional Transnational Government of Tamil Eelam released on March 15, 2010 says as follows:

> [C]ontemporary Tamil nationalism is one that encourages multiple and transnational identities, and is diversified, inclusive, socially beneficial and based on democratic principles. (Page 6).

The full report is available at: www.sangam.org/2010/03/TGTE_Report.pdf. Accessed on February 12, 2011.

WORKS CITED

Cheran, R, Darshan Ambalavanar, and Chelva Kanaganayakam, eds. 2007. *History and Imagination: Tamil Studies in the Global Context.* Toronto: TSAR Publications.

Cheran, R, Darshan Ambalavanar, and Chelva Kanaganayakam, eds. 2009. *New Demarcations: Essays in Tamil Studies.* Toronto: Canadian Scholars Press.

Arivoli's Humanism:
Literacy Activism and the Senses of Enlightenment

FRANCIS P CODY

What meanings does a deceptively familiar idea like "humanism" take on in the Tamil countryside among activists and learners in a self-styled "Enlightenment" literacy movement? The Arivoli Iyakkam, the "Light of Knowledge" or "Enlightenment" movement, is a mass-literacy movement in Tamil Nadu and Pondicherry, India, that began in 1989. It continues in some districts to this day, though on a diminished scale and changed in character compared to its height in the early-to-mid-1990s. The goal of the Arivoli Iyakkam's enlightened literacy project has been to produce human subjects that form themselves by means of the written word in Tamil. Activism in the literacy movement is premised on what volunteers discuss in terms of "*manitaneyam,*" which might be translated into English as "humanism." To learn to read and write according to the tenets of this variety of literacy activism is to become a more modern, and hence a freer and more human, subject. Literacy activism, as an exercise in *manitaneyam,* however, has paradoxically sought to remake the very people that it aims to empower. Arivoli Iyakkam aims to awaken people's sense of their own agency using models of personhood and social action that map only partially onto those that obtain among the movement's villager learners. This article consists of an attempt to make some philosophical and sociological sense of these problems, and also to understand the role of what I take to be a pragmatic orientation to humanism that is similar to, but not at all reducible to, the humanism of the European tradition of Enlightenment.

The Arivoli Iyakkam has been both a grassroots social movement, organized primarily by leftist NGOs, chief among which is the Tamil Nadu Science Forum, and a central government development programme, sustained by funds and support from the National Literacy Mission.[1] Since its very charismatic beginnings, the Arivoli Iyakkam has been somewhat routinized as a volunteer-based social movement and development initiative. But the literacy movement is even now often referred to, in activist and bureaucrat speech, as "*irandavathu cutantirap porattam*" (second Independence Struggle) because of the scale and intensity of mobilization that has occurred under the name of Arivoli. While the Arivoli movement was initially conceived of by largely middle-class academics in the cities of Madurai, Tiruchirapalli, Pondicherry, and Chennai, in the rural district of Pudukkottai, where my fieldwork among activists and learners in the movement was conducted, nearly a quarter of a million people have since participated in adult literacy lessons and associated activities.[2] Most of the participants have been women from among the Dalits or poor sections of the lower and middle castes. It is among the poor in rural regions like Pudukkottai, where the literacy movement has been most popular and most powerful, that activists and learners picked up and transformed ideas that have their origins elsewhere.[3]

What exactly is the relationship between Arivoli and its brand of humanism, an unsatisfactory translation of *manitaneyam* that I will soon correct, to narratives from the European philosophical tradition? In order to develop an answer to this question, that is forced upon us by virtue of Tamil India's postcolonial relationship to the European tradition, by questions of history and social power, I will use two strategies: one is based on a very brief philosophico-etymological examination of Arivoli's version of enlightened humanist *manitaneyam,* a study of the relationship between concepts; the second consists of a slightly lengthier social analysis of the movement's variegated efforts to draw on, or ground itself in, narrative precedents for how one might connect the concept of light to that of progressive knowledge and build a movement based on the notion that humans can and should control their own destiny. This consists of an investigation of actual narrative connections to various forms of humanist enlightenment. Towards the end of producing self-making subjects, activists strategically incorporate aspects of Tamil cultural tradition and global leftist narratives in their efforts to develop a specifically grassroots modernism that can be familiar while still pulling social action towards an imagined future. However, they do so differently positioned with regard to these traditions in question. I will finally bring these two strands together in an attempt to synthesize a social–philosophical approach to the question of Arivoli's humanism in which both lines of analysis are equally implicated.

In pursuing these questions I will attempt to steer a path between the pole of orientalist invocations of primordial Tamil difference on one side, and the equally problematic pole of a historicizing narrative of essential human sameness, in delayed time, on the other. These are the two most readily available narrative structures. Nor am I concerned with the "real" history of Arivoli as opposed to how people narrate their own pasts. Furthermore, this attempt does not consist of an ethnography in any conventional sense of the term. Rather I start with an exploration of semantic meanings of keywords used by activists to describe their work, words that have been artificially abstracted from pragmatic contexts, and then consider who narrates humanism how and with regard to what historical norm, using a range of written, spoken, and visual materials. This is ultimately a study of the very relationship between socially situated structures of narration and the substance of concepts.

The Affective Quality of Arivoli's Concepts of "Social Service" and "Humanism"

The most common response from Arivoli activists, from across the socio-economic spectrum, to the question of why they feel compelled to work for the literacy movement involves an invocation of the desire to perform *camuka cevai* (social service). Most activists will add that they are motivated to do so because of *manitaneyam*, what I provisionally translate here as "humanism" only to unravel any easy conflation in the pages to come.

Let us begin with the first of these concepts. By using the phrase *camuka cevai* activists were drawing on a discourse that probably first blossomed as such under the influence of religious reform movements influenced by the missionary style and Gandhian nationalism, and which much later became incorporated into the vocabulary of a speech genre we might call "NGO-speak." In the idea of *camuka cevai*, "society" itself becomes an object of service *(cevai)* and one might even say of devotion. It is very important to note here which *"camukam"* denotes that object. For many rural speakers of Tamil, *camukam* might well be used to refer to one's caste or religious affiliation in a mode of reference that makes *camukam* operate much in the same way as the English word "community." But as it is invoked in the phrase *camuka cevai*, as used by the Arivoli Iyakkam activists I came to know well over the course of several years, I believe that the *camukam* they invoke is the *general principle of "society"* and not restricted to any particular community—it is purposefully unbound and maximally inclusive, oftentimes sitting at the level of the Indian nation.[4] This usage is in keeping with a notion of society that we might well attribute to the universalisms of post-Enlightenment thought.

I would now like to consider the second "keyword" in Arivoli discourse on motivation and activism: *manitaneyam.* While a moment ago I had translated *manitaneyam* as "humanism," I would now like to complicate the picture here inasmuch as attention to etymology and semantic range reveals a more profound *philosophical* point of difference. That the notion of love or affection is encoded in the Tamil word *manita* (human) + *neyam* (love) is of utmost importance. But first, let us focus on the similarities between *manitaneyam* and humanism which calls for some attention. The ideas of humanism and *manitaneyam* are very much alike with regard to certain precise understandings of ethics, progress, and liberation in the tradition of Euro-Global modernity—deeply shaped by critical Enlightenment thought. At the core of these projects is an ethical stake in humans making their own history. In the modernist task of creating self-making subjects—that is to say subjects who would not rely on any external source of norms (gods, kings, etc.) but rather produce their own normativity—humans would be their own measurers and be cast back upon themselves with all the anxieties and uncertainties such a moral responsibility entails. In this regard, the Arivoli ideal of *manitaneyam* is very much in line with common moral narratives of secular modernity.[5] However, many such narratives, especially those in the Kantian line of thought, locate the limits of the realm of those who would produce their own normativity (the realm of ends) within the realm of reason, abstracted from the senses, the sensual, and the realm of affect.[6]

In Arivoli's *manitaneyam*, however, as I noted earlier, *neyam* or *nesam* is of utmost importance. What ties one to the other and the world, one's duty and motivation, is not an operation of rational logic alone or even primarily, but a question of affect, affection and the density of social relation. In the words of a village volunteer in Pudukkottai, "*Manitaneyam* means that knowledge should be imparted with *anpu* (affection) and that it should be of use to people." Just as the universalizing principle of society—something to which everyone belongs to equally—is the object of *cevai*. Arivoli's humanism offers perhaps an alternative universal, in which affect *(neyam, anpu, cevai)* cannot be separated from the project of self-making. Affect is not a residual category but central to the project. This difference is marked not just in the etymology of words but also in the logic of narrative practice. It is to this logic that we now turn.

Situating Enlightenments, Building Narrative Propulsion

Let this shift to the situated logic of practice begin with a look at explanations of concepts in a minimal social and historical context, and then move, slowly, closer to the ground of experience. In any number of social projects aimed at remaking the world activists must deal with the stuff of history, narratives handed down or imposed, depending on one's perspective, from the past. In the opening paragraphs of the *Eighteenth Brumaire,* Karl Marx famously described the making of history as an act of agency that is nevertheless made, "under circumstances directly encountered, given and transmitted from the past" (1963:15). Like the "borrowing of languages" from the past described in his account, any self-conscious movement devoted to social change must appropriate cultural forms from the past and insert them into a historical present, with eyes towards an imagined future. For Marx, the narrative forms or tropes of the past sit like a weight, indeed, "like nightmare on the brain of the living" who would seek to revolutionize themselves (Ibid:15). However, a look at Arivoli activism reveals that the past need not only appear as weight, a source of pure drag, but the appropriate past can also appear as a *resource* in the project of remaking the social world.

Narrative frames provide crucial lines of propulsion in any modernist attempt to remake the social world.[7] Arivoli volunteers consistently invoke past instances of enlightenment and enlightened social change from a wide variety of sources. For example, one mode of emplotting the Arivoli Iyakkam with reference to a prior text that I have already mentioned is to depict Arivoli as the "*irandavathu c tantirap porattam*" (second Independence struggle). This is a strategy that is used by activists of all sorts and even by bureaucrats affiliated with the movement and by many other villagers in Pudukkottai. In this example, the Indian struggle for Independence is targeted as an event available to all as a template for interpretation through which, and by means of which, Arivoli's struggle for emancipation through full literacy can be grasped as one of world historical significance. In this sense, Indian Independence acts as an intertext, mediating interpretations of the present.

While the text of national liberation is one that is shared by everyone, other narrative pasts are more likely to be used by some participants in the Arivoli movement than others. Some activists draw heavily on specifically Tamil traditions of thought on education as the bringing of light in order to frame or ground their own activism, while some draw on left traditions that they take to be more global in reach and less "culturally" loaded. As we will see shortly, the choice of which past and which cultural forms to invoke in the service of narrative propulsion is conditioned by the activist's place in a social structure and this fact of a less-than-unified narrative framework across classes has led to some contradictions in the project of making self-making subjects—a point I will expand on later. The broader point I would like to note here is simply that invocations of existing discourses or intertexts are acts of agency in the present, and not simply restrictions on agentive action as in Marx's complaint with the weight of the past. By beginning from the present we can focus on how the very idea of "Arivoli" can resonate with a range of narrative structures from different perspectives.

The Social Location of Narrative Grounds for Arivoli

Let us first look at how the idea of Arivoli has been viewed from the perspective of villagers in Pudukkottai, activist and non-activist, before moving on to the movement's leaders and framers. Most of the village-level literacy workers I interviewed claimed that the word "*arivoli,*" a compound of the roots for "knowledge" *(arivu)* and "light" *(oli)*, was coined in 1990 by Science Forum activists in the (then) Union Territory of Pondicherry as they were launching their Total Literacy Campaign.[8] It thus appeared to many as a neologism, but a particularly apt one because the equation between written language and light, or more specifically the power to see, has recognizable roots in the Tamil literary tradition.

For example, in the *Tirukkural* the very well-known kurals 392 and 393 read,

> Two are the eyes of those who truly live,
> One is called numbers and the other letters[9]

> *ennenpa enai ezhuttenpa ivvirandum*

kannenpa vazhum uyirkku

The learned have eyes that see, they say,
The unlearned have but two sores on their face

kannudaiyar enpavar kattar; mukatthirandu
punnudaiyar kallathavar

These lines are taken from the subchapter on education and are learned by heart by students in their formal schooling. They were readily proffered to me by literary-minded activists in Pudukkottai's Arivoli movement when asked about the place of literacy in Tamil culture. The poet Auvaiyar is credited with the very similar verse, "Numbers and letters are equal to eyes" *(ennum ezhutum kannenat takum),* which also serves as an ethical text, emphasizing the virtues of literacy through the idiom of sight. These very memorable texts circulate very widely across the Tamil-speaking world and have been easily absorbed into the Arivoli Iyakkam's grassroots presentation of itself as consistent with Tamil educational traditions of the classical era.

The equation of literacy with eyesight was also familiar to many villagers I interviewed across Pudukkottai District who had had little or no formal education and would not have come across these tropes through their own reading of these classical texts in school but rather through a differently formalized familial oral circulation. There is thus a certain continuity between these models of ethics and everyday formulations of progress and literacy.[10] When I asked a group of Arivoli learners in the village of LN Puram the naïve anthropologist's question, "What does Arivoli mean?," I received the following response from a woman in her forties who had never gone to school:

> Arivoli means like an eye seeing for those who can't read, that's all Arivoli means. If you don't know how to read, it means it's like an eye that cannot see. Arivoli means, we'll read and that eye will see light. That's Arivoli.

Without hesitating, this villager drew on the metaphor of an eye seeing the light and opposed literacy to the condition of being blind, much like the sage Tiruvalluvar had done in his *Tirukkural.* She had done so without quoting the text directly. The *Tirukkural*'s figuration serves rather as a covert intertext. I have received a large number of similar responses from learners and teachers alike. Such responses attest the degree to which the assimilation of literacy and knowledge with light and seeing is in the air, though this trope has undoubtedly been amplified through its use in the literacy movement.

Before becoming the name of the Tamil literacy movement, the word "Arivoli" was already in very limited use as a proper name given in the wake of the Dravidian nationalist movement. The name Arivoli might well also have Christian roots that have been secularized such that the word has been generalized as a modern-sounding

Tamil name.[11] As one village literacy coordinator in Pudukkottai who was aware of the word prior to its use in the literacy movement told me, "It is a beautiful, *Tamil* name," emphasizing the name's Dravidian origins.[12] Indeed, another easily assimilated narrative frame handed down from the past, from the perspective of a number of village-level activists, is that of Periyar's brand of Dravidianist rationalism.

Periyar's rationalist Self-Respect Movement for caste and gender equality lasted from 1926 to 1949 and was, or course, subsequently institutionalized as the Dravida Kazhagam. The DK continues to maintain a high profile in the Pudukkottai region and I had the opportunity to attend many public functions that were jointly organized by the DK and Arivoli Iyakkam village volunteers in their capacity as members of the Tamil Nadu Progressive Writers' Association. During my fieldwork, for example, Arivoli workers worked in tandem with members of the local DK chapter to celebrate Periyar's birthday in public events. Within Pudukkattai's literacy movement there have been a number of secular "Arivoli Weddings," often across castes and celebrated without priests, not unlike DK self-respect weddings. It is also through the DK that the first large network of village reading rooms was established in Tamil Nadu, again providing a model for Arivoli libraries as a place where villagers could meet, read, and discuss pressing political issues. The Self-Respect Movement is responsible for popularizing the thought of many non-Indian scientific and social thinkers, Rousseau, Voltaire, Marx, and Engels included, in the Tamil language through its journal *Kudi Aracu.*[13] Even if there is no evidence that Periyar himself used the world "Arivoli" to refer to enlightenment, his frequent use of the word "*mooda nambikkai*" (superstition or false belief) has been replicated in the discourse of scientific rationalism in the Arivoli Iyakkam, referring to that which obscures the light of knowledge and self-belief.[14] His concept of *manita tarmam* (Human Dharma) is in many senses also quite close to Arivoli's *manitaneyam,* emphasizing duty and not only self-determination.[15] The word Arivoli's contemporary power in circulation, though propelled by central government funds and a robust activist network associated with the broader left, thus also rides on classical literary tropes and the polythetic traces of 19th and 20th century reformist projects, including not only Christianity and Tamil nationalism, but also a more specifically Dravidian rationalism. This is the view from Pudukkottai's small towns and villages.

It is now time to change points of view and look at the Arivoli Iyakkam's urban leadership in the Science Forums. From the perspective of the leaders who initiated Arivoli activism in the late 1980s and early 1990s, they were participating in a global leftist movement that had nothing particularly Tamil about it. Connections to Tamil reform movements and to literary tropes connecting script to the eyes are much more strongly felt at the district level, especially among the Tamil language literati, than in India-wide official ideology of the people's science movement. The Arivoli movement's narrative strategy among many leaders shares much with models developed by the Kerala Shastra Sahitya Parishad (KSSP) brand of left-rationalist activism and by the global socialist movement.[16]

When I asked Dr T Sundararaman, one of the early leaders from Pondicherry whom many credit with coining the very word "Arivoli," about the origins of the idea and possible connections to Periyar's Dravidian rationalist-humanism, he told me that it had not even occurred to him. He attributed the coining of the word Arivoli for the literacy movement to his wife, Sudha Sundaraman, a prominent feminist at the all-India level and general secretary of All India Democratic Women's Association (AIDWA)—the women's wing of the Communist Party of India (Marxist). In contrast to Pudukkottai's literati activists and village learners, the urban intellectuals who had founded the Science Forums were much more likely to refer to models of literacy activism from other countries or to anti-colonial and democratic struggles in India more generally. The European Enlightenment itself is easily invoked as a precedent by many urban activists in the Arivoli Iyakkam as are the Russian Revolution and similar educational experiments in Fidel Castro's Cuba and Julius Nyerere's Tanzania.

The model of education used by the Arivoli Iyakkam to impart a modernist model of the subject by means of literacy lessons is in fact very closely modeled on the *Pedagogy of the Oppressed* (1970) devised by the Brazilian philosopher/activist, and educational advisor to the World Council of Churches, Paulo Freire. The other main intellectual source of theory that was cited by those I interviewed in Chennai and Pondicherry was the Irish scientist and leftist activist JD Bernal, who hoped to spread the revolutionary-Soviet model of science, education, and society across the globe. What I would like to note here is the broad desire on the part of the narrators of Arivoli's importance to attach likeness to and continuity with these people and events, and how different these frames are from those invoked among the poor in Pudukkottai itself. Prior revolutionary events can act as the ground upon which the more recent Arivoli Iyakkam stands and Arivoli can be seen as a translation of the original Enlightenment or prior revolutions into Tamil language and onto Tamil soil.

But the converse is also true as the discourse on enlightenment circulates, and this is a critical point lest we slot this as just another case of postcolonial mimicry: appropriation quickly turns to *retrospective incorporation.* The word "Arivoli" can now, in the wake of mass mobilization, be used retrospectively to refer to the European Enlightenment itself in the Tamil-language cultural and literary press in ways that, I suspect, were not possible prior to the literacy movement. An example of such usage can be found in science activist TV Venkateswaran's review article on the field of cultural studies in the March 2000 issue of the journal *Putu Vicai* (New Force), which uses the word "Arivoli" to refer to the European Enlightenment in the context of explaining critiques of scientific reasoning. For rural activists who have taken to reading journals like *Putu Vicai* through their involvement with the movement, Arivoli acts as a lens through which prior similar events that have happened in India and elsewhere can be interpreted. It thus seemed perfectly natural for village-level activist R Neela from Pudukkottai, who had been reading about theories on modernity in books and journals that circulate among Science Forum members, to state that she had just read somewhere that an "Arivoli Iyakkam" had already happened in Europe in the 18th century. The Enlightenment itself, then, can be rendered as a prior instance of what activists already know through their encounters with science and literacy activism. Note, however, that this sense of priority is temporal and not necessarily prior in the sense of being somehow more foundational in the eyes of village-level activists. The very act of retrospection must be understood as an agentive enlistment, preserving the philosophical priority of the present.

Struck by "The Gap"

This last example of a Pudukkottai village-activist learning about the European Enlightenment and its ideology of humanism through the lens of her own activism in the name of *manitaneyam* demonstrates a sort of circular motion of interpretation that serves as a knitting together of narrative across social contexts—attempts at alignment that can cut across spatial and social divides over time. Discourses on Arivoli draw on different understandings and experiences of the past, but through the cultural work of activism and reflection, these varied pasts can be made commensurate and appear to be leading to a relatively coherent present. The Arivoli Iyakkam is a cultural project of creative translation and localization, provisionally aligning diverse understandings of light, literacy, and knowledge. But sometimes activists are very much struck with the extreme difference in orientations that are both a product and continuing cause of social difference. To the extent that the Arivoli Iyakkam has been a program associated with the state and with urban orientations to personhood, time, and place, it has sometimes failed to resonate across what some activists refer to as "the gap."

In order to end with some very brief examples of the gap in practical action, and to explain what the experience of this gap might mean for Arivoli's concept of *manitaneyam*, let me present a few vignettes excerpted from the writer S Tamilcelvan's memoirs of his days as an Arivoli activist. Tamilcelvan was an activist leader in Tirunelveli District's Arivoli Iyakkam during the Total Literacy Campaign and post-literacy phases of the movement in the early to mid-1990s. Today, he is a prominent short story writer and essayist, and he is the President of the Tamil Nadu Progressive Writer's Association. His memoirs are entitled *Irulum Oliyum (Darkness and Lightness).* Tamilcelvan hails from the small town of Pattamadai and he represents someone who dwells at the intersection of urban leadership and the rural grassroots. His thoughtful reflections thus provide an indispensable window into the class contradictions that were made manifest through the very praxis of activism and insight into what these contradictions might mean for attempts to bring "enlightenment" by means of literacy activism.

Throughout his book, Tamilcelvan describes events that lead him to reconsider his relationship to knowledge and to people. He had sought to teach people their place in world history and in the nation by writing pamphlets and speaking about the struggle for Independence and the problems of contemporary communalist politics, only to find that his activism required him to learn much his own place in relation to the world of rural marginality. For example, on one occasion Tamilcelvan went to a village named Ayiraperi to oversee an Arivoli lesson in which the teacher asked a group of villagers which district they were living in. The students responded they do not live in a district, but that the district (by which the students presumably meant the district office) was in the city of Tirunelveli. Tamilcelvan (2004:41) reports:

> After the lesson I took a walk with Kandasamy [the teacher] and we talked with amazement about our lack of understanding. They had made us understand that the town of Tirunelveli itself was the district. The idea that Ayiraperi [their village] was located within the area of Tirunelveli district had not reached the people even fifty years after independence.[17]

Tamilcelvan was shocked at the villagers' expression of their own marginality with regard to the state, and by extension, to his own world of spatial experience. He had taken it for granted that they would also take for granted his approach to the relation between person and place. Their response raised the question for him of whether these villagers were really living as full members, as fellow citizens, of an independent India if they had no meaningful experience of living in a district called Tirunelveli. For these rural women learners, the district *(mavattam)* and sub-district *(taluka)* appeared to be the name of government offices they had heard of and perhaps never seen; they were distinct places *in* other towns. But these learners expressed no deep sense of themselves *living within* and *being a part of* an encompassing state unit known as the district.[18] Indeed, there is reason to believe that the learners were in fact intentionally marking their difference from the author with regard to access to state services. What is worth emphasizing here, however, is how this incident is taken by Tamilcelvan to be an index of his *own* distance from people's lives and his own ignorance: "we talked with amazement about *our* lack of understanding."

It is in these moments that the book's title, *Irulum Oliyum (Lightness and Darkness),* comes back to remind readers that it might well be *they* who are living in darkness, and not Arivoli's students, insofar as they know very little about village life and what it is to be in such a marginal position with regard to the institutions of government and education. On another occasion, when he was taken by villagers to be just another government officer of whom they could demand better streetlights, Tamilcelvan reports, "I started to hate my pants and shirt. It occurred to me that I could have worn a *verti.* Even if I had come wearing a *verti* I could not have been one with him. After forty years of powdering my face how I could just wipe my middle-classness off?" (Ibid.:19). His powdered face here stands as sign of class difference and the inability to be "one" with the villagers he would seek to serve and empower through literacy. Using a metaphor drawn from the first letters of the Tamil alpha-syllabary, he explains "Like the distance between *'ànà'* and *'aavanna'* there would always be a gap *(idai veli)* continuing between us and the people" (Ibid.:25). Any attempt to depart from the basic stuff of interpersonal relation, in the name of the freedoms that might result from the work of abstraction, seems to lead to a feeling of failure insofar as the movement *must* understand itself as emanating from the very people it seeks to uplift. Otherwise, it could make no claims of being conducted so that people could make themselves.

At an even broader level, then, Tamilcelvan's angst over the gap and his willingness to reflect upon his own lack of understanding produced by the feeling of disconnect tells us a good deal about the nature of *camuka cevai* and *manitaneyam* as these are practiced in the Arivoli literacy movement. To the degree that this variety of humanism is premised on the self-making of people, it must reflect upon the question of what *kind* of self is at stake. Tamilcelvan explains that it was only quite late into Arivoli activism that he understood that people were coming to lessons, not necessarily out of pure self-motivation (the ideal of the self-making subject) but out of a sense of duty in response to the affection shown to them by Arivoli volunteers (Ibid.:24). The desire to connect with people had provoked a reciprocal reaction, but not on the grounds expected by many Arivoli activists. They had built a relationship with learners that required the learners to attend classes, but for the sake of the activists. This is how the questions of affect and duty were forced upon Arivoli volunteers by their very subjects in the context of practice. This was a burden to reciprocate that has everything to do with the centrality of *neyam* in Arivoli's project to make modern subjects who would in turn make themselves and their own history. Such a project required that the framers and the teachers of enlightenment also allow themselves to be remade in the process, but without losing sight of some sort of end goal of universal self-determination.

In Lieu of Resolution

In this short essay, I have used examples from the Arivoli Iyakkam's brand of humanism to address what I take to be larger issues regarding Tamil modernity's engagement with the question of what it is to be human. First came the problem of conceptual relations. In this, we have seen how even such an arch-modernist project as the Enlightenment Movement cannot but adopt a framework premised on the primacy of affective ties and social relations as the foundation of activism. Next, as we moved into the actual historical or narrative connections that protagonists, variously situated, have made in grounding the movement, it became clear that these serve to propel movement in sometimes convergent ways, all the while drawing on varied pasts. Finally, we have brought the question of disconnect or narrative-experiential "gaps" to the fore in order to interrogate the meanings of *manitaneyam* further and to elucidate the accompanying paradoxes of making self-making subjects in the Tamil countryside from the ground of activist practice.

This variety of mass mobilization must be carried in the name of the common person and by means of an affective-reciprocal relationship with those common people it seeks to empower, even if, in the end, the very problematic of auto-production, as developed in the Arivoli ideology, might not be immediately immanent in the everyday practices of rural Tamil life. Arivoli activism is indeed a form of cultural work that is caught between the modernizing desire to pull people to action, providing a vision of what might be through abstractions like "the social" and the "human," and the recognition that activism must also be premised on logics that are representative of, and appropriate to, the habitus of the very villagers they seek to mobilize.

NOTES

1. The Tamilnadu Science Forum also worked very closely with its sister organization the Pondicherry Science Forum. I will henceforth refer to both organizations collectively as the "Science Forums." The Government of India's National Literacy Mission, housed in the Ministry of Human Resource Development, was established under Rajiv Gandhi in 1988 in response to the National Policy on Education of 1986, which first declared a specific plan for full adult literacy in India. The Bharat Gyan Vigyan Samiti (BGVS) is a government-organized body designed to mediate between the NGO, activist side of the movement and the Government of India's education policy.

2. During the Total Literacy Campaign of 1991–92, Pudukkottai's Arivoli Iyakkam had managed to enroll 246,000 learners in literacy classes run by a group of approximately 25,000 volunteer teachers (Athreya & Chunkath 1996; Saraswathi 2000). The Mahalir (Women's) Arivoli Iyakkam that took place while I was doing fieldwork in 2003–04 was expected to reach about 60,000 village women through literacy classes.

3. Other districts that saw great enthusiasm and experimentation in the Arivoli Iyakkam include Virudunagar (formerly Kamarajar District), Sivagangai (formerly Pasumpon Mutturamalinga Thevar District), and Tirunelveli, in addition to the very powerful Pondicherry Arivoli Iyakkam in 1990–02.

4. I point readers to Bhaskar Mukhopadhyay's (2005:44–47) fascinating discussion of how *"samàj,"* was reformulated as "society" in Bengal. See also Gyan Prakash (2002) for a "Colonial Genealogy of Society," in which he analyses the contrast between "society" and "community" in the making of a specifically colonial governmentality.

5. I borrow the phrase "moral narrative of modernity" from Webb Keane (2006) who argues that even secular narratives of modernity have a particularly moral character, which he attributes in large part to their Protestant roots, in that they are a call for humans to act upon their own history through the exertion of their own agency.

6. Of course, a number of thinkers in the Euro-American tradition have conceived of (secular) humanism in more pragmatic, relational, and potentially affect-laden terms.

William James and FCS Schiller are notable among what we might term pragmatist–humanists. My point here is simply to distinguish one humanism in which the worth of humans and their capacity for self-creation are more firmly grounded in their capacity for rational thought from another in which humans are granted the capacity to make themselves under conditions of some deeper sense of affective binding.

7. Jürgen Habermas, writing about Benjamin's thoughts on temporality in relation to the problematic setup by Marx in the *Eighteenth Brumaire*, puts the point quite nicely: "A modernity that has been evaporated into what is actual at any given time, as soon as it attains the authenticity of a now-time, [must] constantly take its normativity from mirror images of pasts whose services are enlisted for this purpose .... Inasmuch as we appropriate past experiences with an orientation to the future, the authentic present is preserved as the locus of continuing tradition and innovation at once" (1987:11–13).

8. Pondicherry has since become a separate state.

9. From the Kavi Yogi Shuddhananda Bharathiar (1995) translation of the *Tirukkural.*

10. I refer readers here to Anand Pandian's work (2010) on the relation between classical Tamil tropes of cultivation and everyday formulations of virtue and progress in Theni District.

11. Prior to its use in the literacy movement, Arivoli was also the name of a small publishing house in Madurai and the name of a relatively famous speaker on the public speaking circuit.

12. Arivoli is a direct Tamil equivalent of the Sanskritic name, "Gyanadeepam," which is more popular among south Indian Christians than among other communities, though "Arivoli" draws from Dravidian etymological roots.

13. See Geeta and Rajadurai (1998) for a fuller account of the Self-respect Movement. Recent research by J Kayalvili Devi (1999:61) on the movement's most prominent and widely read journal, *Kudi Aracu (Republic)*, discusses how Periyar's work is responsible for some of the first translations of Robert G Ingersoll (1833–99). An American critic of religion and slavery, and an advocate of women's suffrage, Ingersoll is associated with what was called the American "Free Thinkers Movement."

14. This is a word he would also apply more generally to religious belief, in opposition to "*pakuttarivu*" (rationalism).

15. For a good account of how Periyar opposed his version of *manitatarma* (Human Dharma) to Brahminical Manu Dharma, again gleaned from articles in *Kudi Aracu,* see MSS Pandian (2007:191–3).

16. The KSSP, whose motto is "Science for Social Revolution," is Kerala's equivalent of the Science Forums and was the organizing agency behind India's first Total Literacy Campaign in Ernakulam District in 1989.

17. This translation from *Irulum Oliyum* and all others cited from this volume are mine.

18. As E Valentine Daniel (1984:61–105) has written with regard to context-sensitive pragmatic meanings of the Tamil "*ur*"—the word I have unsatisfactorily translated above as "village" but which could also be translated as "home"—it must be understood in contrast to the context-free and rationalized government spatial categories of belonging which children learn in school: bounded categories, each one encompassed within a larger one (the Panchayat is nested within the Development Block, which sits in a Taluk within the District, which is in a State, etc.).

WORKS CITED

Athreya, Venkatesh B, and Sheela Rani Chunkath. 1996. *Literacy and Empowerment*. New Delhi: Sage Publications and UNESCO. (See note 2.)

Bharathiar, Kavi Yogi Shuddhananda. 1995. *English Translation of the Tirukkural*. Chennai: Himalayan Academy.

Daniel, E Valentine. 1984. *Fluid Signs: Being a Person the Tamil Way*. Berkeley: University of California Press. (See note 18.)

Freire, Paulo. 1970. *Pedagogy of the Oppressed*. Translated by Myra Bergman Ramos. New York: Continuum Press.

Geeta, V and SV Rajadurai. 1998. *Toward a Non-Brahmin Millennium: From Iyothee Thass to Periyar*. Chennai: Bhatkal and Sen. (See note 13.)

Habermas, Jürgen. 1987. *The Philosophical Discourse of Modernity*. Translated by Fredrick Lawrence. Cambridge, MA: MIT Press.

Kayalvili Devi, J. 1999. *Kutiaracu Italk Kavitaikal*. Chennai: Manimekalai Piracuram. (See note 13.)

Keane, Webb. 2006. *Christian Moderns: Fetishism and Freedom in the Missionary Encounter*. Berkeley: University of California Press. (See note 5.)

Marx, Karl. 1963 [1869]. *The Eighteenth Brumaire of Louis Bonaparte*. New York: International Publishers.

Mukhopadhyay, Bhaskar. 2005. The Rumor of Globalization: Globalism, Counterworks and the Location of Commodity. *Dialectical Anthropology* 29: 35–60. (See note 4.)

Pandian, Anand. 2010. *Crooked Stalks: Cultivating Virtue in South India*. Durham, NC: Duke University Press.

Pandian, MSS. 2007. *Brahmin and Non-Brahmin: Genealogies of the Tamil Political Present*. Delhi: Permanent Black. (See note 15.)

Prakash, Gyan. 2002. The Colonial Genealogy of Society: Community and Political Modernity in India. In *The Social In Question*, edited by Patrick Joyce. New York: Routledge. (See note 4.)

Saraswathi, LS. 2000. Total Literacy Campaign: Pudukkottai, Tamil Nadu. In *Reading the World: Understanding the Literacy Campaigns in India*, edited by Malavika Karlekar. Mumbai: Asian South Pacific Bureau of Adult Education. (See note 2.)

Tamilcelvan, S. 2004. *Irulum Oliyum: Arivoli Iyakka Anupavankal*. Chennai: Bharati Puttakalayam Press.

Venkateswaran, TV. 2000. Panpàttil ayvukal cila arimuka kurippukal. *Pudu Vicai* (March): 76–78.

Glimpses of the Unitary Self in 16th-century Tamil Literature

D SHULMAN

Is there a "Tamil way of being human," as Val Daniels[1] has so beautifully intimated? Is the Tamil person distinctive, in definable ways, from, say, the Telangana or the Malayali person, to say nothing of the Canadian or the Piedmontese? I am, perhaps only impressionistically and superficially, sympathetic to the notion. Life, especially the interactive world of subtle verbal and non-verbal relations, feels very different in Tenkasi and in Kollapuram. But then life anyway feels different from moment to moment. So sympathy apart, can we find some way to mark or measure difference?

I'm an old-fashioned philologist; I work on texts; decades of habit have become instinct, or perhaps it's the other way round. I look for answers in the words left behind by poets of distant centuries. You'll have to forgive me for following this well-trodden path. If I ask myself how I might begin to think about this question, I begin to wonder about issues of autonomy: are we talking about a relatively self-contained, self-driven unit, bounded off from others, more or less autonomous in thought and action, and thus an individual—or, as McKim Marriott has proposed, a "dividual", deeply porous, constantly interpenetrated with others close or far? I wonder about issues of integration: is the Tamil person put together in some specific, patterned dynamic of growth and maturation, as in Margaret Trawick's powerful analogy between the human domain and that of, say, rice cultivation— with strong notions of ripening as softening, an inner maturation conducive to "mixing", *kalappu,* breaching external contours? And then I might brood on questions of internal economy: can we generate a culturally sensitive model of the mind? Are there certain "parts" of the self, if there is such an entity that dominates the inner arena under particular conditions? Are there parts that are more or less accessible than others? Is a word like "part" or "function" appropriate?

But if there really is, or was, a Tamil way of being human, then it has undoubtedly evolved and changed over time. It would be good if our model could be nuanced historically. I think it's quite likely that the Tamil way of being human in the sixth century was rather different from the modes of, say, the 16th century. Here, I'll be sticking mostly to the sixteenth and to a single, monumental literary text, one that has sadly gone out of circulation but was once considered the foundation of a Tamil education: this is Ativīrarāma Pāntiyan's *Naiṭatam*, a Tamil *mahākāvya* version of Śrīhara's famous Sanskrit work, the *Naiṣadhīya-carita*.[2] The Tamil poem was composed at Tenkasi by the Pantiya king, brother to another great poet, Varatunkarāma Pāntiyan. There is good reason to believe that Tenkasi in the second half of the 16th century was the site of a remarkable cultural efflorescence, a kind of Renaissance, in which we can detect—as with the Italian Renaissance of the 14th century—major shifts in very basic concepts and feelings, including notions about what a human being is or could be.

But how can we begin to characterize the brave new world of 16th-century Tenkasi? How can we be certain that we are not simply projecting our own notions onto our texts? Remember, too, that Ativīrarāma had a "parent" text with which he was profoundly engaged; and, since we are interested in the composition of the inner world of feeling and thinking, we have to keep in mind that Śrīhara's *Naiṣadhīya* is by far the most richly psychologized, or interiorized, of all Sanskrit *kāvyas*. In fact, this relation between the Tamil text and its prototype is not a simple matter. Even when the Tamil poet actually translates a particular verse, more or less literally, his relation to his model is in no way mechanical. It is a question of modes of internalization, of a certain conversation taking place in the space between the two intertexts. We will have to put this fascinating problem aside for now, though it calls for new ways of thinking about south Asian textualities. And still the basic question remains.

Say we want to define a 16th-century Tamil notion of "self." The word itself is missing. (Or we could say, following Winnicott: "Self" is a word that knows more about us than we know about it.) What we find is the same somewhat chaotic jumble of terms for various parts and aspects of the inner person that we know from much earlier sources in Tamil: *uyir*, the life-breath or life-force; *nĕñcam*, the feeling organ, situated in the breast, probably the site of *uṇarvu*, that is, consequential understanding or intuitive perception; *āvi*, a near-synonym for *uyir*, but perhaps capable of delicate differentiation in contexts of life-or-death decisions; *maṉam*, the perhaps devalued faculty of derived intellection (but also the usual source or site of desire); *cintai* or *karuttu*, both of them apparently endowed with strong cognitive elements; the metaphysical term *ātma(n)*, relatively rare in Tamil literary texts; and a more general, very common word, *uḻḻam*, the "inside" or "interiority," which also quite often seems to be linked to some kind of thinking-intellection (cf. the verb *uḷku*). There are also sub-categories of *uḻḻam*, such as *uṭpulaṉ*, the inner eye, sometimes identified with the *itayam*, "heart" (Skt. *hṛdaya:* see *Naiṭatam* 3.8). Ativīrarāma has not invented a new word for "person" or "self." He happily recycles all these earlier terms. And yet, if we read attentively, we begin to notice that their semantic range has shifted quite radically away from earlier usages.

Take *uyir*, for example. For the sake of argument, I would like to suggest that in earlier Tamil sources, right through the end of the Chola period, we have an implicit meta-psychology-cum-anthropology organized around the core concept of breath, the life-force that is always in movement, in and out, and that is always, perhaps by definition, a unitary force. *Uyir* flows in and out of bodies that seem to contain it but are in fact only precarious vessels for it. Moment by moment, the person breathes the entire cosmos in and out, and the cosmos itself, infused with *uyir* and moving with its rhythm, is also breathing in and out—so there will be both a transient, internal *uyir* and an external, trans-personal one. The latter is sometimes said to be creative in the out-breath and absorptive in the in-breath; this may also be true, on a lesser scale, of the internal *uyir*. God breathes out the world into some form of existence, and re-internalizes it, de-objectifying it or melting it down. Breathing is, however, much more than breath alone. In a way, it is about differential intensities of living and feeling (not thinking); and thus Tamil *uyir* has surprising connections to Advaita, that school of Indian philosophy most concerned with issues of "aliveness." The world, with its profusion of sense and texture and color, continually goes in and out, opening and closing space within the person; and there is also a profoundly interactive or interpersonal aspect to this unending rhythm. Loving, for example, is at least partly about the merging of breath. Look, for example, at what happens to Rāma and Sītā when they first catch sight of one another in Mithila, according to Kampan's *Irāmâvatāram* (1.10.592–93):

parukiya nokk' ĕṉṉum pācattāṟ piṇitt'
ŏruvaraiy ŏruvar tam uḷḷam īrttalāl
varicilaiy aṇṇalum vāṭka'ṇaṅkaiyum
iruvarum māṟip pukk' itayam ĕytiṉār//

maruṅk'ilā naṅkaiyum vacaiyil aiyaṉum
ŏruṅkiyav iraṇṭ' uṭaṟk' uyir ŏṉṟ' āyiṉār
karuṅ kaṭaṟ paḷḷiyiṟ kalavi nīṅkip poyp
pirintavar kūṭiṉāṟ pecal veṇṭumo//

They bound and tugged at each other's insides
with the noose of that first hungry look,
and thus the lord of the tightly bound bow
and the girl with eyes deadly as swords
entered, by turns,
each other's heart.

The breath in two bodies—that of the girl
with no waist and that of the boy
without flaw— merged back into one.
When the two lovers, once joined
on their bed in the dark sea and then
torn apart, came together again—
was there need for words?

We have three pieces of a person's inner world: the *uḷḷam*, capable of being captured by a look from another person's eyes and thus dragged outside; the *itayam*, which can be penetrated by another person, through strong feeling and sudden desire; and the *uyir* that clearly dwarfs its bodily containers and seeks to fuse with itself, a single, rather impersonal force, the rhythmic breath of life itself. This *uyir*, we might note, tends to be intimately linked to *uṇarvu*, intuitive knowledge or understanding, or to a kind of insight not usually derived from intellection.[3]

Ativīrarāma also knows about the *uyir*; for him it is an internal, alive part of the person, and a rather vulnerable part at that, easily susceptible to destabilization and to death.[4] No one can manage without it. Somewhat surprisingly, however, *uḷḷam* now seems to be the wider, more elastic and comprehensive term. *Uḷḷam* mostly overrides the *uyir* and usually contains and rules it. Quite often this new *uḷḷam* seems to mean something akin to our notion of "mind."

Look, for example, at *Naiṭatam* 4.29:

karum puyaṉ maṟaikku' mati katir veṭṭal kairava malar pĕṟātatu pol
arump' iḷa muṟuval iḷa mulaip pokam aiya nīy ĕytutaṟk' aritāl
virumpiṉar ākiy amararum iruntār viṇavar iṭatt' avaḷ ārvam
purint' iṭāt' uṉatu per ĕḻil ava' ṭan uḷatt'iṭaip pŏṟippal kāṇutiyāl

As the night lily can't enjoy the light of her lover,
the moon, on a night of dark clouds,
it won't be so easy for you, Sir,
to taste the breasts of that woman
whose smile unfolds like a bud.
Also, I have to tell you that the gods
want her, too. To block any passion
for them, I'll paint your great beauty
in the middle of her mind—
just watch!

This is the goose speaking to Nala before flying off to negotiate with Damayantī. He chooses his image carefully: the *kairavam* flower is uniquely suited to the Moon, as, by implication, Damayantī is to Nala; but sometimes there are cloudy nights or other impediments. To ward them off, the goose will paint *(pŏṟippal)* a verbal image of Nala in Damayantī's *uḷḷam* —not her interior in a general way, and probably not even her "heart" *(itayam, maṉam)*, but some part of her mental economy where she can see, visualize, imagine, fantasize, feel desire, deliberate, and make a choice: in short, her mind.[5]

We could easily spend the rest of this hour filling in the contours of the *uḷḷam*. But let's say you agree that this term now, in Tenkasi, means something like "mind." So what? What does the concept of mind offer us for the purpose of defining personhood or self? What does the *uḷḷam* actually do, and in what ways is it different from earlier context-specific usages?

Normally, I would want us to draw out a set of inductive conclusions based on individual verses. Since time is short, however, I am going to offer a tentative list of functions that seem to fit Nala's (or Ativīrarāma's) *uḷḷam.*

1. First, the *uḷḷam* knows how to think, in marked contrast with the *uyir.* This is not a trivial matter. There are different modes of thinking and of knowing, some more complex and far-reaching than others. If we compare the Tenkasi *uḷḷam* with the inner world of the *bhakti* poet (say Māṇikkavācakar, or Cuntaramūrttināyaṉār, or Nammāḻvār), then the latter consistently offers self-images of fragmentation and diffusion in which the mind plays, for the most part, an invidious role; whereas Nala scans his awareness and seems to use his mind to hold the sometimes dissonant pieces of himself together.

2. Second, the *uḷḷam* has an inside, which is to say that it has some sort of external border, however tenuous. It is a bounded entity, full of generative content, welling up continuously, and at the same time apparently in its deeper reaches, unconstricted and spacious. We will want to explore this space.

3. Third, it has parts, some more prominent than others. I believe there is a particular privileging of the imagination, as I will try to demonstrate in a moment. A possible hierarchy of components emerges, with *karuttu* and *maṉam,* for example, like *uyir,* subsumed within *uḷḷam.* Moreover, certain of these parts provide the mechanism for the connectivity of one *uḷḷam* to another and for the possibility that one *uḷḷam* can create novelty in another.

4. Fourth, *uḷḷam* has a pronounced tendency to doubt itself. It easily moves into the ironic. It knows itself, not perhaps in the split-off way that the *bhakti* persona naturally chooses, but in some reflexive mode that allows for an intra-psychic generative emergence of mistakes, illusions, fantasies, hallucinations, and madness. These may, in fact, in some sense constitute the dynamic core of personhood. I stress again: these extreme states, the very stuff of a love story such as that of Nala and Damayantī, are now perceived as wholly internal to the "self" (that word again). Even possession, a particularly powerful displacement, is primarily **endogenic**. The *uḷḷam* is capable of observing its own self-generating fantasies in action, as we will see.

5. Fifth, the *uḷḷam,* where perception happens and is processed, makes judgements about what is and is not real (and also, but not only, about what is and is not "true"—these are not the same judgements).

6. Finally, the *uḷḷam* is a locus for mood, as distinct from emotion/feeling. "Mood" is a discovery. It implies the existence of a minimally integrated, distinctive person. It also implies a certain instability of internal states, a rapid transition among nuanced feelings that can be introspectively articulated in complex fusions or combinations. Perhaps more than anything else, this discovery of mood gives us the sense that we are in the presence of a proto-modern personhood.

Let's begin with this last point, probably the easiest to assimilate. If one reads through the *Naiṭatam* consecutively, trying to get a sense of it as a unified work, one slowly, but inevitably, begins to construct a profile of the two main protagonists. Of course, both of them have inherited features from earlier Nala-Damayantī texts. Nala, as I have argued elsewhere, tends to be more absent than present, a somewhat brittle vehicle for disguise and for displaced awareness. His identity, to use an anachronistic term, is largely vested in Damayantī's recognition of him *as someone*, a human person of distinctive character. His personhood—his self, if you like—is repeatedly at stake in the dice games he plays, in the riddle contests he enters, in his desperate race from Ayodhya to Vidaharba, in his startling mathematical skills, and so on.[6] Words like "integrated" or "unitary" wouldn't seem to suit him very well. At best, he oscillates between relatively extreme states of one kind or another.[7] But in the Tamil *Naiṭatam*, Nala acquires an introspective, even meditative quality. Consider the following moment. On his way to the *svayaṃvara* ceremony in which Damayantī will choose her husband, Nala is stopped by Indra and three other gods; they, too, are in love with Damayantī, and they cruelly request Nala to argue their case before the woman whom he loves.

> Other than you, who have conquered Love,
> for all his power, by your own
> beauty, who is there to heal
> the suffering spread by *his*
> honeyed arrows? (11.26)

Indra's demand is much worse, the poet tells us, than asking Nala to give up his life, *uyir*. Nala at once loses his *karuttu;* forgets who he is *(taṉṉaiyu' maṟakkum)*. He cannot say no to the gods, cannot lie to them—though suddenly "lying" seems to him to lose its terror, and "truth" to expand its register. Uncertainty washes over him

> *kuru maṇi mekalaik kuvaḷaik kaṇ kŏlo*
> *pŏru mataṉ pakaḻiyo pŏymmai tīt' ĕṉṉun*
> *tarumamo vuyir nilai taḷarntu vāṭum ĕṉ*
> *marumam mīt' ūṉṟiya vāḻiṟ poḻvate*

> Is it her eyes (think of her bangles, think of her waist,
> studded with jewels), is it the arrow of hostile
> Desire, is it this dharmic business of lying
> being classed as "bad"?
> Something is eating at my life
> when I'm at my weakest, most vulnerable,
> like a sword twisted in my heart. (11.29)

Tamil poets are fond of such inner states, but Ativīrarāma has pushed the analysis farther than usual—far beyond anything in the parent-text of Śrīharṣa. He seems to see directly into Nala's mind and to listen carefully to the words that this mind produces in an emergency. Nala wavers, protests, debates with himself, briefly turns against conventional morality and its hollow categories, hesitates again, makes silly pronouncements, and ends up complying with external constraints. Doubt colors this difficult moment, which ends in an acknowledged *aporia:* something—Nala doesn't know what it is—is eating at his life, his *uyir-nilai.* Something that is experienced in his *marumam,* his most vulnerable inner place, his guts. Do we not recognize the type? Is he so different from ourselves? Note that this Tenkasi Nala is endowed with freedom of choice and undoubted agency, clearly in evidence in the very richness of his inner monologue and in his doubt.

In passing, let me try to delineate an image of the "new" Damayantī as well. She is rather a far cry from the self-possessed heroine of the *Mahābhārata* or the *Naḷavĕṇpā.* The Tenkasi Damayantī is impulsive, passionate, given to severe hallucinatory, borderline psychotic states, and rather ambivalent about the way language functions in relation to her experience. In particular, she seems to have doubts about the *śleṣa* double-entendres that are her speciality in Śrīharṣa's poem. We'll see one example of how her *uḷḷam* operates in just a moment.

We have time, at most, for only three more examples. I want to begin with an example of the newly conceptualized imaginative faculty. Then we will look at a short passage about (shared) fantasy in relation to the whole person. And I will conclude with a striking verse that examines the mind's perceptual judgments about what is real and that, in effect, draws us a picture, or a working model, of the mind in action. We can then try to outline a few tentative conclusions.

Here is 4.32 (just three verses away from our earlier example of *ārvam,* intense desire, in the *uḷḷam*). Nala is speaking to the goose, who has just finished a rather inventive, detailed verbal portrait of Damayantī in the hopes of arousing Nala's desire for her:

> *vĕṇṇakait tuvar vāy aṇaṅkĕḻil palarum viḷampiṉar niṉ mŏḻi yavaḷ ĕn*
> *kaṇṇ ĕtirppaṭṭāḻ polu' mĕyt tuṇaiyāṟ karuttiṉāṟ kāṇṭale kāṇṭa'*
> *naṇṇi muṟ ṟoṉṟum pŏruḷu' nuṇṇiya'te' ṉāṭutaṟk 'ariyalā mukattiṟ*
> *paṇṇiya nokka' nokkunarkk' aḻaku payappatai yaṉṟi veṟ' uḷato*
>
> Many have spoken of her white smile, her mouth
> red as coral, her overpowering
> beauty, but your words have almost placed her
> before my very eyes. Seeing through
> the mind of one's friend is really
> seeing. Eyes that barely see
> what's right in front of them,
> especially something very fine,
> are only there to impart beauty
> to one's face.

This is one of those verses where Ativīrarāma has taken a thought directly from Śrīharna and developed it in somewhat surprising ways. Let us look at the rather arcane but highly polished Sanskrit verse in question (2.55):

> *akhilaṃ viduṣām an-āvilaṃ suhṛdā ca sva-hṛdā ca paśyatām/*
> *savidhe 'pi na-sūkṣma-sākṣiṇī vadanâlaṅkṛti-mātram akṣiṇī//*

> Everything is lucidly perceived
> by those who see through the heart
> or through a friend. The two eyes
> that sit on our face, that can't detect
> anything fine, however close it comes,
> are only there for ornament.

Nala, perhaps for the first time, but certainly not for the last time, in these two texts, privileges an inner vision over the object-driven, physical act of vision. The goose, by masterful description in language, has made Damayantī present to him. There is an interesting question about the singularity and specificity of this vision and how it is articulated—but we will have to put it aside. What is clear is that *kāṇṭal*, "seeing,"[8] is often at its best when enabled or mediated by what is going on in the mind of a close companion, *tuṇai* (or friend, *suhṛd*, in the Sanskrit). But the two texts differ slightly, in my view significantly, when it comes to what exactly the companion's mind is supposed to do. For Śrīharna, it seems to me a matter of feeling, something transpiring literally in the heart *(svahṛdā)*. For Ativīrarāma, the critical word is *karuttiṉāl*, "[seeing through] the mind"—but *karuttu* here seems to mean not merely "thought" or "mind" in a general way but rather the much more crisply defined faculty of the imagination. When someone close to you imagines something, you, too, can perceive it, perhaps by virtue of the empathic closeness you feel with that person. In short, seeing is believing (the Tamil commentary glosses this interactive process as *nampikkai*, "belief," made evident by the imagination), but seeing is not looking at an external object; it is, rather, a matter of co-imagining.

Then there is the point about the relative incapacity, even uselessness, of our eyes. The test of real perception is what we do with subtlety. Our eyes aren't much good at discerning fine nuances—perhaps the single most important attribute of anything real—even if the fine object is brought very close. The major commentator Narayana, addressing Śrīharna's verse, says: "Eyes can't even perceive the kohl applied to their edges or their own redness, and so on, so how can they grasp something that is more remote?" On the other hand, the imagination—at least as it is conceived in 16th-century Tenkasi—seems perfectly suited precisely for this purpose. The imaginative faculty, we might conclude, is entirely predicated on subtlety and fineness; also, perhaps, as I have already hinted, on singularity.

There is, it seems, an intuitive flash of emotional insight that comes into play when a friend describes something (as Nārāyana says in his gloss). The Tenkasi epistemology takes this notion a step farther, toward the interactive imagination that can make something seem real to us. "Real," even more than "true." Here, again, is the Tamil commentator: our eyes are no more than an ornament for someone who sees with the help of his friend's imagination. The latter is what makes something real. There is also, incidentally, a variant reading for the middle of the verse: *naṇṇi muṟ ṟoṉṟum pŏruḷ uḷam piriyi' ṉāṭutaṟk' ariya vāṇ mukattiṟ paṇṇiya nokkam*, "if your mind moves away from what is right in front of it, then the eyes in your face [are only an ornament]." Our commentator thinks this is an inferior reading, very much opposed to the sense of the Sanskrit original. I agree. Still, even in this variant we see the clear superiority of the mind, capable of undermining direct physical perception and reducing the eyes (once again) to useless ornaments. In either case, what we see stands in a somewhat oblique, and inferior, relation to what we imagine.

So here is one tentative conclusion: a person sees, interactively, by virtue of an active imagination attuned to subtleties. Seeing is not, of course, all there is to it. The *uḷḷam* will have to process what the inner eye shows it. It, the *uḷḷam*, also seems to know where imagination ends and something else begins. But the critical point rests on the complex, interpersonal process of truly seeing and knowing. Nala cannot see Damayantī directly (at this point), just as the eye cannot really see even something quite close; Nala can only imagine her by imagining his friend's imagination of her. There are, apparently, degrees of imaginative force. You have to go through the intimate other's imagination—perhaps through several such receding frames—but you can do this because, as we know from the earlier discussion, you are breathing the same air as the other, in and out. You and your friend belong to a single, living, resonant cosmos connected through the fine tissue of many distinctive imaginations. This way of understanding perception also, incidentally, explains why what the imagination sees is objective, not in the Kantian sense of discretely contoured substances but in the sense that the imagined object is shared, consequential, and thus real. It rides the same rhythmic breath. Damayantī's image—her unique face, eyes, hair, breasts, waist, and feet—exists and is, in fact, moving into Nala, breathed in, as it were, into some reservoir of personal being where it can deepen, grow, and perhaps later re-emerge outward to connect with, or superimpose itself upon, the living presence of Damayantī herself—as we will see. All this depends upon the particular way the goose has chosen to depict her verbally, thereby activating Nala's *karuttu* via his (the goose's) own vision.

But note the profound difference from the earlier, somewhat simpler *uyir*-based anthropology. The internal breathing in and out is no longer isomorphic with the external breathing. It is no longer a matter of the cosmic imagination recycling itself over and over, so that everyone is, in effect, breathing in the same cosmos. Now the internal breath moves in accord with its own imagination as nurtured or motivated by the resonant imagination of the friend. Somehow, here, there is an autonomy to the person that regulates the transition, so that what comes from outside and what comes from inside create something else, something new, that is connected to the imagining other and therefore real (indeed, far more real than a direct perception).

We could also describe this process as an opening into depth, a resonant internal depth—but remember that the outside is also deep if it is breathing in and out. Indeed, the cosmos out there adjusts itself to your creative act: Damayantī's image exists, it is moving into you and back out of you—which is the only way you have or hold it—because through your friend you are able to imagine it, in all its singularity. Without this friend, you are blind. One could say much the same thing about the necessary presence of the poet.[9]

This entire process seems to be rather ordinary, a normative, everyday, moment-by-moment experience. But what about more extreme mental states—say love-madness, or possession, or delusion? Much of the *Naiṭatam* is given over to exploring such states. Here is one striking example.

Nala has been infiltrated into the women's quarters of the palace where Damayantī lives. No one can see him, thanks to the gods' magic. He undergoes some unsettling experiences as he makes his way through the courtyard. He brushes against women, glimpses them in states of dishabille; they see his reflection on various surfaces, his footprints on the ground, their own hovering reflections off the jewels he wears. For his part, he sees an infinite series of Damayantīs, the hallucinatory, obsessive products of his mind—what is called *uruvĕḷittoṟṟam*, an externalization of an inner vision. Damayantī, too, thinks she sees him everywhere. The stage is now set for a meeting.

In the midst of all these women, Nala stumbles upon Damayantī herself—but he fails to recognize her because of the endless Damayantīs that fill his mind (11.59). She's just like all the others. She is holding a garland, and of course she can't see Nala in front of her; but she does see an imaginary Nala, who is so real to her that she casts the garland around his neck, anticipating her bridegroom-choice that still lies ahead. As it happens, this garland actually falls around the neck of the real Nala—and at once disappears from sight, since everything that touches him becomes invisible. Clearly, something rather remarkable has happened, and both of the lovers try to think it through:

uruvĕḷiyāka yāṉ kaṇṭav ŏṇṇutal
maru malar mālikai vaṉaintat' ĕṉ ĕṉav
aracaṉum ĕṇṇināṉ avaḷuñ cūṭṭiya
tĕriyal kāṇkilaṉ ĕṉa tĕrumāntāḷ aro (11.61)

muruk'aviḻ kuḻaliṉā' ṭaṉaiyum muṉṉ uṟum
uruvĕḷiy ĕṉav iṟai uvantu pulliṉāṉ
arivaiyum aṉṉavāṟ' ĕṇṇiy āṅk' ĕtir
puravalaṉ mārp' uṟap pulliṉāḷ aro (11.62)

cŏll' arum iṉpa' mīṭūṟat toṉṟalum
pullu viṭṭ' avvuruppŏlivu nokkiṉāṉ
mĕll iyal avvuru viḻiyiṟ kāṇkuṟāt'
allal uṟṟ' aṇi vaḷaiy aṅkai nīkkiṉāḷ (11.63)

karun taṭaṅ kaṇṇiyaik kaiyiṟ pulliyum
pŏruntiyav uruvěliy ěṉṟu pokki nall
arun taṉam pěṟṟ' iḻantāril aiyaṉum
varunti věn tuyarŏṭu mati mayaṅkiṉāṉ (11.65)

"This garland came from a woman
whom I saw—as an illusion!"
That's what *he* thought while
she lost sight of the garland
and was bewildered.

He happily embraced her—the all-too-familiar
delusion. She clung to his chest, thinking
that was as it was.
Indescribable ecstasy welled up.
He let go of her, staring
at the brilliant vision.
She, grieved that she could see
no form, gently withdrew
her bangled arms.

Though he had held the dark-eyed woman
in his arms, he had let her go,
for to him she was illusion.
Now sorrow tortured him
like a man who has found great wealth
only to lose it.

Nala's first thought is that a totally real, concrete garland has been given to him by a woman who, he is quite sure, is an illusion. Note that he knows very well that his mind has gone wild, that he is seeing things under the pressure of impossible desire (doubly impossible now—for not only is Damayantī not with him, but he is also committed to persuading her to marry one of the gods instead of himself). Damayantī, like Nala, is perfectly aware that her mind is generating images of her absent beloved; what she can't understand is how the garland she cast on one of these images could suddenly disappear into thin air. For our purposes, the key point is that both lovers seem to think of their own minds as bounded, individualized entities that naturally, in certain circumstances, will give birth to illusions. Moreover, these illusions can, in theory, be distinguished from non-illusory reality. The ability to know that you are hallucinating, however compelling the delusion might seem, implies a theory of mind or consciousness as in some sense integrated, active, and whole.

But now comes a further surprise. Nala happily *(uvantu)* embraces the *uruvěli* delusion. Why not? He thinks he knows what he is doing. He also has a specific, possibly rather positive relation to his apparently self-generated, interior image of his beloved. (We might keep in mind that this inner image was originally nurtured and made concrete by the friendly imagination of the goose.) He thus thinks he is embracing an internal, imaginary person, in effect a part of himself, which he has projected outside. Damayantī has her own parallel or complementary conclusion. She, too, embraces the image. But the poet's phrasing is ambiguous. She thinks "that was as it was," *aṉṉavāṟ' ĕṇṇi.* This could mean that she simply reproduces, on her own terms, the chain of thought that Nala has just produced. But our 19th century commentator thinks otherwise: *tamayantiy āṉavaḷ naḷaṉ uṇmaiy ĕṉṟ' uṉṉi pulliṉāḷ ĕṉṟuṅ kŏḷka,* "Thinking that [this] Nala was real, Damayantī embraced him." I think this way of reading the verse is persuasive and very much in line with the whole tenor of the passage and with the *Naiṭatam*'s implicit meta-psychology. Damayantī cannot see Nala with her eyes, though he is right beside her; but she sees the inner image with so overpowering an intensity that she trusts it more than she trusts her own eyes. All this fits well with the verse we just read about the vivifying power of the imagination, especially an interactive imagination, and its superiority over purely physical perception.

Put more generally, these verses allow us to trace a continuum that stretches from actual external perception via the mental act of the imagination to abnormal states of possession, hallucination, and delusion, with various gradations along the way. All these states are internal to the mind, which has both an inside and an outside. A strong notion of hierarchized levels of knowledge accompanies this discovery. There are things that we know, there are things that we think we know (but may not be sure), and there are things that we know we know. Sometimes we also know without knowing that we know. Look at the final verse in this short section. Nala is still convinced that he is embracing an illusion (this despite the indescribable ecstasy welling up), so he lets her go and is at once overcome by sadness, "like a man who has found great wealth only to lose it." On some level, he knows he has lost something real. This last verse, incidentally, is an innovation of Ativīrarāma's vis-à-vis the Śrīharṣa original. A rather modern-sounding irony infuses the sad statement of our poet.

We thus have an interesting symmetrical (complementary) inversion. Nala sees the real Damayantī but thinks she is unreal. She sees empty space before her, filled with what she knows to be her own mental image, and thinks the latter is real. Note the language of "real" versus "unreal," in contrast with "true" and "untrue." *Uṇmai* can have either meaning. For reasons I can't elaborate here, I would want to argue that the contextual distinction between these two registers is a diagnostic feature of the late-medieval or early-modern discussions of the mind in south India. Within the ongoing debate about the mind and its powers, the reality (and not merely the truth) of the imagination as an active, creative, and ultimately very personal force with effects outside itself is a major theme. I tried earlier to say something about the objective status of an imagined subject and the metaphysics of breath and deep innerness that explain it.

Nala lets go of the real Damayantī but goes on staring at her *pŏlivu*—the radiant vision that he thinks has been produced by his mind. We, on the other hand, outside the text, know the *pŏlivu* to belong to the real person. In terms of a more general theory of the imagination, we are very close at this point to a notion of "real" (that is, existentially demanding) fiction. Such a notion depends upon gradations of knowledge and their distribution over the standard set of poet, characters, and readers. In the new epistemic regime, we, the readers, generally have privileged access to a wider kind of knowing than that available to the characters and even, in some cases, to the poet, who is often lost in his own fictions. This differentiation in modes of awareness seems to be intrinsic to the notion of a relatively unified person as well.

If there were time, I would want to show you how Ativīrarāman has transformed this passage as a whole. To put the matter very simply: where Śrīharna offers us a subtle psychology predicated on the notion that for a meaningful embrace to take place between two lovers, their two mental illusions of one another must also (first) embrace,[10] Ativīrarāman takes us in the direction of two well-defined, autonomous individuals, each with his or her own perspectives built into their perceptions, who complement one another in both the images and the ideas they project outward into space. As I have said, this external space is only too happy to confirm the projection. For our part, we, the readers or listeners, know perfectly well that the embrace is entirely real. We know it through the intimate words of the poet, as if whispered in our ears.

I want to look at one last example, which happens to be taken from an introductory section of the *Naiṭatam*—it is the first verse of the *Nakarappaṭalam* (though part of this verse recurs, to interesting effect, in 4.8). As is well known, these opening verses of a *mahākāvya* are thought to encapsulate major thematic or conceptual concerns that will emerge later in the text. A whole anthropology is implicit in this complex, overdetermined, captivating poem:

kuṭa vaḷaik kulam vayiṟ' uḷaint' iṉa maṇi kŏḻikkum
maṭuvil vāṉakar uruvu kāṭṭiyatu poṉ matil cūḻ
kaṭi kŏṇ mānakar an niḻal katuviṭāt' akaṉṟa
puṭai kŏ' ṇīr nakar uṭutt' alai pŏṅku per akaḻi (2.1)

In a pool teeming with pearls
spilled in pain from the wombs of conch
swollen as pots, you can see
the great city circled by walls,
a perfect image of the Heavenly City.
And the water that is not swallowed up
by that image is the moat,
ruffled by waves, that surrounds
that city.

The "great city" is Māvintanakaram, Nala's city, probably something like Tenkasi.

Outside the walls there is a pool *(maṭu)* that catches the reflection of the whole city, which thus looks to the beholder like the true form *(uruvu)* of Amarāvatī, the city of the gods, brought down to earth. But this reflection takes up only part of the expanse of the pool. The left-over watery surface is just that—a liquid, shimmering mass. Or is it? Maybe it, too, reflects something, for example the moat surrounding Māvintanakaram, in which case we have water revealing water: the same eye that takes note of the moat circling the city, outside, sees this same liquid expanse in the peripheral part of the pond, the part not occupied with the city's reflection. Another possibility, the first that comes to the commentator's mind, is that the Heavenly City, Amarāvatī, must have a moat around it, too, and that it is that celestial body of water that is, as it were, visible in the pond's periphery. In this case, since the core image is, after all, that of Nala's mundane city + moat, we would have water (of the pond) reflecting water (of that city's moat) that is as if reflecting yet more water (of the moat in heaven)—a triple vision that includes a double superimposition. A vertical axis, imaginative and figural (Amarāvatī descends to earth in the pool), transects the horizontal axis of immediate, physical reflection (Māvintanakaram in the same pool). In a way, this vertical axis displaces the horizontal one.

The *Naiṣadhīya* is, famously, a book of reflections and shadow images *(chāyā)*; Nala himself is a kind of mirror-image, perhaps of the god of love, Manmatha (among others), and we all remember that four mirror-images of Nala turn up at the critical moment of the *svayaṃvara.*[11] We might think of the entire text as an extended meditation on the metaphysics of mirrors. Something of this fascination with reflected images carries over into Ativīrarāma's text.[12] Yet it seems that we are being offered a new theory of reflections, one strongly linked to the Tenkasi epistemic world of which I've been speaking. What can we extrapolate from the way this verse formulates the dynamics of mirrors?

Caravanappĕrumāḷaiyar aptly tells us that mirror surface and reflection are mutually exclusive. When you look at your face in the mirror, the image takes up a certain space; beyond or around that space, you see the mirror itself. Similarly, when you look in the pond at Māvintanakar, you see a reflection—identified by an imaginative leap *(utprekṣā)* with Amarāvatī—and all around it, the reflecting surface itself. On the other hand, this reflecting surface, as we have just seen, may itself be multi-layered, a palimpsest of limpid and largely coincident images. There is a certain thickness or depth to the mirror. The one-to-one reflection that we see on the surface may, in fact, be the most superficial perception of all. Better to look deep inside. What is more, that surface reflection somewhat aggressively swallows up or seizes *(katuvu)*[13] much of the available space. In a way, one might prefer to look beyond, outside, the reflection; that part of the radiant surface that is not preyed upon by the image may actually be the more promising element, the richest in potential being and, for that matter, the more real. There is something irreducible about the watery remnant with its waves washing over the edges of the reflection.

Let's not forget that it is the mind that brings the Heavenly City into play. Some imaginative move, probably existing *a priori*, seizes upon the surface reflection and uses it to project the inner vision outward. A boundary has been crossed. Actually, what is physically perceived is the water of the pond and, in part, the reflection of the earthly city—that and the rest of the pond-mirror. How easy it is to forget that Amarāvatī is nowhere near. Once the imaginative projection has been articulated and externalized, it more or less takes over.

But we have failed to pay attention to the opening line of the poem. This pond is filled with pearls that are swept away by the waves, or cast on to the shore, or that somehow rise to the surface, or that can be sifted and examined and ultimately polished—all these are possible meanings for Tamil *kŏḻi*. You can take your pick. These pearls are all born from conches, one of the standard sources for pearls in Indian literature (along with the joints of the bamboo, the temples of elephants, etc.). The conch grows the pearl inside itself, just like any other pregnancy, and gives birth to it in pain. But we are talking about reflections and coming to the surface. It seems that the seemingly innocent metaphor is, as usual, deliberate and expressive. This is how mirrors give birth to reflections. The process may have rather little to do with the external object waiting to be reflected; indeed, this object is probably both secondary to and later than the germinating process inside the mirror. The reflection predates its object. The reflection is held, complete, inside before it emerges in pain.

I want to suggest that this whole set of interlocking images, in their specific logical organization, shows us one possible picture of the *uḷḷam*, that inner space that more and more coincides with the mind and that is, in 16th century Tenkasi, the true site of the imagination. By implication, a verse like this also speaks to the analytical profile of the person in his or her more creative aspect. The *uḷḷam* is primarily a domain of limpid depth. It can, of course, be churned up by various internal, endogenic forces such as thought and desire. It generates pearl-like images that may come to the surface and even take over that surface. Imagination drives this unending process. "Reflections"—that is, imaginative projections, rich in existential potential—are conceived, held, and nurtured inside. Giving birth to them exacts a cost. They never exhaust the rich resources of the depth. Moreover, the pool—that is, the depth of *uḷḷam*—is not passive. It can also *not reflect*. That is the degree of real autonomy for any person. External reflections may enter into this deep reservoir, may even swallow up a portion of its surface; such reflections come in with the breath and are then breathed out. Or the pool may swallow them and make them disappear. In any case, the pool never gives itself over completely to its reflections. Something here speaks to the capacity of the human being to create worlds inside himself or herself without exhausting the left-over potential of non-reflective being, and also to breathe these worlds out into an elastic cosmos, which may then reflect them back inside.

The generative *uḷḷam* we are observing is at once bounded, or autonomous, and infinitely creative. You will by now not be surprised to hear that, in my understanding, the "pearl-like" reflections in the pool are always singular and tend also to be highly individual. The notion of singularity should include possible shifts in the terms of their internal composition, that is, in the relations among their component parts or among further, perhaps superimposed or interlocking reflections. Indeed, the *uḷḷam* is often preoccupied precisely with mapping out these relations, which may underlie experiences such as falling in love or choosing the right word or trying to decide what is real. Each reflection, whether internally generated from the depths of the reservoir or originating outside, involutes differently. Once alive in the mind, these reflections for the most part no longer actually reflect anything; nor do they represent. They are, however, the stuff of what we see.

Conclusion

In the old days, the *uyir* was almost enough, the essential core of the personality. Life, in the *uyir*-based model, is a struggle between processes of hardening, encrusting, or crystallizing into form and countervailing processes of melting down, softening, mixing, loving, understanding. As I have already said, this struggle comes down to a question of differential levels of "aliveness." The Śaiva Siddhânta formalizes the same tension in patterns driven by epistemic concerns—what we might call issues of self-awareness, first and foremost, but also the corresponding linguistic acts that move the *uyir* along either of the two vectors, for example by using the words "yes" or (preferably) "no."

A more complex paradigm of innerness emerges from Tamil *bhakti* literature. Here the elements comprising the inner person tend to be at war with one another. Māṇikkavācakar defines the word "I" *(nāṉ)* as *irumpiṉ pāvai*, an iron doll; he thinks of his *něñcam* as a corpse *(piṇam)*.[14] What part of him is truly alive? The *uyir*, once again. But this *uyir* may have rather little of the empirical personality attached to it. The latter has, in the best scenario, melted down, thereby allowing contact with god. Moreover, the warring parts of the inner person are rather loosely integrated in these poems. Personhood rests, in a way, on experiences of being overpowered *(āṭkŏḷḷutal)*, on the one hand, or of agonizing in a rich and nuanced series of emotional states, with their precise linguistic counterparts, on the other. Tamil, like Greek, has a remarkable semantic profusion when it comes to states of mental suffering.

By the mid-16th century, a new paradigm has emerged. The old terms are still very much in use, but they now mean something quite different. I have concentrated tonight on the *uḷḷam*, but we would find in the *Naiṭatam* no less interesting new usages of *maṉam, uṇarvu, aṉpu, pāvaṉai*, and so on. A meta-psychology, implicit in everything that the characters say to one another and to themselves, presupposes a relatively self-aware, quite singular individual who knows his or her mind as a unitary entity capable of generating from within a striking range of images—from straightforward (devalued) seeing that is outwardly directed to a hypertrophied imaginative vision that may spill over into hallucination and compelling fantasies. This individual is also given to self-doubt, irony, and rapid shifts of mood. I have argued that the imagination serves as the primary index of this re-organized person, as his or her defining feature, and that this imaginative faculty is understood as active, creative, heavily inter-subjective, and probably superior, in more ways than one, to external perception. It is also linked to fresh discussions of the question of what is real and, in the context of this question, to a strong notion of fiction. Such a person inhabits a cosmos far more complex than anything that came before. It is a cosmos that is more specifically infinite in range because of the singular imaginations at work upon and within it. The Tamil cosmos was probably always a domain of vast potentiality and endless configurations, but as such it was also relatively undifferentiated; whereas now it is permeated by all these singularities, each creating its own versions of itself that it breathes out into the world. These versions also interact with each other, enabling imaginative process in the other, generating novelty in the other. It is no wonder that, faced with this explosion of difference, the Tamil poets and poeticians are now fascinated by the question of what is or is not real.

I wouldn't hesitate to characterize the complex Tenkasi person who emerges at this time by a word like "modern." To understand this person more fully, however, we have to look beyond Tenkasi to contemporaneous developments in Kerala and in Telugu literary production, since both these cultural worlds impinged on the southern Tamil country in important ways. Indeed, there is surely something wrong about limiting the discussion to the area bounded by Tamil speech; Tamil, Telugu, Malayalam, Kannada, south Indian Sanskrit—by this period, all these belong to a single culture of many local variants. So perhaps my point of departure was also wrong. Still, I would want to check our conclusions against Tamil texts like Muttutāṇṭavar's *padams* and Tāyumāṉavar's passionate poems. So far, we have made only a small beginning.

NOTES

1. E Valentine Daniels. 1984. *Fluid Signs: Being a Person the Tamil Way.* Berkeley: University of California Press.

2. Ativirarama Pantiyan. 1962. *Naitatam.* Madras: South India Saiva Siddhanta Works Publishing Society.

1986. *Naisadhiya-carita of Sriharsa.* With commentary of Narayana. Delhi: Meharchand Lachhmandas.

3. See Trawick, Margaret (1990). *Notes on Love in a Tamil Family.* Berkeley: University of California Press. 133–134, 273–274; examples in *The Wisdom of Poets. Studies in Tamil, Telugu, and Sanskrit* by D Shulman. 2001. New Delhi: Oxford University Press. 302–307.

4. See *Naiṭatam* 11.29, 31.

5. For *uḷḷam* in this or some closely related sense, see e.g. 4.79; 11.8, 16, 18, 19, 32.

6. Shulman, D (2001): 131–158. See note 1 above.

7. Shulman, D. 2008. "Nala Unhinged" In *Damayanti and Nala: The Many Lives of a Story*, edited by Susan Wadley. New Delhi: Chronicle Books.

8. Cf. *Maṇimekalai* 27.9.

9. I want to thank Don Handelman for extensive discussion of these points.

10. Look at *Naiṣadhīya* 6.51:

> *anyonyam anyatravad īkṣamāṇau parasparenâdhyuṣite 'pi deśe/*
> *āliṅgitâlīka-parasparântas tathyaṃ mithas tau pariṣasvajāte//*
> They kept seeing one another / as if they were elsewhere, / though together they occupied one / shared space. / And while their two fantasies, / false, mutual, and internal, / gripped one another, / these two people / truly embraced.

11. See Malamoud, Charles. "Shadows in the *Naiṣadhacarita*." In press; Dayan, Maya Tevet. 2008. "The Unseen Man Who Saw Himself in Mirrors: Metaphysics of Reflections in the *Naiṣadhīyacarita*." In *Karmic Passages: Israeli Scholars on India,* edited by Shalva Weil and David Shulman. New Delhi: Oxford University Press.

12. *E.g.* 3.15.

13. *Katuvu* also means "to reflect."

14. *Tiruvācakam* 5.22,32.

Shulman, D (1995). "Hipus hasubyekt bashira hametafizit hahodit." Israel Academy of Sciences and Humanities, *Igeret* 13.

Gender, Language and the Quest for a Tamil Identity: A Study of the Politics and Persona of Neelambikai Ammaiyar

VIJAYA RAMASWAMY

The politics and persona of Neelambikai Ammaiyar can be seen as the site of an encounter between emerging personhood, resurgent Tamil identity as well as women's agency in society and politics. The inherent tensions in negotiating one's identity as a woman and one's understanding of personhood with one's identity as a Tamil is compounded by the larger picture of the nationalist struggle. The Tamil quest for identity and self-expression vis-à-vis the English colonial masters as well as the Sanskritic/Hindi domination implicit in the Congress ideology was met primarily by the *tani thamizh iyakkam*. In the case of Neelambikai the site of emotion, cultural identity and conflict, is clearly perceived as that of the body and emotions of Neelmbikai located primarily within the ambience of the *tani thamizh iyakkam* of which she was the co-founder.

The nomenclature '*tani thamizh iyakkam*' can be translated literally as 'separate Tamil movement'. The *tani thamizh iyakkam* was marked chiefly by emotional in fact passionate worship of Tamil personified in the 'Tamil Tai' (literally Tamil Mother). In fact the term *tani thamizh iyakkam* can be defined as the Tamil ethno-nationalist movement which did not merely claim separateness from the 'mainstream' Congress-led nationalist struggle but in fact moved parallel to it and represented 'a counter culture'. It can be perceived as the beginnings of Tamil personhood which has persistently struggled against the domination of the centre in terms of Congress ideology, linguistic chauvinism of the Hindi belt and unequal resource allocation.

Tani thamizh iyakkam represented not only the major strand in the transitional years in Madras politics but emerged as the most important postcolonial discourse in Tamil Nadu. It foregrounded the Dravida Munnetra Kazhagam and the Anna Dravida Munnetra Kazhagam as well as the intensifying anti-Hindi, anti-Brahmin agitations that persist to this day. In a sense then, the sense of personhood of the Tamils during the transitional years between colonialism and postcolonialism in Tamil Nadu was dominated by this movement which perceived northern domination and the use of Hindi as internal colonialism and juxtaposed Tamil language and Tamil cultural identity against it as much as against British colonial colonialism.

Gender-related issues and women's participation/non-participation in the political movements within the region had formed a major plank of all political and social agencies. This was as true of the Theosophical Movement in the later part of the nineteenth century as it was of the Congress and non-cooperation or the Justice Party and the Self-Respect Movement. Gender politics within Tamilaham presented a fragmented picture. Some Tamil women took recourse to what they considered the progressive potential within Westernization and avidly read 'progressive' writers of the West and expressed their views in English. Operating primarily though not entirely, within the Theosophical Movement, these women rejected the British colonial rule at one level but at another level sincerely believed that British liberal ideas were crucial for India's progress in general and Indian women's emancipation in particular.

In the case of Tamil women, the quest for personhood and identity was complicated by the mediation of patriarchy in the overall discourse of culture and identity. Those Tamil women who wrote and perhaps thought in Tamil came largely under the influence of the Justice Party and the Self-Respect Movement.[1] These women eventually came under the influence of the *tani thamizh iyakkam*. A strong nexus thus became established between anti-Brahmanism and women's issues. And yet these women were themselves the products of a patriarchal society and hence unable to articulate entirely in the voice of women. The resultant tensions get reflected in a peculiar situation, where they constantly express their anguish over women's miseries, arising out of a patriarchal order such as destitution, widowhood, illiteracy and so on. Yet they continue to sing the paeans of wifely devotion and modesty and chastity in women. Thus they seek imaginary solutions for gender inequality, rather than locating the cause in the social structure itself. A close look at gender politics and literature at the moment of 'transition' would then seem to suggest that the problem with Tamil society in general and Tamil women in particular was not so much 'cultural amnesia' as cultural schizophrenia.[2]

This study attempts to situate intellectually alive and politically active women who seem to have stood at cultural cross-roads in the decades preceding independence. The life of Neelambikai Ammaiyar, one of the more enigmatic figures of those times is used as the template for such a study. I have explored the writings of Neelambikai Ammaiyar, her politics and persona as the site of such a cultural cross-roads of personhood, identity and women's agency.

This essay is at one level, an attempt to deconstruct the life of Neelambikai Ammaiyar from a hagiographic text, that of Tirunavukkarasu. At another level it seeks to situate the subject within the problematic of her times through the medium of her political and social commitments as seen through the quasi-biographical text by Sarada Nambi Arooran titled *Neelambikai Ammaiyarin Samuga Chintanaigal*.[3]

Lastly, the gender concerns of Neelambikai Ammaiyar's generation and her own personal predicaments have been explored through her subjectivity revealed in her prolific biographies of women.

Neelambikai Ammaiyar was born at Nagapattinam on 6 August 1903 to Vedachalam Pillai (Maraimalai Adigal) and Saundaravalli Ammaiyar. She was named Neelambikai after the presiding deity of the temple known as Neelayathatchi. The emotional fragmentation she would undergo throughout her life was reflected in the first days of her birth. After naming her 'Neelambikai' her father, the co-founder and great votary of the *tani thamizh iyakkam,* tried his best to Tamilize her name as 'Karuppamma' but to no avail. Neela whom her brother fondly calls 'The Mother of *tani thamizh iyakkam*' in his biography of her,[4] was caught in the trap of nomenclature and despite her loyalty to Tamil, would respond only to 'Neela' and not 'Karuppamma'. In an interview with Mangaiyarkkarasiyar, the sister-in-law of Neelambikai Ammaiyar, (9 December 2002), I was told that the change of name officially never occurred in the case of Neelambikai although her father had made a successful transition from Vedachalam to Maraimalai.

Neelambikai Ammaiyar's writings and political opinions have survived the cruel silencing of women's voices which has largely been their fate in history, thanks ironically and perhaps inevitably to three men—Maraimalai Adigal her father who enabled her to publish '*Tani Tamizh Katturaigal*' her first collection of articles in 1926, Tiruvaranga Pillai her husband who published the rest of her prolific writings (amounting to thirteen books) and Tirunavukkarasu her brother who became her biographer. This short biography published in 1946 is no more than a hundred odd pages in sharp contrast to Tirunavakkarasu's biography of his father which runs into 877 pages! His work published in 1945, the year she died, is hagiographic in nature and in fact prefixed by adulatory condolence messages. The brief profile hides much more than it reveals although the personal and political predicament of Neelambikai Ammaiyar is present as a palimpsest throughout the text. Sarada Nambiarooran, who obtained her M.Phil degree from Bharatidasan University working on Neelambikai Ammaiyar, restored this gender imbalance by publishing her partial biography in 1990. Obviously, however, a thesis devolving around the ideas of Neelambikai cannot become a substitute for a full-fledged biography.

Neelambikai Ammaiyar's difficult times and more difficult choices are therefore best recovered from her own biographies of both Western and Tamil women, both the choice of subject and the framing of each facet of the biography in terms of her own experience as a woman and a political thinker. These writings are to be seen in conjunction with the sub-text of Tirunavukkarasu's narrative. Tirunavukkarasu's biography of his sister Neelambikai Ammaiyar as well as her own self-reflexive writings, provides the most perceptible site of the inter-play of conflicting emotions and fragmented identities that characterized her personality.

To be a Woman and a Tamil at the Turn of the Century: Neela's Early Years

Neelambikai had an excellent education at home necessitated by her withdrawal from school due to ill health. She was grounded almost equally well in English and in Hindi as she was in Tamil. She was an avid reader of Shakespeare and the poems of Tennyson and Wordsworth. Her interest in the Hindi languages leaned largely towards devotional literature and the songs of Kabir, Meera and others, which she sang before appreciative Tamil audiences.

In many of her attitudes, opinions and anxieties regarding women, her writings partially conflate the literary and social self-expression of Subbalakshmi Akka and Panditai Krishnaveni Ammaiyar both of whom guided her education through school. In fact, Neelambikai stayed in the women's hostel and later in the widows' home run by them and studied in the girl's school which they had established. Her almost fanatical devotion to Tamil language and literature, and correspondingly her animosity towards Hindi and English, both of which represented alien domination to her, was undoubtedly influenced by these two women, although Neelambikai in her quest for Tamil purity went even further.

Neelambikai's sound knowledge of English accounts for her many translations from English to Tamil. As early as 1937, she compiled a Hindi-Tamil dictionary in which more than 7000 technical terms in Sanskrit/Hindi were provided with a Tamil equivalent. She undertook a difficult exercise—the publication in 1931 of *Six Hundred Parallel Proverbs in Tamil and English*—to show that the English language did not have anything more to offer than the Tamil language in terms of the richness of its vocabulary, its idioms or its literary traditions.

The inter-textual influences clearly perceptible in the writings of Neelambikai draw their sustenance from such diverse sources as the writings of Harriet Beecher Stowe in the United States and Harriet Martineau in England (who is credited with having authored as many as 1624 essays!); the Tamil devotional traditions of the Tevaram, Tiruvachagam and the spiritual writings of Ramalinga Adigal; the political and social treatises of EV Ramaswami Naicker and the training in Tamil language and tradition provided by her father Maraimalai Adigal.

Passages in Tirunavukkarasu's biography about Neelambikai's early training in Tamil texts by her father are both moving and revealing. There were no fixed hours of study and the days Neela cooked his favourite dishes well, (including '*milaku rasam*'), she would be taught a few lessons from Tamil classics like *Silappadikaram, Purananuru, Nannul, Villiputhurar Bharatam* and the like. This too, only after her enthusiasm had dissolved into tears. The biographer's chapter on Neela's education is aptly titled 'Father's Mischief and Daughter's Sorrow' (p.8–11). Learning against such odds Neelambikai Ammaiyar delivered her first public lecture in 1916 when she was thirteen on the theme of 'Parental Duties'. The script was the father's. Emotional rupture between father and daughter occurred when, not content with scripting her early lectures, Maraimalai Adigal sought to script her personal life as well.

Cultural Loyalty and Assertion of Linguistic Identity

The strong anti-Hindi, Tamil chauvinist tone of Neelambikai's essays shows the influence of women such as Ambujammal, Krishnaveni Ammaiyar and Akka Subbalakshmi as also the conflation of ideas drawn from Maraimalai Adigal and Periyar. Neelambikai's anti-Sanskrit/Hindi and pro-Tamil/Dravidian essays earned her the honorific *Tani Tamizh Tiruvatti.* Her essays reflect her antagonism not only towards Sanskrit or Hindi as a language, but also to the entire processes of Sanskritization and Brahmanization which she looks upon as the cause of Tamil decadence. Making the point that intrusion of an alien language is inextricably linked with cultural invasion, Neelambikai shows that while the texts of the 'Second Sangam' such as *Tolkappiyam, Kalithogai* or *Ahananuru* and *Purananuru* contain a miniscule percentage of Sanskritic terms, the texts of the later Sangam period like the entire *Kizhkanakku* literature contain Sanskrit words in abundance. *('Tani Tamizh Padukappu'* in *'Tani Tamizh Katturaigal'* pp. 46–47 ff).

The repeated emphasis of Neelambikai and others involved in the *Tani Tamizh Iyakkam* on the *Tolkappiyam* and other indigenous texts is to be explained by the fact that Tamil has always had its own tradition of poetics. For example, the use of *aham* (the interior) and *puram* (the exterior) as the primary literary modes and the systematic use of poetic themes or moods in consonance with the five *tinais* (eco-zones) enumerated in the *Tolkappiyam* and elsewhere are strongly rooted in the Tamil *bhasha* tradition.

Neelambikai gives a number of examples such as *bhasha, brahmanar, jati, raja, manithar* and so on to show how Sanskritic terms and Sanskritic notions have intruded into the Tamil language. She adds that Brahmins began to define Sanskrit as *'girvani'* and *'deva vani'*, to reflect the cultural superiority of Brahmins ('Tani Tamizh Padukappu' literally 'protection to pure Tamil' in *Tani Tamizh Katturaigal* – pp.50–54: 1925). If one were to logically extend Neelambikai's argument in feminist terms, the beginnings of patriarchal notions like the purity–pollution polarities, women as ensnarements and the virtues of female chastity *(karpu)* are found in abundance in the *Kural* and *Naladiyar.* Both belong to the late Sangam period when Brahmanical-Sanskritic influence was contending for social space with the indigenous Tamil culture. In contrast, the literature of the early Sangam age which has a sizeable contribution by women coming from diverse social backgrounds (Auvaiyar [Panar minstrel caste], Kakkai Patiniyar, Ilaiveniyar, Venni Kuyattiyar [potter caste], etc.) reflects the values of a matrilocal society ('Kalviyum Taimarum' [Literacy and Women] and 'Ozhungana Kalvi' [Right Education] in *Tani Tamizh Katturaigal:* 1925: pp.1–12).

It is obvious that Neelambikai herself was the product of a cultural pastiche. She had a deep knowledge and admiration of both English and Hindi literature and yet her ideological/political commitments enjoined upon her the condemnation of both. This results in what can best be described as cultural schizophrenia.[5] Interestingly, the same cultural tension is to be perceived in her father Maraimalai Adigal. He was an avid reader of the English Classics and corresponded with GU Pope who has been responsible for some of the finest translations of Hindu religious texts including the *Tiruvachagam.* Tirunavukkarasu in his biography of Neelambikai comments that Adigal looking upon the face of his infant daughter would say, 'Neela's face has the brilliance of geniuses like Shelley and Shakespeare' (Tirunavukkarasu: Neelambikai:1945). It is also noteworthy that the co-founder of *Tani Tamizh Iyakkam* translated Kalidasa's Sanskrit play *Shakuntalam* into Tamil! The tricky problem of cultural negotiation between an admiration for English as the signifier of Western rationality and of Sanskrit as the language of Indian classical tradition on the one hand and the location of one's own Tamil identity in one's Dravidian roots on the other, gets carried into the persona of Neelambikai. Her own upbringing in a culture that was more pastiche than pure makes her a prime example of cultural fragmentation and cultural negotiations.

As early as 1937, Neelambikai compiled a Hindi-Tamil dictionary in which more than 7000 technical terms in Sanskrit/Hindi were provided with a Tamil equivalent. She undertook a somewhat similar exercise to show that the English language did not have anything more to offer than the Tamil language in terms of the richness of its vocabulary, its idioms or its literary traditions. Her long essay 'Tamizhil Vadamozhi Kalakkal Agathu' (Eschewing the Use of Northern Languages in Tamil) states her ambivalent situation:

> 'Is it better to use Tamil in its pristine pure form or to use the common parlance which is an admixture (of Sanskrit and Tamil) to create literary pieces? .... The water we drink contains germs which are **naturally** found but we **artificially filter it to remove these germs.** So the language we speak **which spontaneously acquires alien vocabulary (emphasis mine)** must be distilled to produce pure literary Tamil.[6]' (*Tani Tamizh Katturaigal:* p. 25. Translation mine)

She realizes that the Sanskritization of one's vocabulary and the Brahmanization of one's culture was the 'natural' result of the prolonged historical association between Tamil and Sanskrit, between the 'Adi Dravida' Tamils and the 'Aryanized' Tamil Brahmins. Although *this composite culture is reflected in her own thinking and writing,* she still attempts the painful transition to 'pure Tamil' in her politics, social philosophy and literary writings. The degree of pastiche can be seen in the fact that despite her fanatical zeal to purge Tamil of any Sanskritic traces, her own name, Neelambikai, continued to be palpably Sanskritic.

Condemning the metaphor used by some of her contemporaries of Tamil and

Sanskrit as constituting the eyes of the Tamil literary face, she feels that Brahmins have patronized and monopolized Sanskrit to their exclusive social advantage. Hence she further argues in her essay 'Tamizhnadum Tamizh Mozhiyum Munneruvathu Eppadi?' ('How can Tamil Nadu and Tamil Language Develop?'), that the emergence of a tradition that is a confluence of Sanskrit and Tamil would be detrimental not only to the cause of Tamil but to Tamilians.

Perhaps Neelambikai's major contribution to the enrichment of the Tamil language was her Hindi-Tamil Dictionary *(Vadatchol-Tamil Agara Varisai).* One of the verses lamenting the untimely death of Neelambikai says:

> Neelambikai,
> The one who sowed the seeds of pure Tamil
> in Tamil soil, harvesting good texts,
> through prolific use of Tamil
> subduing, crushing the pride of northern language . . .[7]

However, apart from her anti-Hindi tirade Neelambikai does not seem to have done any political writing. Surprisingly, she does not attack British imperialism with the same vigour with which she attacks 'Northern' domination.

Gendering Personhood, Tamil Identity and Social Concerns in Neelambikai

Neelambikai's writings that are concerned with women's issues are however quite prolific. She expresses her strong faith in education for women and states that women should aim at the level of erudition that someone like Auvaiyar possessed—a wisdom that enabled her to write normative texts for the broad guidance of Tamil society. Her essay on the process by which the land of the Tamils and the Tamil language could move forward[8] contains extensive passages on women's education where she lays stress on Tamil. She says that modern Tamil women should emulate the example of the Sangam poets such as Auvaiyar, Kakkai Pattiniyar, Ponmudiyar, Vellividiyar and others *(Tamizhnadum Tamizhmozhiyum Munneruvathu Eppadi:* 23). To quote Neelambikai:

> 'Our language is called Mother Tongue, our land is Mother Land,
> knowledge is [feminized] as Kalaimagal and wealth as "Tirumagal"'. (p.12)

Neelambikai emphasizes, in particular, the need to wean Tamil women away from western education and to familiarize them with women in spiritual literature.[24] This is the avowed purpose of her text *Muppenmanigal Varalaru.*

These sentiments are seminal to the emergence and gendering of Tamil nationalism. The iconic representation of Tamil as a woman was crucial to the whole issue of gender participation in the freedom struggle in Tamil Nadu. The feminizing of the language gave women an advantage over men in taking a lead role in the *Tani Tamizh Iyakkam.*[10] In fact it was in the 1940s, the years of transition from colonialism to freedom, that Neelambikai was conferred the title 'Tani Tamizh Tiruvatti'.

Neelambikai in her essays *(Tani Tamizh Katturaigal)* also opposes the re-marriage of widows over twenty, although she, like her father Maraimalai Adigal, does support the re-marriage of child widows. Condemning the practice so widely prevalent in the West, Neelambikai holds forth to her women readers the example of Harriet Martineau who never married on losing her fiancée but chose to devote herself to literature. Neelambikai advocates a similar career in education and authorship to young Indian widows.[11] However, she condemns the practice of Sati in unequivocal terms and in an essay titled 'Irandor Veetitrkku Chelbavarum Avveetinarum' in *Tani Tamizh Katturaigal* ('The Living in the House of Death and Their Visitors') she strongly attacks the attitude of a woman who sells all her resources to placate Brahmins and perform rituals in order to procure salvation for her husband and ends up destitute.

A major aspect of Neelambikai's life that is discussed by both Tirunavukkarasu as well as Sharada Nambi Arooran is her political activism in women's causes. She participated in virtually all the women's conferences held in Tamil Nadu, both before and after her marriage. In fact she founded the 'Saiva Madar Sangam' in 1942 in Palayankottai, Tirunelveli, which despite its religious garb actively engaged with women's issues, especially education and social reform. Her outstanding essay on 'How can Tamil Nadu and Tamil Language Develop' was originally a long speech delivered at the women's conference in 1938.

Emotion and Angst in Neelambikai—Humanitarian Concerns

While she uses the biographical mode as well as public speeches (printed subsequently as essays) to express her concern for the plight of Indian women as shown by her biographical sketches in *Menaattu Penmanigal* (Book I and II) as well as *Muppenmanigal Varalaru,* Neelambikai's broader concerns go beyond women's issues. Her anguish over child labour comes through in her biographies of Elizabeth Browning as well as Harriet Beecher Stowe. The issue of slavery, which Stowe tackles through factual reporting (as in her account of the Dred Scott case) as well as fiction *(Uncle Tom's Cabin)* not only receives a sympathetic handling in her biography by Neelambikai, but also finds an echo in her own writings in Tamil. In her strident anti-Aryan essay titled 'The Ancient inhabitants of Navalan Teevu' *('Navalanteevin Pazhaiya Kudigal',* in *Tani Tamizh Katturaigal:* pp. 79–86), she wonders what construes cultural superiority. What justified the Aryans stigmatizing Dravidians as dasyus' or the Brahmins denigrating the hunting, meat-eating tribals as barbarians? (pp.79–86).

Sarada Nambi Arooran effectively reconstructs the social persona of Neelambikai

Ammaiyar. Her text is a meticulous analysis of the various writings of Neelambikai Ammaiyar classified under such heads as 'Reflections on Language', 'Observations on the Feminine', 'Thoughts on Religion' and so on. There is also for the first time an attempt to place her within the historical canvas in the chapter on 'The Historical Times of Ammaiyar and the Beginnings of the *Tani Tamizh Iyakkam*'. Unlike the other histories of this movement which marginalize the role of Neelambikai she redresses the imbalance in her doctoral thesis on the *Tani Tamizh Iyakkam:* Emergence and Growth' published by the Chekkizhar Press, Chennai in 1994. However, Sarada Nambi Arooran's text fails to bring a critical perspective to this study of Neelambikai Ammaiyar and borders on the hagiographical. The main reason for this is that the text developed out of an M.Phil dissertation where biographical chiaroscuro has no place. As with the narrative of Tirunavukkarasu, the muffling of all personal nuances of Neelambikai's life is understandable in view of the proximity of both to the subject of their research. However, the author expressed the view (Interview with the author, 9 December 2002) that there must have been a lot of personal pain in Neelambikai's life. She made the interesting admission that perhaps she (that is Dr Nambi Arooran) had not been allowed to interact with Neelambikai's children (while researching on this book) because of the unpleasant truths that may come out.

Neelambikai's emotional identification with maternity on the one hand and her strong urge towards political activism on the other such as participation in long marches in women's anti-imperialist rallies, resulted in much physical suffering. Mangaiyarkarasiyar said (interview with the author, 9 December 2002) that when Neela went for the women's conference and subsequent anti-British, anti-Hindi demonstration in 1938, she was holding her four-month-old daughter in her arms.

Neelambikai herself found great emotional satisfaction in her 11 children and her biographer Tirunavukkarasu writes that her books were written while she was carrying one child and cradling another in her arms *(Neelambikai Ammaiyar:* 1945:39 to 42 Translation mine). The particular passage is worth quoting:

> 'Herewith an example of Ammaiyar's patience. One day Ammaiyar was researching material for her writing. Four or five (sic) came running towards her. One climbed on to her lap clamouring for milk; one asked to be fed rice; one complained that he (her brother) pulled her hair and one ran away with her pen; a lot of noise, shouting and crying. Marai Tirunavukkarasu [i.e. The biographer] came down the stairs on hearing the racket and asked in an angry tone, "what's all this going on here, sister?" She responded with a smile, "Aren't they charming? This is true happiness, the fruit of all my prayers."'

In a moving passage Tirunavukkarasu describes how Neelambikai in her advanced state of pregnancy completed one of her books and delivered her baby within a few days of it. When he advised her not to strain she is purported to have said, "who knows? I might deliver tomorrow and this book needs to be finished now"

(*Neelambikai Ammaiyar*:1945:78).

A strong autobiographical tone is perceptible in her life of Harriet Beecher Stowe. She admires the manner in which Stowe negotiated between her social concerns, her many political writings and the upbringing of six children. Her books were written after her children went to sleep. Neelambikai paraphrases Stowe as writing to her husband:

> 'You want me to be a successful writer. Will I be able to do so with small children to look after *and no room of my own?*'
> (Harriet Beecher Stowe Ammaiyar in Mennattu Penmanigal: 82)

In concluding the life of Harriet Beecher Stowe Ammaiyar, Neelambikai writes that her book *Uncle Tom's Cabin* and her many writings (including the celebrated Dred Scott case) on the horrors of enslaving mothers by forcibly separating them from their infants transformed public opinion in America. The very first print of her book sold three thousand copies! Here was a shining ideal of a woman who was a loving wife and mother and a tireless campaigner against slavery. It would, perhaps, not be out of place to comment that during her 15 years of marriage Neelambikai conceived thirteen times. She took care of her home and children and wrote thirteen books.

Parting Ways—Political and Personal

Tani Tamizh Iyakkam started by Neelambikai Ammaiyar and her father Maraimalai Adigal became the signifier of Tamil identity. In it crystallized the Tamil quest for its own distinctive self-expression vis-à-vis the English speaking, westernized intellectuals and the Sanskrit/Hindi-oriented Congress followers. The *Tani Tamizh Iyakkam* did not merely claim separateness from the 'mainstream' Congress-led nationalist struggle but in fact moved parallel to it and represented 'a counter culture'. Its apparent manifestation was linguistic separatism or 'a movement towards purification of Tamil'. Its political and cultural dimensions take off from this crucial point of difference. The origin of this movement is romanticized by Tirunavukkarasu in his biographies of both Neelambikai Ammaiyar and Maraimalai Adigal. To quote him from his book 'Neelambikai Ammaiyar':

> 1916.
> Neelambikai may have been around thirteen years of age. One evening father and daughter were walking in the garden. Neela sang the song composed by Ramalinga Adigal which begins with the stanza:
> 'Even if the child forgets its mother or
> the mother the child born from her womb,
> Even if the life spirit forgets the body,
> Or the body its life force.....'
> The learned heart its learning

> The eyes forget to blink
> I will never forget Namashivaya
> Which shines forth in the hearts of sages.'
>
> Adigalar interrupted the singer to ask 'Neela, do you not think that this poem would sound so much better if the Sanskritic (vadachol) word deham was replaced by the Tamil word yakkai?'...At this juncture Neela said with spirit, 'let's from this moment give up the use of Sanskritic words and expunge them from our vocabulary. Let's learn to speak in pure Tamil. Her father immediately changed his Sanskritic name Swami Vedachalam *('Swami of the Unshakeable Mountain')* to the Tamil version Maraimalai Adigal.'
>
> (p.13 Translation mine)

The *Tani Tamizh Iyakkam* by its attack on Sanskrit/Hindi logically extended its struggle to encompass anti-Brahmanism in all its manifestations. It therefore became associated with the South Indian Liberation Front started in 1916 which then led on to the foundation of the Justice Party, the Dravida Kazhagam and so on. The Justice Party with its anti-Hindi anti-Brahmanical programme formed the government in Tamil Nadu after the 1920 elections. The Self-Respect Movement of EV Ramaswamy Naicker followed immediately after. Ironically both the words 'svaya' and 'mariyadai' meaning 'self' 'respect' are Sanskritic in origin! EV Ramaswami Naicker in spearheading a movement for the self-respect of those he called the indigenous Tamils discarded the negative description of them as non-Brahmins, a description which still moves within the Brahmins and the Other polarity and instead popularized the notion of 'Dravida'.

In attacking Brahmins he also attacked patriarchal institutions perceived as social representations of Brahmanism. It is noteworthy that it was at the First Tamil Women's Conference (Tamil Nattu Perumagalir Manadu) held on 13 November 1938 that its chairperson Neelambikai Ammaiyar conferred on EV Ramaswami Naicker the title of 'Periyar' in recognition of his support to women's causes. Both 'Viduthalai' and 'Kudiarasu', the journals run by Periyar carried fiery articles by him such as 'Why did Women Become Enslaved?'[12] He argued that it was the emergence of private property that led to a situation in which women themselves became property (Anandi:1991:25). He also condemned in print the despicable practice of old men marrying young girls. Yet Periyar's life itself seem to contradict these principles when he married Maniamma, a party worker young enough to be his daughter.

A short story by Neelambikai's contemporary Tamarai Kanni Ammaiyar was in fact an apocryphal representation of this incident (Lakshmi:1984:78). The disenchantment with Periyar led to women like Moovalur Ramamritham Ammaiyar who had been a staunch supporter breaking away.[13] Neelambikai Ammaiyar and the *Tani Tamizh Iyakkam* also parted ways with Periyar although neither biography written by Tirunavukkarasu, either that of Neelambikai Ammaiyar or of Maraimalai Adigal, goes into the cause of the rupture.[14] It is not unlikely that this as well as the larger issue of his distancing himself from gender issues especially the Devadasi bill influenced Neelambikai's disenchantment with the Periayar movement.

A major factor in the parting of ways was perhaps the avowed atheism of the Svaya Mariyadai Iyakkam in contrast to the strong religious foundations of the *Tani Tamizh Iyakkam.* Both Maraimalai Adigal and his daughter Neelambikai were steeped in Saiva Siddhanta philosophy as well as the devotional aspects of the Bhagavata movement such as the singing of Tevaram and Tiruvachagam hymns. The iconoclastic acts of the Periyar group such as garlanding the image of Ram with slippers must have offended the religious sensibilities of Neelambikai as well as her father. It is significant that out of the 15 essays in the '*Tani Tamizh Katturaigal*' not one is a direct attack on Brahmins although both Brahmanical rituals and Sanskritic textual traditions are under fire.

The hagiographical and utterly inadequate biography of Tirunavukkarasu leaves out both the celebration of EV Ramaswamy Naicker's movement by Neelambikai by conferring on him the title of 'Periyar' at the women's conference in 1938 and the break with his Svaya Mariyadai Iyakkam that followed soon after. What he does talk about at great length is her religiosity and her pilgrimages to renown Saivite shrines in Mylapur (the Kapaleesvara temple where her marriage took place in 1927) Tiruvanmaiyur, Trisulam, Tiruvorriyur, Tirukalahasti and Kanchipuram (pp.33–34; 48–50 etc.). Her differences with Periyar are in many ways obvious although unstated by the biographer.

The tension with Periyar is cradled within larger complexities in the relationship between movements such as the Svaya Mariyadai Iyakkam and the Dravidian movement and Tamil women such as Neelambikai, trapped between the public and the private domain. Women within the *Tani Tamizh Iyakkam* had a predominant concern with Tamil identity and Dravidian renaissance. The spin off from these primary concerns was the rejection of Brahmanical/Sanskritic patriarchy. At the same time they faced the immediate problem of negotiating between political and social activism on the one hand and their own location and role as mothers/wives/daughters-in-law within Tamil patriarchal society. The idea of wholly 'liberated' Tamil women therefore becomes an oxymoron for Neelambikai as well as for many of her contemporaries given their own placement within the patriarchal structure.

This social predicament formed the unfortunate basis for the parting of ways between Neelambikai and her father Maraimalai Adigal. The early chapters of her biography written by her brother Tirunavukkarasu, glorify the father–daughter relationship. It says that she met and fell in love with V Tiruvarangam Pillai (referred to as 'Aranganar') in 1918 with the blessings of her father who hailed him as "the sixty fourth Adiyar" (p.11 of the biography. The reference is to the 63 Saivite Nayanar). However, the professional relationship between the two men soured over the publication of some of Adigal's articles on *Tiruvachagam* by Aranganar's publishing firm. Maraimalai Adigal forbade their marriage and Aranganar went away to Tirunelveli where he started the 'Saiva Siddhanta Kazhagam' in 1920 which continues to be one of the oldest and most respectable publishing firms in Tamil Nadu.

For nearly ten years Neelambi Ammaiyar was not allowed to meet her fiancé. It was however during these years that her father encouraged her to write articles in Tani Tamizh which were published in various journals such as *Dravidan, Deshabhimani, Anandabodhini, Ottrumai* and *Tamilnad.* These were eventually published in 1925 as *Tani Tamizh Katturaigal* in 1925. The biographer says that she spent the nine years between 1918 and 1927 in teaching in various schools, writings and going on pilgrimages. It was also during these years that she developed chronic asthma, which today is seen as a psychosomatic illness and may have been occasioned by her personal frustrations. In the teeth of Maraimalai Adigal's opposition she and Aranganar got married in 1927 in the Mylapur Kapaleesvaram temple. The biographer writes that the marriage had the blessings of her father (p.37). Thiru Muthukumaraswami, the son-in-law of Subbaiyya Pillai contradicted this in an interview (Interview with the author, 9 December 2002), categorically stating that Maraimalai Adigal refused to even attend her wedding despite being in the same town and that it was K Subhramanya Pillai who blessed her marriage. After marriage Neelambikai moved with her husband to Tirunelveli and it was the Saiva Siddhanta Kazhagam started by her husband which published 12 of her books.

Neelambikai lived another 18 years after her marriage. The biography says nothing of the relationship between the co-founders of the *Tani Tamizh Iyakkam,* post Neelambikai's marriage. It was Neelambikai's sister-in-law Mangaiyarkarasiyar who at 86 recalled that father and daughter never met after her marriage. Her mother seems to have seen her twice (Interview with the author 9 December 2002). The startling truth is present as a sub-text in an appendix to the biography of Tiruvarangam Pillai by Pulavar R Ilankumaran *(Kazhaga Amaichar Tiruvaranganar varalaru* published by the *Saiva Siddhanta Kazhagam,* 1982). The appendix is a five line condolence letter written by Maraimalai Adigal in 1945 to his son Tirunavukkarasu, Neelambikai's brother and biographer. Formal in tone, it acknowledges the receipt of the letter informing him of your sister Neelambal's death'. It is clear that he had not visited her at her bedside during her prolonged illness. Nor does the letter even acknowledge Neelambikai as his daughter (p.121 of Aranganar's biography). It is amazing that Tirunavukkarasu's biography which lauds the support the father extended to his daughter (pp.55–56 ff) nowhere mentions this surgical break between the two!

Negotiating Multiple Identities

To conclude, Neelambikai Ammaiyar's life and times which comes through diverse discourses, the writings of others as well as her own highly subjective biographies, is a textured one. Her life provides us with a rich historical tapestry of multiple identities, emotional tensions and cultural negotiations. The *Tani Tamizh Iyakkam* which foregrounds the life of Neelambikai reflects the deep-seated anxiety of the Tamils to re-assert their identity in their life and in their writings in the wake of onslaughts on their culture both from English colonialism from outside and Hindi domination from within. In her persona, writings and politics Neelambikai becomes the cultural site of fragmented identities and emotional negotiations, representing in a microcosm the larger predicament of Tamil women in those historic years of transition.

Neelambikai as a product of cultural pastiche, appears to be the site of ambivalences and paradoxes both at the personal and at the political level. Yet she had clearly generated a space within her mind which enabled her to engage with an extremely complex situation of imperial dominance, Brahmanical hegemony and patriarchal oppression without opting out of her own location within the Tamil patriarchal framework. Given my own feminist logic when I repeatedly asked Neelambikai's biographer Sharada Nambiarooran and others whether repeated child birth (which eventually led to her premature death) did not indicate sexual exploitation, the unequivocal response was an emphatic 'no'. She was a happily married woman and people spoke of them as an ideal couple (Interview with Mangaiyarkkarasiyar, 9 December 2002). Yet the same informant told me that Neelambikai never wore a *tali* which is a symbol of the marital status which every Tamil woman must wear! This seeming paradox seems to have found an uneasy coexistence in Neelambikai Ammaiyar. Clearly, for Neelambikai and her ilk, the journey towards personhood—being human, being a woman and being a Tamil—lay through untrodden paths confronting these intrepid travelers!

NOTES

1. The gender politics of Periyar has been dealt with in a few articles – S Anandi, 'Women's Question in the Dravidian Movement', *Social Scientist* 216–217, Nos. 5–6 (May–June, 1991); V Geetha, 'Gender and the Logic of Brahmanism: EV Ramaswamy Periyar and the Politics of the Female Body', in *From Myths to Markets: Essays on Gender,* edited by Kumkum Sangari and Uma Chakravarti. Shimla, Delhi: Manohar Publishers and the Indian Institute of Advanced Study, 1999, pp. 198–236; CS Lakshmi, 'Mother, Mother Community and Mother Politics on Tamil Nadu', *Economic and Political Weekly* 20 (October 1990); and S Anandi, 'Women's Question in the Dravidian Movement', *Social Scientist* (1991): 216–217; and K Vijaya, 'Role of Women in Self-Respect Movement', Proceedings of the Indian History Congress, 1994 (54th Session, Mysore, 1993). The most comprehensive treatment of the theme from a feminist perspective is V Geetha. The citation from Periyar's essay is from Anandi's article, p. 25.

2. See GN Devy's thesis in his book, *After Amnesia: Tradition and Change in Indian Literary Criticism.* Hyderabad: Orient Longman Ltd., 1992.

3. This was published in 1990 by the Saiva Siddhanta Nool Padippu Kazhagam, Tirunelveli as Neelambikai Ammaiyarin Padaippugalil Samuga Chintanaigal (in Tamil).

4. T Tirunavukkarasu. 1946. *Neelambikai Ammaiyar* (biography in Tamil). Tirunelveli: Saiva Siddhanta Kazhagam. Preface, p.4.

5. This notion is an extension of GN Devy's argument in *After Amnesia: Tradition and*

Change in Indian Literary Criticism, op.cit., passim.

6. Neelambikai Ammaiyar. 1925. *Tani Tamizh Katturaigal (Essays on Pure Tamil).* Tirunelveli: Siva Siddhanta Kazhagam.

7. Elegy composed by Erode Siva Kuppusami Pillai in Tirunavukkarasu's Neelambikai p.18. Translation mine.

8. 'Tamizhnadum Tamizh mozhiyum Munneruvadu Eppadi', Neelambikai's address before the Tamil Women's Conference, published by the author through Kazhagam, Tirunelveli, 1938.

9. Muppenmanigal Varalaru (1940), Introduction.

10. The feminization and deification of Tamil is specifically explored by Sumati Ramaswamy in two articles—'Daughters of Tamil: Language and the Poetics of Womanhood in the Tamilnad', *South Asia Research* 12.1 (1992): 38–59 and 'En/gendering Language: The Poetics of Tamil Identity' in *Comparative Studies in Society and History* 35, No. 4 (October 1993): 683–725. This aspect is dealt with in detail by her in *Passions of the Tongue: Language Devotion in Tamil India, 1891–1970*, Berkeley: University of California Press, 1997. Also see CS Lakshmi, 'Mother, Mother Community and Mother Politics on Tamil Nadu', *Economic and Political Weekly* (20 October 1990).

11. Neelambikai Ammaiyar. 1940. *Menattu Penmanigal,* Tirunelveli: Saiva Siddhanta Kazhagam. 107 ff.

12. The references to Periyar's essays are from Anandi's article, op.cit, p. 25. See also V Geetha's various articles on this theme besides the article in *From Myths to Markets,* op.cit. fn.1. For instance, V Geetha and Rajadurai, SV, 'DMK Hegemony: The Cultural Limits to Political Consensus'. in *Region, Religion, Caste, Gender and Culture in Contemporary India*, Volume III, edited by TV Satyamurthy. New Delhi: Oxford University Press, 1996.

13. Incidentally it was also largely responsible for Annadorai, Karunanidhi and others breaking away from the Justice Party of Periyar and forming the Dravida Kazhagam which later became Dravida Munnetra Kazhagam (DMK). This discussion is still a very touchy issue with Periyar loyalists.

14. K Nambi Arooran's book *Tamil Renaissance and Dravidian Nationalism* in fact has a whole section on Periyar, the Svaya Mariyadai Iyakkam (Self-respect Movement) and the Justice Party. Despite this the book does not go into the conjunction and disjunction between the two leading Dravidian movements of the day—the Tani Tamizh Iyakkam and the Svaya Mariyadai Iyakkam.

SELECT BIBLIOGRAPHY

A chronological listing of Neelambikai Ammaiyar's writings published by the Saiva Siddhanta Kazhagam, Tirunelveli, used in this text:

Tani Tamizh Katturai. 1925. Fifteen essays on the need for pure Tamil, women's education, the epistemological fallacy of equating westernization with culture, etc.

Six Hundred Parallel Proverbs in Tamil and English. 1931.

*Airopiya Mathar Eruvar.*1933. Biographies of Joan of Arc and Florence Nightingale.

Pattinaththar Paratiya Moovar. 1934. Hagiographies of Tiruneelakantar, Sirutondar and Kannappar, Saivite Nayanar saints.

Tamizhnadum Tamizhmozhiyum Munneruvathu Eppadi? (How May Tamil Country and Tamil Progress?). 1938.

Muppenmanigal Varalaru. 1940. Hagiograhies of three spiritual women: Karaikkal

Ammaiyar, Tilakavatiyar and Mangaiyarkkarasiyar.
*Chiraichalai Chirthituttiya Elizabeth Fry Perumatti. (On the Prison Reformer.)*1939.
Menattu Penmaniga. 1946. Biographies of Queen Victoria, Elizabeth Barret Browning, Harriet Beecher Stowe and Harriet Martineau. This also contains translations especially of Elizabeth Browning's poems on child labour in the coal mines.
Vadachol Tamizh Agaravarisai (Sanskrit-Tamil Dictionary).1965. Third Reprint (date of first print not known).

OTHER SELECT REFERENCES

Anandi, S. 1991. Women's Question in the Dravidian Movement 1925–48. *Social Scientist* 19, Nos. 5–6 (May–June): 24–41.

Arooran, Nambi K. 1980. *Tamil Renaissance and Dravidian Nationalism*,1905–1944. Madurai: Koodal Publishers.

Arooran, Nambi Sharada. 1990. *Neelambikai Ammaiyarin Padaippugalil Samuga Chintanaigal* (Tamil). Saiva Siddhanta Kazhagam, Tirunelveli.

Dharmambal, S. 1990. *Nutrandu Vizha Malar (Centenary Souvenir in Tamil) 1890–1990.* Madras: Privately published by M Karunanidhi.

Krishnaveni Ammal, S. 1939. *Kavi Malar Maalai* (in Tamil). Madras (publishers not known).

Lakshmi, CS. 1984. *The Face Behind the Mask: Women in Tamil Literature* in the Women in Society Series. New Delhi: Vikas Publishing House.

Lakshmi, CS. 1990. 'Mother, Mother-Community and Mother-Politics in Tamil Nadu.' *Economic and Political Weekly* 20–29 (October).

Pandian, MSS. 1993. 'De-nationalizing the Past: Nation in EVRamaswamy's Political Discourse.' *EPW* 28, No. 42 (16 October): 2282–87.

Pandian, MSS. 1994. 'Notes on the Transformation of Dravidian Ideology: Tamil Nadu 1900–1940.' *Social Scientist* No. 252–53 (May–June): 84.

Radhakrishnan, P. 1993. 'Communal Representation in Tamil Nadu: The pre-Non-Brahmin Movement Phase–1850–1916.' *EPW* 28, No. 31 (July): 1585–97.

Rajeshwari Ammaiyar. 1945. *Vanakkappal.* Madras (publishers not known).

Ram, Mohan. 1974. Ramaswamy Naicker and the Dravidian Movement. *EPW* 9, No.6–8 (February): 217–24.

Ramaswamy, Sumati. 1993. Engendering Language: The Poetics of Tamil Identity. *Comparative Studies in Society and History* 35, No. 4 (October): 683–725.

Ramaswamy, Sumati. 1997. *Passions of the Tongue: Language Devotion in Tamil Nadu – 1890–1970.* Berkeley: University of California Press.

Sri, P. 1971. *Nan Arinda Tamizhmanigal* (in Tamil). Madras: Vanathi Padippagam.

Tirunavukkarasu, T. 1946. *Neelambikai Ammaiyar* (Biography by Neelambikai's brother in Tamil). Tirunelveli: Saiva Siddhanta Kazhagam.

Nature, Identity, and Tamil Literature

A VELUPPILLAI

Introduction

Tamil identity is defined in South India mainly by the Dravidian movement, while in Sri Lanka it is expressed directly as Tamil identity. The identity in both countries has much in common with a major difference: In South India, the Dravidian movement started as a social and political anti-Brahmin movement, whereas in Sri Lanka the Brahmins did not dominate the social and political field and there was no necessity for an anti-Brahmin movement. Except for this difference, national feelings in both countries seem to almost overlap. In South India, the Dravidian movement looks back to an age before the sectarian bhakti movement appeared by about the 7th century. This bhakti movement entrenched Saivism and Vaishnavism which popularized a religion that made heavy use of Puraa'nangka'l and Itikaacangka'l. Brahmins played a leading role in the bhakti movement, which was a huge success among the Tamils; they gradually consolidated their hold on the Tamil society. Some Brahmins identified themselves as descendents of Sanskrit-speaking Aryans and they dominated the society in early 20th century. They asserted that it was they who brought high culture to the Dravidians who included the Tamils. The non-Brahmins started a Justice Party and ensured some political success. Very soon, there emerged a Self-Respect Movement, to make non-Brahmins conscious of their equality as human beings with Brahmins.

Periyaar and Arignar Return for Revenge

EV Raamacaami Periyaar, who was associated with the Justice Party and who founded the Self-Respect Movement, started the Dravidian movement, challenging the authority and dominance of the Brahmins and some elements in Hinduism who seemed to downgrade and oppress the non-Brahmins. Arignar Annathurai, who was once his lieutenant, has criticized many Puraa'na stories vehemently and also, founded the DMK as a political party. It is interesting to deeply explore Tamil tradition and examine who used these titles periyaar and arignar and in what context. There is epigraphical evidence that three Jain monks from Kazhukumalai in Tirunelvely district had the periyaar title in the eighth or ninth centuries.[1] In early Tamil, arignan had the form arivan. It seems to have denoted the omniscient Jain fordmaker in many places. It can also denote the enlightened Buddha. *Vaalarivan*[2] in the first chapter of the *Tirukkural* could be considered the modern day equivalent of the title *peerarignar.* A'rivan and periyaar suffered a lot at the hands of the Brahmin-led bhakti movement. These titles have come back to the Tamil society to honor social reformers who challenged and haunted Brahminism, but under another ideology and not to revive Jainism.

Dravidian Movement Looks Back to a Glorious Past

Other people who speak Dravidian languages such as Telugu, Kannada, and Malayalam find it difficult to participate in the Dravidian movement as those languages do not have anthologies such as the *Edduttokai* and *Pattuppaaddu,* narrative poem like the *Cilappatikaaram,* didactic work like the *Tirukkural* and grammatical work like the *Tolkaappiyam.* Kerala, which too had a very oppressive caste system, used the Marxist movement to effect social and political reforms. The three last mentioned works reveal Jain influence, even though they are not Jain texts as such. The DMK, under Kalaignar Karunanitni, its charismatic leader for almost 40 years, and its splinter groups such as ADMK, MDMK, and DMDK, which dominate Tamil Nadu politics, have high praise for these books. It is difficult to imagine Tamil identity disowning these three works. Tamil identity has to be defined as predominantly indigenous characteristics of the Tamils, preserved and fostered mainly by the early Jain authors.

Nature in Akam and Puram Tradition

Tamils have a linguistic identity of not less than two millennia. They have a remarkable classical literature, generally referred to as *Cangkam* literature. *Tolkaappiyam porulatikaaram* has some sections dealing with the literary theory of that literature. *Akam, interior,* and *puram, exterior,* are the main themes of that literature. *Akam* deals with *mutal, ultimate; karu, base;* and *uri,* "appropriate:" a three-tier structure. *Mutal* and *karu* deal with the environment. *Mutal* deals with space and time—space referring to the particular landscape. Nature is also defined by variations due to six seasons annually and six periods of time daily. *Karu* deals with, among other things, animals (including insects, reptiles, etc.), birds and plants of each landscape. *Karupporul* seems to have had a huge impact on the activities of the people. Each of the five landscapes takes its name from an important flower in that landscape. The name of the landscape also becomes the name of the particular aspect of love. Relatively, *Puram* is not so closely connected with the *mutal poru'l* and *karupporu'l* of each landscape. But a specific kind of fighting in each landscape is associated with the name of another flower, which fighters in each landscape used to wear when they go to war, either aggressively or defensively. It is important to note that there is no poem exclusively on nature or on elements of nature, as people did not differentiate their lives from nature.

Nature and Tamil Identity During Classical Times

The fact that Tamil identity and Tamil literature are very closely connected appears from the colophon attached to the *Ku'rigncippaaddu,* one of the *Ten Idylls,* an anthology of Cangkam literature. The colophon records that it was composed by Kapilar to instruct Tamil to Pirakattan, an Aryan king. What Tamil/Tamilness means in this context is clearly Tamil *akam* tradition and especially *ku'ringci* tradition. Kapilar is one of the greatest and most prolific *Cangkam* poets. He specialized in *Ku'rinjci akam* poetry which treated the union of lovers and incidents relating to it. He has composed a 261 line long *Ku'rignci* poem. What is very interesting about this poem is that it tries to list more than ninety flowers when the heroine and her lady-friend went on to pick flowers as a pastime. As already noted, *anpin ainti'nai,* "five-fold situations based on love," as well as *aintu pu'ratti'nai,* "five exterior (war) situations," were indicated by names of different flowers. Flowers appear to be a favorite of ancient Tamils. They become very important in Saiva and Vaish'nava temple worship at least from the beginning of the bhakti movement. Flowers still have a hold on Tamil girls and women in Tamilnadu. This poem also illustrates the importance of nature and its description to identify Tamilness and how Tamil literature helped in this identification even during the Classical period. This is also a perfect example to establish the relationship between nature, identity, and Tamil literature.

Were the Ancient Tamils Secular or Pluralistic?

Ancient Tamils are claimed by some scholars to be secular and by some others to be pluralistic. The *akam* tradition can give some clues here for a clearer understanding. *Mutal poru'l* and *karupporu'l* mean very different things to people who have come through strong theistic traditions. The Tamil lexicon reflects the view of such Tamil scholars. It glosses the earlier term and gives God as its first meaning and *akam mutal poru'l* definition as its second meaning.[3] It also glosses the *karupporu'l* and states—God, as the efficient cause, the originator of all things—as its first meaning and *akam* karupporu'l definition as its second meaning.[4] *Tolkaappiyam,* in its enumeration of *karupporu'l,* mentions *teyvam*/God along with seven other items for each of the landscapes. There were Gods among the Tamils but their importance has been downgraded. This probably reflects Jain attitude to a creator God. Jains do not accept that there was a God who created the world and who could redeem human beings through grace. They do not encourage but accept the existence of these downgraded Devas/Gods, who have supernatural power and who can bring relief, help or guidance to people in worldly life. Each of the landscapes has a different God. *Tolkaappiyam* mentions a different God for each of the four regions and omits mentioning one for the arid landscape. There is no pan-Tamil God in this scheme. Ancient Tamils appear to have been pluralistic given this background, as Tamils worshipping different Gods from different landscapes must have been interacting frequently. Each king must have been ruling over people of various landscapes; capital cities and ports must have had mixed populations along with foreigners. Jains, Buddhists, and Brahmins might have felt comfortable in this Tamil social set-up, may be for centuries. Modern Tamils wonder whether they could go back to the spirit of that age which could accommodate Christians, Muslims, and others within the overarching Tamil identity.

Nature seems to have played a very important part in the life of the early Tamils. *Marapiyal,* "chapter on the traditions," the last chapter of the third section of the *Tolkaappiyam,* has much material to illustrate the very close relationship Tamils forged with literature. This chapter starts listing nine designations of young ones in Tamil usage. Then it lists 15 designations of males, followed by 13 designations of females. Tamils have been choosy in using a particular name from each list for the young one, male or female of each kind of living being. The usage could not have been standardized throughout the Tamil land. Tolkaappiyar has made provision for these exceptional usages. This kind of usage must have been based on some pattern, which is worth taking up for study. These usages are not confined to domesticated animals and domesticated poultry. Wild animals such as the tiger, boar, fox, buffalo, and camel; aquatic animals such as the crocodile; marine animals such as shark; and birds such as the peacock also have multiple designations.

What is noteworthy is that some of these usages also extend to plants. Tolkaappiyar says that *pi'l'lai, kuzhavi, ka:n'ru* and *poattu* apply for plants also (24). The first three also figure among the nine designations of young ones (1). The word *kuḻavi* was also used for human babies in his time (23). The fourth is a male designation, referring to palms and plants that don't bear fruit. The male name *ea'ru* is used for pigs, three different kinds of deer, buffalo, Indian elk, and cattle (40, 41). It is also used for the shark, which lives in the sea (42). Tolkaappiyar also mentions that strong males of all beings can be called *ea'ru* (50). This tells us that ancient Tamils have been guided by reason in giving these names and Tolkaappiyar also took care in recording his observations. Four male names—*moattai, takar, uta'l* and *appar*—are confined to *yādu,* goat, sheep(48). In Tamil literary usage, goat and sheep are not specified. But still, it is not possible to explain why four names were used. It could be either dialect variations or indicators of different stages in the life-cycle of these beings. The female name *peddai* is used among camel, horse, ass, and Indian elk (53). He then says that it is also used among birds (54). He adds that if investigated, *peedai* and *peddai* usage would correspond to each other (55).

Subramanya Bharathi sang that, kaakkai kuruvi engka'l caati, "crow and small bird belong to our caste." But ancient Tamils seem to have gone further and embraced even plants. They classify plants too into two as grass (including palms) (86) and trees (87). There are separate words – different sets of words for each of these categories. Scholars say that *toadu, madal, oalai, eadu, ita'l, paa'lai, iirkku* and *kulai* are used among grass (including palms) (88). It is mentioned that *ilai, ta'lir, mu'ri, toadu, cinai, kuzhai, poo* and *arumpu* are used among trees (89).

Six Classes of Life Sharing the Environment

Origin of Six Classes of Life, Based on Senses and Mind

The usage of these designations among living beings could not have been introduced by one or more grammarians. They indicate how the life of ancient Tamils has been integrated with nature. But what Tolkaappiyar may have introduced from Jainism could be the classification of living beings into six classes, based on sensory knowledge. He acknowledges that this six-fold classification is not his but of enlightened persons.[5] he sense of touch makes for a one-sense life and he cites the example of plants;. Having, in addition, the sense of taste makes for a two-sense life and he gives as examples the snail and shell-fish. Adding the sense of smell makes for a three-sense life, and he gives as examples termites and ants. The additional sense of sight gives crabs and bees a four-sense life. Having in addition, a sense of hearing makes for a five-sense life, and he gives as examples animals and (irrational) humans. The sixth sense, mind, creates (rational) humans.

Could this classification of living beings by senses be that of Tolkaappiyar or that of the Tamils? Tolkaappiyar himself says that it was a classification of somebody else, even though he did not specify the name. He himself says that there were other items in each category, besides those which he mentioned. Among ancient Indian religions, Jainism alone had such a classification based on senses of life. Jainism was also the only ancient religion to include plants among living beings. This is further confirmed by what Tolkaappiyar regards as mutal nūl (primary source) and vaḻi nūl (secondary works). According to aphorism 96, mutal nūl is produced by "a striver who has become omniscient, having rid himself of karma." The Tamil wording can be translated to apply to the Buddha, but Buddhist influence has to be ruled out as there is no tradition of connecting the author of the book to that religion. This description will fit in to a Jain fordmaker and not to Hindu Gods.

Jains and Ancient Tamils: Who Were More Environment Friendly?

On the basis of this classification, some Jains make the claim that their religion is the most environment friendly religion. This classification occurs in ancient Jain sources when they deal with ahimsa, "non-violence." Their aim seems to be to keep away from all living beings in order not to hurt them but not positively to sustain them. But when this classification occurs in *Tolkaappiyam,* it seems to have a more positive tone to partaking and identifying with nature. The *Encyclopedia of Religion,* the latest of such publications, edited by Mircea Eliade, has an entry on Tamil religion. The distinctiveness of Tamil religion has, among other features, some close association with nature which, of all religions among Tamils, reflects at least in their Tamil texts.

An attempt by a Jain author to write an ethical work as well as a sizeable work on ancient akam tradition is seen in Ka'ni Meataavi/ Ka'ni Meatai. Both books are included among the *Eighteen Minor Works* which are considered Post-Caṅkam works. He has written *Ealaati,* "Cardamom, etc. ," an ethical work under a medical term, compressing six or seven rules in each verse in a book of 80 verses. He has also written the biggest *akam* book (in those *Eighteen Minor Works*) of 150 verses under the title, *Ti'naimaalai noo'r'raimpatu,* "Garland of Landscapes One Hundred and Fifty." Each of the five landscapes has about 30 stanzas.

*Nature/*akam *Tradition in Bhakti Literature*

Campantar, a Brahmin, who spearheadied the Saiva bhakti movement during the 7th century, in his signature stanza found in almost all his hymns, identified closely with Tamil and claimed to be an expert in Tamil. Only a very small number of his hymns can be identified as dealing with *uripporuḷ*—love themes in relation to Siva. But he was singing about nature—*karupporuḷ,* drawing heavily from classical landscape descriptions. It has been aptly pointed out that the subject matter of his hymns were "half nature; half God." His identification with Tamil tradition appears to be his appropriation of nature from the Tamil tradition and linking it to Siva temple worship.

The *akam* tradition seems to have influenced the Vaishnava bhakti movement much more than the Saiva bhakti movement. The stories about Krishna's childhood and youth appear to have given lot of scope for *āḻvārs* to introduce many themes from *akapporu'l* tradition in their bhakti poetry in relation to Krish'na. Tirumangkai, Aa'ndaa'l, and Nammaazhvaar have excelled in such poetry. Landscape descriptions of nature, along with love themes related to devotion to Krish'na, occur in many of their stanzas. Tirumangkai's well-known *tirumadal,* "sacred horse made of jagged palmyra stems," poems could be characterized as *peru:nti'nai,* "improper love," and not commendable. The poems of the other two could be characterized mainly as *anpin ai:nti'nai,* focused on Krish'na/Vish'nu bhakti. Aa'ndaa'l is raised to the level of a Goddess, a consort of Krish'na/Vish'nu. In addition to a big temple in Sreevilliputtoor which is in her name in her home town, she has earned a shrine in many Vish'nu temple complexes. Nammaazhvaar is celebrated as the greatest *aazhvaar. Tiruvaaymozhi,* his magnum opus, is celebrated as the fifth Tamil Veda.

Saivite Assertion of Sharing of Life with Plants and Animals

Maa'nikkavaacakar, who was a Saiva bhakti poet of the 9th century, attempted a synthesis of classical *akam* tradition and bhakti. The *Kōvai* literary form, which is the classical *akam* tradition in the form of a narrative, had already made its appearance before his time. His *Tirukkoavaiyaar* was a very difficult synthesis of the bhakti and *akam* traditions, with a lot of material about nature thrown in. Even the very first verse, which mentions Tillai/ Cidambaram, brings in nature-elements from all the five landscapes of the Tamil tradition. He was also referring to his previous births as *'pullaaki ppoodaay ppuzhuvaay maramaaki … ppaampaaki kkallaay … taavara cangkamattu'l,* "Within the immoveable and moveable (realm) … having become grass, shrub, worm and tree, … snake and stone" *(civapuraa'nam,* lines 26–30). He must have been influenced by the *Tolkaappiyam marapiyal. Kal,* "stone," was not mentioned in that text, but Jainism includes the stone too as having life. This seems to be a special feature of Tamil religion, especially in Tamil Saivism. That plants have life as do animals and human beings, but that it constituted a different variety of existence was also one of the arguments put forward by Aru'nanti Civaaccaariyaar in the *Civagnaanacittiyaar (parapakkam*—129,130) to reject Buddhism because Buddhism lacked that insight. Aru'nanti Civaaccaariyaar, of course, could have been influenced by Maa'nikkavaacakar in asserting that plants had life and that the plant category has some basic differences from the animal category. But both these authors could have had their inspiration from the Tamil tradition, as portrayed in the *Tolkaappiyam.*

The *Paa'ndikkoavai,* profusely quoted in the commentary of *I'raiyanaar Ka'laviyal/Akapporu'l,* is the earliest example we have of the *Koavai* literary form. This form appears to string various themes of the classical *akam* tradition into a continuous narrative of 400 stanzas in which the same couple figure as hero and heroine. A kind of synthesis is attempted of the classical *akam* tradition and praise of the glory of a Pandya king. Almost all *Koavai* works have this dichotomy. Each stanza deals with an anonymous hero and heroine acting out a theme in the classical *akam* tradition, with *uripporu'l* as the central theme. *Karupporu'l* of different landscapes is thrown in as background. In addition to this, each stanza praises someone indicated: a king, a God, a patron, an honored person, and so on. The portrayal of the latter seems to be the main purpose of each author.

The *Koavai* literary form seems to have led to the need for new treatises on

Akapporu'l. Sectarianism seems to have raised its head there. Saivites claimed that Siva was the author of *I'raiyanaar Akapporu'l.*[6] There was *Maa'ran Akapporu'l* where the lovers live as good Vaishnavites. The best expository treatise, in contrast to later sectarian Hindu traditions, is *Akapporu'l Vi'lakkam* by Naa'rkaviraaca:nampi, a Jain author. His exposition of akapporu'l vilakkam is remarkably non-sectarian.

Landscape Descriptions in Kaappiyams *of All Religions*

Jain Authors Were Trend-Setters

The subject of nature has become so important in Tamil literary tradition that Tamil poets have elaborate descriptions of nature when they compose narrative poems which fit in the *perungkaappiyam/kaappiyam* according to *Ta'ndiyalangkaaram,* a Tamil treatise on rhetoric. When Tamil poets borrow stories from Sanskrit/ Prakrit themes and then write Tamil narrative poems, they do not describe the natural scenery of the land where the story was located. For the description of the country and city, they appear to go back to classical Tamil literary tradition. *Ciivaka Cintaama'ni,* the pioneer *perungkaappiyam* (according to *Ta'ndiyalangkaaram* description) by Tiruttakkateavar, a Jain author of about the 10th century, has some nature-descriptions, but they were included within the first chapter of the book which has another theme. Toalaamozhitteavar, the 10th century Jain author of *Coo'laama'ni,* was the first author to compose a separate chapter for the country and the city at the beginning of his book. Tamil tradition counts this work as one of Five Minor *Kaappiyams,* even though this could be considered a *perungkaappiyam.*

Tamil poets may have introduced these classical Tamil nature-descriptions as a kind of indigenization of outside or foreign sources. Tamil authors enabled Tamil readers and listeners to savor nature-descriptions that they were familiar with and with which they identified, and then to identify and appreciate characters in their narrative poems. This feature also indicates that nature continued to be important for the Tamils. Ceakkizhaar, the 12th century Saivite author of the *Periyapuraa'nam,* was narrating the story of many *naayanaars* who lived within Tamil Nadu. They lived in different naadus and nakarams. Influenced by Toalaamozhitteavar, he too introduced Coazhanaadu country and Tiruvaaruur city at the beginning of his narrative poem. His Coazhanaadu description begins with a description of the Kaaviri river whose delta provided for the fertility and prosperity of the country.[7] Kampar, the famous 12th century Vaishnava author of the Tamil *Raamaaya'na,* creates a utopia when he describes Raama's Kosala country and Ayodhya city. Ceakkizhaar's description seems to have influenced Kampar to have a separate chapter for a description of the *Sarayu* river, flowing by Ayodhya. He has also utilized a great deal of classical Tamil nature-descriptions, following the examples set by Jain authors.

There was a *kaaviyam—Irakuvammicam*—an adaptation of Kalidasa's *Raghuvamsa* by Aracakeacari, a 16th century Tamil poet from Sri Lanka. He was an admirer of Kampar. From his primary source which lists Rama as a member of the Raghu dynasty, he omits the portion of the Rama story which Kampar handled so eloquently. Like Kampar, he too had three chapters on descriptions of the same river, country, and city, though he described them differently. It is surmised that some of his landscape descriptions were influenced by what he saw in the northern part of Sri Lanka.

Christian and Muslim Authors Follow Suit

The 18th century sees Christian and Muslim poets introducing landscape nature descriptions in describing the lands of the founders of Christianity and Islam. Constantius Beschi, an Italian Catholic missionary in Tamil Nadu, who had taken the pseudonym Veeramaamunivar, has made multi-faceted contributions for the development of Tamil. His Tamil narrative poem *Teampaava'ni* on the life and teachings of Jesus, introduces Tamil landscape descriptions in portraying Israel. This is remarkable because he himself was a native of Italy from the Mediterranean region and he might have had some basic ideas about the geography of Israel. But he decided on bringing the message of Jesus to the Tamils in the nature descriptions to which they were accustomed. Umaru, a Tamil Muslim poet, began writing *Cii'raappuraa'nam,* a narrative poem on the life and teachings of Mohammed, the founder of Islam. He was said to be indebted to another Islam scholar for many of the ideas in his book. But he was not describing in his book Arabia as it was. There too, it was Tamil landscape descriptions that were utilized to describe the geography of Arabia.

This characteristic seems to have continued even into the 19th century. HA Krishnapillai, who was a Protestant Christian convert from Vaishnavism, wrote *Iradca'niya Yaattirikam,* a Tamil narrative poem, based on *Pilgrim's Progress,* authored by James Bunyan. One of the ways in which it goes beyond translation is in introducing Tamil landscape descriptions.

Conclusion

It was Subramaniya Bharathi who broke this tradition. In his introduction to *Paagncaali Capatam,* which he describes as a kaaviyam/narrative poem, he pleads for a new type of literary genre, influenced by modern ideas that came to him through English literature. But Bharathi's innovation was no loss to Tamil landscape nature descriptions. UV Caaminaataiyar's edition of *Cangkam* classical literature and some other masterpieces of Tamil literature, along with CW Damodarampillai's edition of *Tolkaappiyam* and some other Tamil texts led to a revival of classical Tamil studies. Classical Tamil literature and the Tamil literary tradition have a new life both among Tamil scholars and an increasing number of western scholars. A reawakening of the Tamils has come about in the 20th century and many Tamils seem to consider their pre-bhakti sectarian movement period to be a glorious period that maintainedtheir secular Tamil identity.

NOTES

1. The names of the three Jain monks are Caanticeanap periyaar (316); pava'nantip periyaar (380); and tayaapaalap periyaar (383) in South Indian Inscriptions, Vol. 5, pp. 122, 130 and 131. This information is available in Veluppillai Alvappillai, "Jainism in Tamil Inscriptions," pp. 315–335. Erodu V Ramaswamy gets the title *periyaar.* Erodu had Jain influence for many centuries, especially under the Gangas of Talakkad. Jainism is not extinct from the region even now.

2. According to the *Cilappatikaaram*, Kavunti made up her mind to accompany Ka'n'naki to Maturai, as she would have an opportunity to worship A'rivan there and to listen to leading Jain monks. Tamil Lexicon explains the phrase *vaal a'rivan* as 'God as pure intelligence'. This looks like the equivalent to *pear a'rignar.* A'n'naaturai, the founder of the DMK, has both titles: *a'rignar* and *peara'rignar*. Conjeevaram N Annadurai was from Kanchipuram, a portion of which was recognized as Jain Kanchi for centuries. Jainism survives there even now.

3. *Tamil Lexicon*, Vol. 6, p. 3261.

4. *Tamil Lexicon*, Vol. 2, p. 760.

5. *Tolkaappiyam, marapiyal*, 24–33.

6. The traditional story explaining the origin of this book is unconvincing. *Ka'laviyal/ Akapporu'l*, though important, covers only a small portion of *poru'latikaaram.* If Siva was the author, did he know only so much of it? I'raiyanaar must have been the name of a human poet. What he did was to write an innovative treatise for *akam*, distinct from *Tolkaappiyam*, based on *koavai* literary genre.

7. Ceakkizhaar might have been influenced by Kapilar's Ku'rigncippaddu. The importance of stream for the flourishing mountainous settlement might have inspired the former to glorify the *Kaaviri* river.

WORKS CITED

Islamic and Christian Contributions. Online material. See http://ckrishnamurti.tripod.com/chap10a.html. Accessed in March, 2008.

Kamparaamaaya'nam. Online material. See http://tamilnation.org/literature/kamban/kambaramayanam.htm.

Project Madurai (PM). Online texts. The following texts were accessed:
http://tamilnation.org/literature/projectmadurai/indexpmsubject.htm#
PM100 part 3, *Tolkaappiyam poru'latikaaram;* PM 001 *Tirukku'ra'l;* PM073 *Ku'rinjcippaaddu;* PM029 *Ealaati;* PM056 *Ti'naimaalai nuu'r'raimpatu;* PM046 *Cilappatikaaram;* PM150,151,157,162,173,179 *Campantar teavaaram;* PM003 *Maa'nikkavaacakar Tiruvaacakam;* PM054 *Tirukkoavaiyaar;* PM007 *Aa'ndaa'l;* PM008 *Tirumangkai Aazhvaar;* PM005 *Nammaazhvaar;* PM301 *I'raiyanaar Akapporu'l/ Ka'laviyal;* PM145 *Ta'ndiyalangkaaram;* PM035 *Cuu'laama'ni;* PM209 *Periyapuraa'nam;* PM167 *Cii'raappuraa'nam.*
All of them accessed in March–April 2008.Tamil Lexicon, Reprint, Madras: University of Madras,1982.

Veluppillai, Alvappillai. 2003. Jainism in Tamil Inscriptions. In *Jainism and Early Buddhism*, edited by Olle Qvarnstrom. Fremont, California: Asian Humanities Press.

Veluppillai, Alvappillai. 1969. *Thamizh Ilakkiyattil kaalamum karuttum*. Chennai: Paari Puththakaalayam.

Veluppillai, Alvappillai. 1988. *Aracakeacariyin Irakuvammicamum atu ezhunta intu pa'n-paaddu ccuuzhalum*, Sir Pon. Ramanathan Memorial Lecture. Jaffna: University of Jaffna.

Zvelebil, KV. 1974. *Tamil Literature. A History of Indian Literature*. Edited by Jan Gonda. Vol.10, Fac.1. Weisbaden: Otto Harrassowitz.

Zvelebil, KV. 1992. *Companion Studies to the History of Tamil Literature*. Leiden: EJ Brill.

Translating Literary Beauty and Some of its Ugly Consequences: The Case of Some of the Real People in *Thiru-k-Kutrala-k-Kuravanji*[1]

DAVID C BUCK

The primary aim of this paper is to trace the development of Kuṟavar people as literary figures from their appearance in the earliest available Tamil literary works down through the ages to a famous stage drama that features them, dating from only a few centuries ago, and then to relate those literary figures to some real people living their lives today. I believe that we can see a clear progression from early portrayals of Kuṟavar people at or near the centre of Tamil social structure, through various incremental steps of marginalizing, to a current situation that places Kuṟavar people on the outer edge, the very periphery of Tamil society.[2]

The paper has a second aim as well. It raises questions about the roles that literature and literary translation have played, and are still playing, in abetting or resisting the ongoing marginalizing of real-life Kuṟavar people, and by extension, of other similar people as well. In the end, the paper is about being conscious of some of the ongoing life-and-death social realities that contextualize any translation project.

Most specifically addressed in this paper are people of a certain *iṉam*,[3] the Kuṟavar people, the Kuṟavaṉ and the Kuṟatti figures who appear first in Sangam Era literature, and remain as literary figures in every succeeding literary era down to, and including, the present. Let us pose the question, "Who are these men and women?" That is, who are they as figures who appear in literature, and who are they in real, down-to-earth life? And what is the connection between real people and their literary portrayals?[4]

Sangam literature is built on the division of poetic themes into two major categories: the inner *akam* and the outer *puṟam.* Of those two, we focus here on the inner type, the *akam* poems, and later developments from them, as the centuries have rolled by one after the other. Within this *akam* classification are the five—actually seven—types, based largely on geographic representations of the emotional content of poetry. The Kuṟavaṉ and Kuṟatti figures, named as they are in some of these ancient poems themselves, but most especially as they are highlighted in the commentaries on *Tolkāppiyam* and on *Iṟaiyaṉār Akapporul,* are the people who live in the mountains, and it is to them that the Sangam tradition metes out the theme of "first love." That is to say, in ancient Tamil tradition, love at first sight most definitely occurs, and poems concerning this particularly exquisite moment for any of us human beings are to be set in the mountains with people called Kuṟavars as the lovers. For that matter, Kuṟavar, and other names such as Iravul ar and Kuṉṟavar, apply to these lovers' families and friends as well. However, the separate literary identity of a Kuṟavar *iṉam* seems not to have developed in sharp detail at this point. While the setting may be mountainous, there is no hint of any social separation between the Mountain Kuṟavar people, the heroes and heroines of the first-love theme, and any other class of people.[5]

Hyperbole in praise is a common literary form through much of the world, I suspect. At least it is common in ancient Tamil literature: just listen to the commentator Nakkīraṉār as he describes these lovers who meet and fall hopelessly in love, there in the mountainous setting:

> "He travels with a retinue of many hundreds of thousands of youths with sharp lances and the strength of lions and yalis . . . And she, too, is surrounded by many hundreds of thousands of women, among whom she was born and raised, . . . who have excellent character. . . . . It is to be concluded that she moves as the cool moon in the midst of these stars. . . . All about her are sandalwood trees, champak trees, sweet mango trees, [with] jasmine and Arabian jasmine combining their fragrances. . . . She sees a kino tree brushing the sky and blooming pure gold with its intoxicatingly aromatic blossoms yielding their honey as bees buzz by. At the very sight of it, she feels a swelling love. . . . Meanwhile, the hero also came to the cool mountainsides to hunt, with his many hundreds of thousands of young men with sharp spears. He chased after a lion that sprang up there, and left the youths who were protecting him. His warrior's anklet jangled, and he tied up his dark curly hair with a golden cord. . . . he moved like the god of love reincarnate and entered the great grove where she was."[6]

The excellent characters of these Kuṟavar lovers are summed up in four traits. For him: wisdom, constancy, investigation, and resolve. She has modesty, innocence, fear, and loathing. But under the influence of each other in this spectacularly beautiful mountain grove, all of these characteristics "are overwhelmed by desire and lie bent, as grass lies bent in the path of a flooding stream."[7] They regain their essential characters only when they come to, remembering who they are, and what their social positions require of them.

This is surely one of the world's most beautiful and delicately developed settings for the poetry of first love. It is sweet and good, tainted with none of ordinary life's inescapable, but long, dark, and intrusive shadows. In fact, some of those long, dark shadows do descend upon the blissfully happy literary couple, but the worst of them are saved for poetic portrayals in geographic regions other than the mountains: sad separation is to be experienced poetically against a seaside backdrop; patient waiting is reserved for non-mountainous forest settings, harsh separation and the uncertain fear in elopement are set in hot deserts, and married life replete with unfaithful husbands is to be portrayed in settled agricultural regions near rivers. Kuṟavar people figure only in the first of these, however: the mountainous regions, and their poetic appearance is always as new, young lovers—she is twelve years of age, and he is sixteen.

But is it real? In fact, it is *not* supposed to be real. None of it is, but particularly, according to Nakkīraṉār in his classical commentary on *Iṟaiyaṉār Akapporul,* the first meeting of young Kuṟavar lovers is not supposed to be portrayed in realistic terms. He put it this way as he commented on the phrase, "among the...eight nuptials, the Kantaruva Convention."[8] He said, "Those eight exist in the real world, but this one does not; it is a conduct established by poets as 'the nonexistent, the sweet, and the good,' and he does not add it to the world's customs."[9] Technically speaking, this is not *ulaka-v-iyal,*[10] but rather *ilakkiya-v-iyal,*[11] a purely literary construction.

He reiterates this point later as well: "One might object that this does not accord with the ways of the world.... But to him we reply, 'You speak with no comprehension. You asked earlier about the nature of the world, didn't you? Must we repeat that at times this does not agree with the ways of the world, even though the author explicitly stated that [this] is established as the non-existent, the sweet, and the good?'"[12] And yet again, he says, "Now this is not the sort of thing that occurs between a boy and a girl in the world.... Here we have a stipulated conduct, established by poets."[13]

Altogether, Kuṟavar people are portrayed in exceedingly beautiful terms in ancient Tamil Sangam convention. They are strong, beautiful people with control over their lives except that when they fall in love as teenagers they are swept away by that lovely but overwhelming emotion. Yet even in those early days of Tamil Classical literature,[14] literary portrayals of Kuṟavar people were not to be taken as word-pictures of real life, but rather as figures upon which to hang utterly beautiful, delicate, attractive, happy poetic imaginings. It raises the question of what relationship these early poems might have had with people who at that time were called Kuṟavar people. But it does not answer that question.

Kuṟavars then continue as important figures for literary portraiture. For example, it is Kuṟavar people, called by that name,[15] who are called upon to introduce *Cilappatikāram,* the great epic that followed on the heels of the Sangam age and brought a new and very grandiose style into the mainstream of Tamil literature. *Cilappatikāram* still paints them as people living in the mountains, but by now they have lost some of their literary lustre. They seem much less on top of things as, for example, they cluster around the Chera monarch to tell him about the magical ascension of the single-breasted Kannagi into the heavens.[16] They are encountered as a separate kind of people, an *iṉam* of their own, by urbane city people as they travel from one metropolis to another.[17] In all instances Ilango Adikal, the princely author of *Cilappatikāram,* portrays Kuṟavar people as outsiders to the urban, settled state-organized society that held sway in those days, and in which he lived as a royal heir.

Then, following close after the period of grand epics such as *Cilappatikāram*, the story of Murugan and his two wives became canonized. God Murugan, who appears alone in the earliest of the Sangam-age works, now has two wives, and they are explicitly described as representing two opposite poles in divinity. While one, Devayanai, is the epitome of propriety and decorum and is often connected with Murugan's Brahminical side, Murugan's second wife, Valli, is the epitome of wild, untamed, mountain life. Although most official stories insist that she was actually descended from divine, clearly non-Kuṟavar, ancestors, many people gloss over that claim. In any case all agree that, at the very least, she was raised as a Kuṟatti by a Kuṟavar chieftain's family in the mountains.[18] In this story, Kuṟavar people in general, through Valli, are set clearly outside the core of Tamil society, yet again through the very same Valli, they are tied into its very centre, this time through adoption and marriage, though, not directly as their own birthright.

Fast-forward now through about a thousand years of more and more developments in the history of Tamil—developments that brought with them a myriad of new forms and feelings. Kuṟavars and people from similar mountain-hunter communities appear occasionally, and in varied placements, but always outside the power centres of the by-now clearly state-organized social structure.[19]

Then about three or four hundred years ago, there appeared a masterful literary form based explicitly on Kuṟavar people and their interaction with high-born families and with kings. This is the Kuravanji literature, of which there are well over 120 examples. Here the literary portrayal of people called Kuṟavars comes centre-stage—literally so, as these works were composed for the stage. Actually all Kuravanji works focus on a Patron—either on god in one of his aspects, or on a king or other important and wealthy man. But those people do not appear on stage. Who does appear on stage are two distinctly different types of people: the high-born[20] and the Kuṟavars—specifically a high-born heroine and a Kuṟatti who reads her signs and tells her fortune. The Kuṟavars are still painted in some ways that draw heavily on the ancient Sangam portraitures: Kuṟavar men are still hunters, and the main Kuṟavar woman and her Kuṟavar husband do exhibit considerable love interest in each other. But now they are poor people, not masters of their own land and destinies. And by this time they are unquestionably described as an *iṉam* of their own.[21] One of the most beautiful and most famous of these Kuravanji dramas is Melagaram Tirikutarasappa Kavirayar's *Thiru-k-Kutrala-k-Kuravanji*, which is centred around the town of Kutralam in Tirunelveli District. And in fact there are today Kuṟavar people living right there who claim direct connection to the Kuṟatti heroine of that stage drama.

Kuṟavar people in *Thiru-k-Kutrala-k-Kuravanji* are said to lead happy but poverty-stricken lives, with homes in the beautiful mountains. The Kuṟavar woman who is one of the two central characters in the drama is described as a widely travelled fortune-teller, independent and very quick-witted, if a bit on the coarse side, who has collected a lot of glamorous jewellery through her art. Her husband and other Kuṟavar men are portrayed comically, as silly bumpkins—audiences are expected to laugh when they make their appearance on stage. They are still hunters, as were their Sangam forebears, but now, instead of lions, they are said to hunt egrets, crows, and sparrows.

Today, in the early years of the 21st century, Mountain Kuṟavar boys in Melagaram eagerly described the ways they make traps to catch little birds to eat, in ways that sounded very reminiscent of the birds-traps described in the stage drama. And Kuṟavar women whose homes are in Melagaram still travel far and wide to tell people's fortunes. The main fortune-telling Kuṟavar woman I met in Melagaram spent several days in Thiruchendur while I was visiting. When she came to tell my fortune, she was dressed and adorned almost exactly as described in the stage drama, and she uttered some of the very same words and phrases.

Mainstream scholars of Tamil literature seem to be divided in their opinions about the connections between modern Mountain Kuṟavar people and Kuṟavar literary figures as seen in this famous stage drama, or in earlier Tamil literary works. Some have facilitated my contacts with present-day mountain people so that I could better understand the literature as well as the people. Some have said that modern Kuṟavars are a different *iṉam* altogether from the people who inspired Kuṟavar literary figures long ago. Quite a few have recommended that I not discuss this literary work with modern Kuṟavar people at all, as they could not be expected to understand it. Indeed when I did discuss the drama with contemporary Mountain Kuṟavar people, they told me that whatever literary interpretation the commentators came up with was fine with them. However, they insisted that I accept them as the direct inheritors of the Kuravanji tradition described in the play and its commentaries. For that matter, too, some who discount modern Kuṟavars' literary understandings tacitly accepted their position as the inheritors of ancient Kuravanji tradition, even to the point of referring, jokingly, to real people by the names given to the Kuṟavaṉ and the Kuṟatti in literature, Singan and Singi.

But the rather rough literary portrayals of Kuṟavar people in the stage drama contrast sharply with the elegantly drawn portrait of the other central character, a beautiful and proper high-born girl, and with admiring portrayals of the only non-fictional characters in the drama, a number of very important men, and a local ruler, from the rich agricultural lands around Kutralam. These men are described as controlling lands and resources in the area, but not particularly in the nearby mountains, which are portrayed as home to the Kuṟavar people. Many readers equate the high-born heroine with the goddess herself, as she appears in the nearby Kutralam temple. Significantly, the entire first section of the drama, where we find descriptions of this girl and her friends as she surrenders herself to god, is often described as the spiritual portion of the work; the second section, which is centred upon the Kuṟavar figures, is often described as worldly, and has even been omitted from certain major productions of the drama by sophisticated urban institutions of the arts. Adult women in these high-born communities are not described. Also conspicuous by their absence from Kavirayar's drama are all of the people who worked the land and created the wealth of those high-born landowners.

By Kavirayar's time, the literary portrayal of Mountain Kuṟavar people clearly had lost a great deal of the lustre that surrounded Sangam-era Mountain Kuṟavar lovers, and what sort of lives real Mountain Kuṟavar people led during those days is not known. Yet, perhaps even in Kavirayar's time, the Mountain Kuṟavar people who lived in the mountains around Kutralam could still claim rights to live in those mountains and to use mountain resources to make their lives and their societies work.

Now we turn to some of the interactions between this kind of literary and social history and the project of literary translation. Note, for example, what is possibly the most famous of all stanzas in Kuravanji literature—certainly one of the most beautiful. It comes in a section of the work in which the Kuṟatti figure describes the glory of the Kuṟavars' mountain homes:

Vāṉarangkal kaṉi kot uttu mantiyot u kon cum

Manti cintu kaṉikal ukku vāṉkavikal ken cum
Kāṉavarkal viḻi eṟintu vāṉavarai aḻaippār
Kamaṉa cittar vantu vantu kāyacitti vil aippār
Tēṉaruvit tiraiyeḻumpi vāṉiṉvaḻi oḻukum
Cen○ katirōṉ parikkālum tērkkālum vaḻukum

Kūṉalil am piṟai mut itta vēn i alan○ kārar

Kuṟṟālat tirikūt a malai en○ kal malaiyē!

Or, in translation,

Mountain monkeys pick fresh fruit
to give to their ladies, and then
they cuddle up and hug them.
Gods up in heaven just beg
for pieces of fruit those ladies let drop.
Forest people raise their eyes to invite
those heavenly gods. Mystics who know
how to fly through the sky alight
right here in these mountains, and here
they cultivate bodies that never decay.
Honey Falls boils up from the earth
and flows on a course through the sky,

so the red-rayed sun's horses' hooves,
and his chariot wheels, slip down into
Mount Tirikutam of Kutralam's Lord,
Him who bedecks His matted hair with
the bent young crescent moon.
That mountain is ours![22]

This glorious stanza is unambiguous—even to the point of utilizing the emphatic final particle *–ē* in "That mountain is ours!"[23] as do all six of the poems in this section. They all assert that the mountains belong to the Kuṟavar people. But what does that mean? I do not know what the poet might have meant by it, himself a high-born man of fame and fortune who certainly saw himself as quite different from the Kuṟavar people he described. It seems highly unlikely that he intended to showcase the Kuṟavars as private-property owners of mountain lands, yet it is also the case that Kavirayar does ascribe to his literary Kuṟavar people the right to live in the mountains, and to use mountain resources in making their living. Perhaps, though, the ownership aspect should have been downplayed; the translation might indeed more appropriately read,

That is the very mountain where we live.

Or perhaps the Kuṟavars' rights to living there should have been emphasized even more strongly, as for example,

That mountain is really our own mountain!

Given the varied accepted grammatical interpretations of final *–ē*, any of these might be seen as defensible translations, yet their implications differ significantly in terms of the social scenarios they assume as a backdrop.

But perhaps even these literary portrayals of Mountain Kuṟavar people and their homes amount, at least in part, to yet another example of "the non-existent, the sweet, and the good;" perhaps their lives were more destitute than the famous song would portray. Even Kavirayar himself certainly does describe Kuṟavar people as living in poverty. For example, as she prepares to tell the fortunes of the high-born girl, the Kuṟatti figure is made to say,

I am a Kuravanji whom
even kings admire, Ammé!
Just pour me out a little gruel
to go in my stomach: that's enough, Ammé!

Bring it to me, whatever it is,
even if it's only porridge, Ammé!
When it arrives I will drink enough water
to fill this big belly of mine, Ammé![24]

That is to say, while she has had her dealings with plenty of high-born people, up to and including kings, the Kuṟatti fortune-teller is so poor she needs to ask for rice-gruel and water to fill her belly.[25]

Today Kuṟavar people in the area are officially prohibited from even going into the mountains to collect materials for basketry and broom-making, an occupation that provides a large portion of their meagre income, and successful hunting has become extremely difficult. Life is very hard. As one Mountain Kuṟavar woman put it in 2004, "We Kuṟavar women may lead relatively more independent lives than high-born women, but we have no financial security. The roof leaks, and we can barely afford a cup of tea now and then."[26]

Problematic questions like these arise at every turn. One final example may be useful here. Like the earlier example concerning ownership and usage rights to life in the mountains, this example also has to do with the varied effects of differing approaches to translating the same words. Very near the end of *Thiru-k-Kutrala-k-Kuravanji* there is a rapid-fire set of bantering exchanges between Singan, the Kuṟavaṉ, and his wife Singi, the Kuṟatti. Some of these exchanges come quite close to being bawdy. For example, at one point Singan declares,

> My tongue is quivering for the petals of your pretty mouth, dear Singi.

To which she replies,

> All that your mouth really enjoys is the taste of your evening wine, right, Singan?[27]

My question here is how properly to translate *mālai-k-kal,* the "evening wine" to which she referred. By all the dictionaries it would indeed be "evening wine." But at least to western readers that translation might easily evoke relatively elegant, staid, upper-middle class visions of nice glassware and good wine—or at least not the cheapest of wines. But "wine" here, *kal,* is not an elegant drink at all. Perhaps to be more accurate in presenting this scene to a western English-language reader, Singi ought to be made to say,

> All your big mouth really likes is an evening slug of cheap beer, right, Singan?

This translation could easily evoke an image of a western man coming home from a working-class job and guzzling a six-pack of beer in front of his TV. And in a sense that is the type of situation our poet wants us to visualize; at the very least, he probably did not want us to imagine nice glassware and good wine. But today Kuṟavar people are under fire. They are often the targets of low-grade harassment, and of jokes about drinking and behaving in low-class ways, all of which eventually feed into justifications for dispossessing them from their mountain homes and resources. In this context, is a translator justified in departing from dictionary definitions and playing up the "six-pack" sort of image since it seems so likely that the playwright intended something along those lines? I decided that it would be a cruel political statement, in today's context, to follow that line of thought, and that it might even feed into yet further troubles for real Kuṟavar people, as well as fuel more misunderstanding on the part of western, English-language readers. Furthermore, the arguments in favour of the "six-pack" translation were based on having a westerner as the English-language reader. How does either the "evening wine" or the "slug of cheap beer" translation strike an Indian English-language reader—especially when we acknowledge that such a person will quite likely already know the current, and extremely low, status of the Kuṟavar *iṉam*, a fact that most westerners simply do not know about? And there is the additional problem with anachronism: if the "slug of cheap beer" phrase really does evoke images of six-packs and TV, then fitting those images into the drama's 18th-century setting would surely be an impossibly discordant task. In the end, I opted in favour of the "evening wine" translation. How one translates something is indeed affected by political considerations, and vice versa: the political impact of a work can be affected by its translation.

Have the differential literary portrayals, over the course of millennia, of Kuṟavar people and of wealthy, powerful landowners really played into justifications for dispossessing people from their ancestral homes? Literature and entertainment styles and forms from other times and places have clearly played such a role in justifying dispossession. One such example would be the blackface minstrel shows that were popular in my own country, the United States, during the 19th century, but which went hand-in-hand with the widespread disenfranchisement and dispossession of African-American people.[28] Another example, this one involving my home state of Kentucky, would be the feature news stories, the cartoons, and the cinematic portrayals of Appalachian people as culturally un-evolved semi-savages that went hand-in-hand with their dispossession from their mountain homes during the 20th century.[29] And then, of course, there is the entire history of the United States, built as it has been on the dispossession of Native American peoples from their homes, also helped along by portrayals, both popular and academic, of untamed independent cultures, unworthy of rights to live there.[30] Might Kavirayar's portrayals have served the expansionist needs of little kings and big landowners by painting Kuṟavar people as so markedly different from those powerful people, indeed painting them as untamed, independent, and silly, that they might seem unworthy of rights to mountain lands which could generate wealth for big landowners? How do literary portrayals like these factor into the continuing process of alienating so-called tribal people, like today's Mountain Kuṟavar people, from their ancestral homes?

Further, questions relating to the continuing political role of a piece of literature do not disappear when a work is translated into another language. Quite the contrary. If, for example, a translation into English of *Thiru-k-Kutrala-k-Kuravanji* presents an English-language reader with a picture of Kuṟavar people as "simple mountain folk," it would have done justice to a big part of what clearly was Kavirayar's intent, but it would also miss the classical background from which literary portrayals of Kavirayar's Kuṟavar people developed, and it would miss the social and political implications for people living today under the shadow of these earlier portrayals. And if the English-language reader is not an Indian, then the background knowledge of Kuṟavar people's current social standing also would be lost. On the other hand, if a translation into English were to bore in on the social aspects of the work, how could it do justice to "the non-existent, the sweet, and the good"?

My hope here is to have laid open one area of interest, one that translators face whether consciously or subconsciously. When there is a parallel between literary portrayals and damaging power relations in social history, whose voices are brought into the understandings that become, eventually, the text that a translator presents to the reading public? In particular, when people are at the receiving end of those damaging social forces, how shall their voices be included? What parallels or counterexamples can be brought to bear on these questions from other areas of Tamil studies—other times, places, and contexts in Tamil Nadu or elsewhere? But most particularly, where does a translator's responsibility lie in the midst of all this?

NOTES

1. An earlier version of this paper was presented at the International Symposium on Tamil as a Classical Language in Chennai, January 2008, and subsequently published as "Translating the Tamil *Akam* Tradition through the Ages: Literary Beauty and the Kuṟavaṉ and Kuṟatti Figures," in the *Journal of the Institute of Asian Studies* 21, 1 (September 2003): 9-21.

2. In fact, within living memory were the days when Kuṟavar people were not allowed through the massive temple gates into the outermost courtyard areas of Hindu temples in places like Tenkasi. Interestingly, some token changes in that situation have begun to appear. For example, it is Kuṟavar men who now perform the music for worship at the important Siva-temple in Tenkasi, and who perform at festival times in other, smaller temples in the Tenkasi area.

3. An *iṉam,* in this context, is a social grouping of people who share something in common with each other. The word has been variously translated into English, sometimes by the words "race," "caste," "class," "tribe," or "clan." For the past few centuries Kuṟavar people have been designated in official English as Tribal people, but it has not always been so. It is hoped that the Tamil word *iṉam* here will convey a more general, and a less legalistic, sense of Kuṟavar identity than any of its dictionary definitions would do.

4. Considerable confusion surrounds the relationships among various contemporary real-life groups of people to whom the Kuṟavar name is attached. The contemporary *iṉam* that is the particular focus of this paper is that group of people called Mountain Kuṟavar people. One young man from that community said quite clearly that his people were to be called either *Mountain Kuṟavars (Malai-k- Kuṟavar)* or *Mountain Hunters (Malai Vēt uvar)*. In any case there is another, quite distinct group of people called Fox Kuṟavars, *Nari-k-Kuṟavar*, who are not the same group at all. Many Fox Kuṟavar people do not speak Tamil as their native language, and they often dress in a more or less North Indian style that definitely sets them apart from most Tamil people. Mountain Kuṟavar people speak Tamil among themselves,

and also told me that they know no other language. Their clothing is often indistinguishable from Tamil mainstream clothing, but sometimes it is slightly different; in any case it is never as distinctively different as that of the Fox Kuṟavar people. Additionally, there are other Kuṟavar people in many villages and towns who do various kinds of work for their villages, often work that deals with public sanitation. Many mainstream Tamil people do not see much difference in all of these various *iṉams.* A commonly expressed view is that all Kuṟavar people eventually trace their lineage back to Mountain Kuṟavar people of long, long ago.

5. Interestingly, tradition holds that some of these Sangam poems were composed by mountain chieftains. Whether such mountain chieftains might or might not have been Kuṟavar people is never discussed and must be left an open question. Still, that some of the very literature treating of Kuṟavar lives might have been created by Kuṟavar people themselves is not impossible to imagine. Contrast this observation with later literary developments, in which it would be impossible to imagine Kuṟavar authors. See, for example, comments on the authorship of *Cilappatikāram,* and of *Thiru-k-Kutrala-k-Kuravanji,* later in this essay.

6. Translations from David C Buck and K Paramasivam, trans. 1997. *The Study of Stolen Love: A Translation of Kalaviyal eṉṟa Iṟaiyaṉār Akapporul with Commentary by Nakkīraṉār.* Atlanta: Scholars Press. 30–32.

7. Buck and Paramasivam (1997), pp. 32–33.

8. Buck and Paramasivam (1997), p. 1. The text of *Iṟaiyaṉār Akapporul* sets up the discussion of this first-love meeting in the context of the eight types of marriage envisioned in Brahminical texts, and likens it to one of those called "the Kantaruva Convention." It is the commentator Nakkīraṉār, then, who says that the experience of these literary young lovers is not part of "the world's customs."

9. Buck and Paramasivam (1997), p. 26. "…the non-existent, the sweet, and the good" is our translation of Nakkīraṉār's phrase *illatu iṉiyatu nallatu.*

10. a "way of the world."

11. a "way of literature."

12. Buck and Paramasivam (1997), p. 38.

13. Buck and Paramasivam (1997), p. 78.

14. That is to say, as early as we have currently existing Tamil literature, leaving open the question of poetry composed before the Third Sangam, but no longer available for modern-day readers.

15. *Kuṉṟa-k-Kuṟavar.* See the Patikam, lines 1–9.

16. Ibid.

17. There may be room to question whether people called Maṟavars and Ēyiṉārs are also referred to as Kuṟavars—commentators have used these terms together in some instances, but separately in other instances.

18. In fact, tradition has it that it was in Ilanji, a town very close to the home of the Mountain Kuṟavar people referred to above, that Murugan took Valli as his wife. See David C Buck, trans. 2005. *Melagaram Tirikutarasappa Kavirayar's A Kuravanji in Ḳutralam.* Chennai: Institute of Asian Studies. 212–213.

19. One example would be the Saiva Saint Kan n appa Nāyaṉār, a rough mountain hunter who comes to be accepted as a Siva devotee. The *iṉam*-name "Kuṟavar" is sometimes used as a generic term referring quite broadly to mountain-hunter people; sometimes *Kuṟavar* is even used quite interchangeably with *Vēt uvar,* •"hunter." See, for example, footnote 4, above, and also V Visvanatha Pillai, 1963, *A Tamil-English Dictionary,* 6th ed. Madras: Madras School Book and Literature Society. 253.

20. Although the term is not used in the text, people referring to these characters usually

characterize them as being from high families, *mēt t u-k-kut i.*

21. There is, however, still some confusion about two *iṉam*-names: Kuṟavar and Kul uvar See Buck (2005), pp. 24–25.

22. Translation by David C Buck.

23. *[anta malai] … enȯ kal malaiyē!*

24. Translation from Buck (2005), pp. 246–247.

25. High school Tamil teacher S Manickam amplified this passage by explaining that the Kuṟatti's own life and experience did not include the fine foods enjoyed by wealthy people, so she knew only to ask for the poor-people's food she was used to.

26. See Buck (2005), pp. 51–52.

27. Buck (2005), pp. 364–365.

28. There is a great deal of literature on this subject. See, for example, Eric Lott. 1993. *Love and Theft: Blackface Minstrelsy and the American Working Class.* New York: Oxford University Press.

29. There is a great deal of literature on this subject. See, for example, numerous reports of feuding "hillbillies," and the "Lil' Abner" cartoon series. Also of note is this documentary: Appalshop Films (1984) *Strangers and Kin: A History of the Hillbilly Image,* produced by Dee Alvin Davis III and directed by Herb Smith. Videocassette.

30. There is a great deal of literature on this subject. See, for example, Susan Lobo and Steve Talbott, eds. 1998. *Native American Voices: A Reader.* New York: Longman, particularly pages 173–177. Also see Robert F Berkhofer. 1979. *The White Man's Indian: Images of the American Indian from Columbus to the Present.* New York: Vintage Books.

WORKS CITED

Appalshop Films. 1984. *Strangers and Kin: A History of the Hillbilly Image,* produced by Dee Alvin Davis III and directed by Herb Smith. Videocassette.

Berkhofer, Robert F. 1979. *The White Man's Indian: Images of the American Indian from Columbus to the Present.* New York: Vintage Books.

Buck, David C and K Paramasivam, trans. 1997. *The Study of Stolen Love: A Translation of Kalaviyal eṉṟa Iṟaiyanār Akapporul with Commentary by Nakkīraṉār.* Atlanta: Scholars Press.

Buck, David C, trans. 2005. *Melagaram Tirikutarasappa Kavirayar's A Kuravanji in Kutralam.* Chennai: Institute of Asian Studies.

Lobo, Susan and Steve Talbott, eds. 1998. *Native American Voices: A Reader.* New York: Longman.

Lott, Eric. 1993. *Love and Theft: Blackface Minstrelsy and the American Working Class.* New York: Oxford University Press.

Visvanatha Pillai, V. 1963. *A Tamil-English Dictionary.* 6th ed. Madras: Madras School Book and Literature Society.

Nāyaka Elaborations of Personhood: A Reading of *The Descent of Gaṅgā* by Nīlakaṇṭha Dīkṣita

GIL BEN-HERUT

Introduction

This paper[1] discusses the Sanskrit poem titled *Gaṅgāvatarana* ("*The Descent of Gaṅgā*," *GĀ* henceforth), which was composed during the seventeenth century CE by Nīlakaṇṭha Dīkṣita.[2] This highly esteemed poet was also, during a considerable period in his life, the chief minister *(mantrin)* for King Tirumala Nāyaka, the famed ruler of the city of Madurai at that time. *GĀ* retells the well-known myth of the descent of goddess Gaṅgā in the form of a river onto Śiva's head and then down to earth. *GĀ* is a *mahākāvya,* or courtly poem, and it adheres to this genre's stringent poetics: it focuses on the heroic deeds of a kingly figure; the plot is adopted from a famous mythical tale; the poem has eight chapters using various meters; it contains nature descriptions and descriptions of different seasons; and so on.[3] Being a late *mahākāvya, GĀ* is a product of a long and developed tradition of pan-Indian courtly literature composed in Sanskrit. At the same time, *GĀ* is also a product of a rich local tradition of literary production; a tradition which operates in a multi-lingual and inevitably dynamic culture. It is with these two circles of reference—the pan-Indian expressivity of Sanskrit and the specific historical context from which this poem emerged—that I explore it in this paper in order to elaborate about the *imaginaire* of seventeenth-century Tamil land.

As already stated, the Nāyaka kingdom in Madurai, as well as in other cities, was a multi-lingual center for prolific literary creation.[4] It is well known that King Tirumala was a polyglot and encouraged literary production in several languages, (Tamil, Telugu, Sanskrit), and that Nīlakaṇṭha Dīkṣita himself was a descendant of a renowned dynasty of Sanskrit *kavi*-s (poets) and the grand-nephew of the famous polymath Appayya Dīkṣita (who, as the tradition tells us, directly passed his poetic competence to his grand-nephew) (Unni 1995: 18; Nīlakaṇṭha 1967: 4). Nīlakaṇṭha composed several *mahākāvya* works based on famous mythical narratives from the classic epics and the Purāṇas. These mythical adaptations were composed by

Nīlakaṇṭha in a descriptive, playful, and amusing manner, and *GĀ* is no exception to this trend.

GĀ tells us about Gaṅgā's descent from heaven; a story which was, of course, already well-known by the seventeenth century CE. The story appears in many variants in the epic literature, as this descent marks, all over the South-Asian peninsula, an entry of a godly wealth into the world of man. Apparently the earliest written accounts of this story appear in the *Mahābhārata* 3.104–108 and in the *Rāmāyaṇa* 1.38–44.[5] In the *Rāmāyaṇa,* this story is a part of a collection of stories that Viśvāmitra tells Rāma in order to exhibit the greatness of Rāma's royal dynasty (Goldman and Sutherland Goldman 1984: 77), as Gaṅgā's descent was invoked by King Bhagīratha, one of this dynasty's kings.

The basic plot of this myth tells us about the descent of goddess Gaṅgā, in the form of a raging river, from the world of the gods onto earth, where she filled the then-empty ocean. With little doubt, the peak of this story is Gaṅgā's landing on the head of god Śiva; and act with which Śiva absorbed the lethal might of Gaṅgā's water. This act enabled her to flow down gently to earth without destroying it completely. As already mentioned, the catalyst for Gaṅgā's descent was King Bhagīratha, a descendant of the royal lineage of Raghu. Since the ashes of his ancestors were held in the underworld (called Rasātala), only the moistening of the ancestors' ashes with Gaṅgā's water could enable their release into heaven, as the water finally did. Thus, it was Bhagīratha who, through ardent *tapas* (austerities), successfully initiated Gaṅgā's descent and reestablished his dynasty's fame.

There are many *stotras* (eulogies or hymns of praise) for Goddess Gaṅgā from the second millennium, as her worship gained popularity throughout the peninsula during this time,[6] but only few Sanskrit compositions in the second millennium actually tell us the story of the descent of Gaṅgā. This state of affairs might have served as an incentive for Nīlakaṇṭha to choose this theme for his work. At the same time, we should not assume that Nīlakaṇṭha's decision to retell the story of Gaṅgā was trivial, as a meaningful correspondence exists between this story and Nīlakaṇṭha's immediate environment, and I dedicate the rest of this paper for the purpose of this correspondence.

Reading the GĀ *in its Locale*

My research begins with a question: what is the relationship between a poem that is composed in Sanskrit, and in the highly conventionalized, restrictive genre of a *mahākāvya,* and this poem's immediate cultural environment of seventeen-century Nāyaka Madurai. As a preliminary note, it should be acknowledged that, by this time, Sanskrit was no longer the foremost medium to compose literature, as the vernaculars had already long ago inherited Sanskrit as the preferred medium for literary composition. In the Madurai area these were mostly Tamil and Telugu. At the same time, it is equally clear that Sanskrit composition still maintained some kind of cultural significance, as is clear from the case of Nīlakaṇṭha—who was a central political figure in the court of King Tirumala. There is even an explicit connection between Nīlakaṇṭha's public persona and his mastery over Sanskritic poetry: Tradition tells us that Nīlakaṇṭha won his lucrative position at King Tirumala's court because of his ability to versify in Sanskrit.[7]

The early scholars of Sanskrit poetry tend to overlook the immediate cultural ecology of Sanskrit poets, presupposing that Sanskrit composition simply does not exercise any relationship with its surrounding. Such scholars perceive Sanskrit literature, all through its two thousand years of compositions, as a static idiom which is trapped within a complex net of conventions and mythical narratives that are ubiquitous and monolithic throughout South Asia.[8] In recent times, scholars contest this premise and re-examine the negotiations between the pan-Indian and local mediums, as reflected in the second millennium Sanskrit literature. Sheldon Pollock writes that we need to—

> . . . think in a historical–anthropological spirit: trying to understand what the texts of South Asian literature meant to the people who wrote, heard, saw, or read them, and how these meanings changed over time (2003: 14).

The nature of the relationship that the *GĀ* exercises with its environment shapes this paper on two axes: The first is temporal and vertical—examining *GĀ* in light of the earlier pan-Indian versions and looking for differences and for their possible meanings. The second is spatial and horizontal—examining the contemporaneous broader culture and its influence on this specific work; a cultural context that contains religious and political dispositions as well as specific vernacular and literary sensibilities. The cultural environment of seventeenth-century Nāyaka kingdoms is, indeed, very rich, partially because it continued the ethos of the late Vijayanagara Empire; an ethos which was highly invested in rich literary production in multiple languages. Furthermore, in the Vijayanagara Empire the king was elevated to a divine stature and new conceptions of gods and goddesses emerged. Later, these cultural configurations were relegated onto the smaller post-Vijayanagara kingdoms, and Nāyaka Madurai was one of these. It is with this background that I approach *GĀ*.

The Poet and the King

Nīlakaṇṭha served the renowned ruler Tirumala Nāyaka, who was the most important ruler of Madurai's Nāyaka kingdom. Tirumala Nāyaka ruled for 36 years, from 1613 CE, and under his reign Madurai reclaimed its former glory as an important commercial and cultural center in the Tamil area (Unni: 15). We know quite a lot about this period, which was recorded by Portuguese and Dutch Jesuits and merchants, and was also portrayed in the literary production of Telugu and Tamil, as well as in

Sanskrit (Narayana Rao, Shulman, and Subrahmanyam 1992: 334-37).

Among other enterprises, Tirumala Nāyaka renovated and expanded the famous Mīnākṣī temple of Madurai. He lived in a large palace, protected by Turkish guards, and developed a specific liking for lucrative paraphernalia, such as a fleet of elephants. We know that this was a time of a new economy that was based on commercial connections with Bengal and Europe (p. 57-112) and that a new class of rich elite emerged in various centers throughout the empire; an elite that served as a new audience for courtly poetry. Accordingly, the Nāyaka kings displayed a sincere interest in poetry of different languages, including Sanskrit.

Nīlakaṇṭha arrived to Madurai following the presage of his grand-uncle, the famous Appayya Dīikṣita. Traditional accounts tell us that on his deathbed, Appayya bequeathed to the 12-year-old Nīlakaṇṭha his own copies of *Devīmahātmya* and *Raghuvaṃśa,* his *pañcaliṅga* (the five Śiva emblems he worshiped), and then prophesied that the young Nīlakaṇṭha would become the minister of the Pāṇḍya king (Unni 1995: 18; Nīlakaṇṭha 1967: 4). And so, by becoming Tirumala's minister, Nīlakaṇṭha fulfilled his famous grand-uncle's prophecy.

According to the following story Nīlakaṇṭha was an important figure in Tirumala's court:

> The Nāyaka king ordered the court sculptor to carve a statue of his queen. As the sculptor was carving the thigh, his chisel slipped and a mole-like blemish appeared. The sculptor immediately discarded the statue and began another statue from scratch, since the queen's statue could have no defect. Then again, to his surprise, as he was carving the thigh on the second statue, the same thing happened and another mole-like cavity was formed. And again. And again. When this had happened for the fifth time, he went to Nīlakaṇṭha seeking advice. Nīlakaṇṭha closed his eyes for a few moments and then told the sculptor "go, finish your statue and submit it to the king. It will be so, since the queen indeed has a mole on her thigh."
>
> When the sculptor presented his masterpiece to the king, the king was enraged on seeing the familiar, initmate mole-like blemish on the thigh, and demanded an explanation from the nervous sculptor. The sculptor then blurted out the entire story.
>
> Suspecting that Nīlakaṇṭha had had the audacity to see the queen's thigh, the king immediately ordered his soldiers to ride out and bring Nīlakaṇṭha, who had retired and was living in a village near the court, for the king intended to blind Nīlakaṇṭha in public, as an example to all.
>
> When the soldiers reached Nīlakaṇṭha, he said to the soldiers, "go tell your master that I have done what he wanted to be done."
>
> When the soldiers relayed this message to the king, he rushed to see Nīlakaṇṭha, and found that he had blinded himself with a pair of burning coals. The king was immediately filled with remorse and presented Nīlakaṇṭha with a village called Palamadai, where Nīlakaṇṭha retired to.

Interestingly, the village of Palamadai exists to this day. It is situated south of Madurai, and its people still commemorate the village's founder, Nīlakaṇṭha.[9] With regard to the tragic ending of the story, the tradition mollifies it applying to it a fantastic twist: The Blind Nīlakaṇṭha went to the Mīnākṣī temple and, standing in front of the goddess, composed on the spot his poem in her praise, *Ānandasāgarastava* ("Eulogy for the Ocean of Bliss"). When he reached the sixty first stanza and sang "with which eyes will I see your lotus feet?", he immediately regained his eyesight (Nīlakaṇṭha 1967: 5-6, in French).

This story bears several interesting characteristics. First, the story marks the locality of the poet and his work. The poem mentioned in this story, *Ānandasāgarastava*, was composed inside a specific temple, and Nīlakaṇṭha is remembered through this story as the local advisor for the local king. Indeed, local heritage commemorates him. Second, this story illustrates Nīlakaṇṭha's rich and complex relationship with the local king and court life. Regardless of how we read the fantastic events in this story, we still learn something about how Nīlakaṇṭha conducted himself in day-to-day politics: his ability to handle crises both large and small, his position as an advisor to the court people, and his intimate knowledge of court gossip and the daily lives of those involved. Third, this story also echoes the typical inner conflict of a *kavi*—whether to live and create in the worldly life at the king's court, or, alternatively, to retire from society to secluded surroundings; a paradox which was very apparent in Nīlakaṇṭha's life. Indeed, as the story tells us, Nīlakaṇṭha despaired at some point of political life and retired to a secluded temple he built in his village Palamadai (Unni: 19).

Nīlakaṇṭha's intimate familiarity with court life is also mirrored in his poetic work. One aspect of this acquaintance is Nīlakaṇṭha's satires *(viḍambana)*, where his ironic descriptions portray a world in which being a poet was considered a worthwhile and acclaimed occupation. Nīlakaṇṭha describes common public gatherings at the king's court in which the king would reward the poet according to his enjoyment from the poem that was recited. One poet would be awarded an entire village; another would be seated on an elephant; a third poet would merely be served a meal at the king's court; the fourth would only receive a dot on his forehead. Nīlakaṇṭha often describes how incompetent the poets of his time were—he talks of plagiarism which was commonly practiced, and he even complains that at one time he heard a poet recite verses he himself had composed.[10]

The first unit of the first chapter of *GĀ* contains a meta-poetic passage that is full of such sarcastic observations. To quote one such verse:

dūyāmahe duṣkavibhir dattakarṇajvarā vayam /
na vā vadāmo vāgdevi nanu tvam api tair hatā //
vijñaptiḥ śrūyatām ekā vidhātaḥ karuṇā yadi /
mūkān sṛja kavimanyān badhirān viduṣo 'thavā //

We are tortured by the bad poets who cause distress to our ears. We do not complain about this to you, Goddess-of-Speech, for you, no doubt, are also hit by them. Brahma, if you have any mercy in you, respond to this humble request: Either make these plagiarists dumb or make all learned people—deaf (*GĀ* 1.33–34).

The sarcastic tone in this verse, as well as in many others in *GĀ*, brings to mind another poem by Nīlakaṇṭha called *Kaliviḍambana* ("Mockeries in the Age of Kali"), in which he mercilessly ridicules people from all sections of society.[11] Nīlakaṇṭha's well-known capability to invoke laughter in the reader is easily noticeable throughout the *GĀ*, oftentimes ignited by the frequent use he makes of rhetorical questions and *arthāntaranyāsa*-s (poetic embellishments, or *alaṅkāra*-s, in which the poet alludes to a similar, general case). All these techniques contribute to the overall cheerful tone of the poem, as the verses below exhibit. The following verse, for example, is a part of a long description of the hot summer, during which Bhagīratha was performing his *tapas* (ascetic practices):

> *svāpakālam anupālya gurūṇāṃ vipralabhya ca cireṇa sapatnīḥ /*
> *prasthitāsu kulaṭāsv api gharmaiḥ pātakī kimapi nānucakampe //*
>
> Waiting for hours for their old husbands to fall asleep, deceiving their co-wives, and sweating to reach their tryst—won't the sinner feel something for these unfaithful wives? (*GĀ* 2.52)

Here, Nīlakaṇṭha couples the king's extreme asceticism with a lovers meeting, since both occur during the hot season. Such comic and at times sensuous and even erotic interludes are quite axiomatic for the *GĀ* and in general for Nīlakaṇṭha's work.

Human and Divine: the Nāyaka King

Moving from the general introduction to Nīlakaṇṭha's mode of writing into the specificities of *GĀ*, let us try to conceptualize this work in thematic terms. The most apparent element in this regard is that the story about Gaṅgā's descent in the *GĀ*, compared with the early versions of the story, is completely reconstructed. In the classical versions, the chronological unfolding of the story of Gaṅgā starts with Bhagīratha's great grandfather, King Sagara, and his untamed sons. In sharp contrast, *GĀ* begins with King Bhagīratha himself. The sections of the story about Bhagīratha's ancestors, as well as other scenes of the original story from which Bhagīratha is absent, become completely peripheral in Nīlakaṇṭha's version. Bhagīratha is present practically throughout the story; he has the most prominent role in the poem; and so, evidently, he is the character that Nīlakaṇṭha is most interested to tell us about. Consider, for example, the opening verse of the story:[12]

> *āsīd bhagīratho nāma rājā ravir ivāparaḥ /*
> *yena sākṣātkṛtaḥ śambhur yena gaṅgāvatāritā //*
>
> Once there was a king named Bhagīratha who, much like the sun, was second to none.

By whom Śiva appeared in this world and Gaṅgā was brought down to earth *(GĀ* 1.60).

This verse, as an interlude for the whole narrative in this work, structures the story around Bhagīratha. The opening section that follows this verse meticulously describes King Bhagīratha's fine conduct, his limitless benevolence, and his flawless nature. These descriptions, with their specific details, generate a general sense that Nīlakaṇṭha was inspired by his own life experience when creating them. Consider, for example, the depiction of this king in the following verse:

avitīrṇamahāgrāmair akṛtasvarṇavṛṣṭibhiḥ /
kaṭākṣair na babhūve 'sya kavivaktranipātibhiḥ //

His eyes never fell upon the faces of poets without showering them with gold and granting them great villages *(GĀ* 1.77).

Apart from receiving a salary from his patron and boss King Tirumala, (both as a poet and as a minister), we already know that Nīlakaṇṭha was granted an entire village by King Tirumala. It seems then, according to these descriptions, that Nīlakaṇṭha is genuinely familiar with kingly behavior and is sometimes even intimated with the way in which a king *thinks:*

jātaḥ kopo na bhṛtyeṣu jāto 'pi na nigūhitaḥ /
nigūhito 'pi na ciram āsta citte 'sya komale //

Anger due to his servants' deeds was never born in the king's delicate mind. And if such anger was born, it was never concealed. And if it was concealed, then just for an instant *(GĀ* 1.70).

Such intimate, vivid, and original descriptions succeed in maintaining the mythical register of King Bahgiratha, while at the same time suggesting a more immediate king as a reference. And that is Nīlakaṇṭha's king, King Tirumala Nāyaka. If we accept this implicit reference, then our reading of *GĀ* can become a reflection of how the human king in seventeenth-century Tamil Nadu was imagined.

And how is the king imagined in *GĀ?* The following examples illustrate the his grandeur. This verse is part of a long passage describing the king's unyielding *tapas:*

nānnam ādriyata nāmbu na mūlaṃ kā bhaviṣyati kathāpi phalānām /
mārutaṃ param abhuṅkta nidāghas taṃ ca hartum iva tasya tad abhūt //

[King Bhagīratha] did not care for food, nor for water, nor for roots. What would be the deal with fruits! He only ate wind, and so appeared the summer, as if to deprive of him even that *(GĀ* 2.30).

Clearly, the summer and the winter fail in their despicable efforts to obstruct King

Bhagīratha's *tapas.* In this manner, the poem is full of heroic descriptions of him. He is a *vīra,* a true hero, or better yet, a *siddha,* one who attained the highest objective of becoming divine. Here is the depiction of Bhagīratha as compared with Kṛṣṇa:

> *govardhanadharasyāpi yadi tāvad yaśo hareḥ /*
> *kiyan na varṇyaḥ bhuvaṃ bibhrat sagirikānanạ̄m //*
>
> If Kṛṣṇa's fame is so great for carrying just one small mountain—how much fame should there be for this king, who carries the earth together with its mountains and forests? (*GĀ* 1.62).

Such grandiose, hyperbolic descriptions of a king are typical of south India's small kingdoms of the late medieval period. In these kingdoms, the logic behind this literary vogue dictates that the smaller the kingdom in actuality, the more fabricated and inflated is its pretense of grandeur. Hence, the description of the king as carrying the entire earth was not unfamiliar to Nīlakaṇṭha's immediate audience, an audience that included, of course, King Tirumala Nāyaka himself.

Notice in the verse above King Bhariratha's superiority over God Kṛṣṇa, and the implicit insinuated diminution of the latter. Such tongue-in-cheek descriptions of the gods are hardly an exception in Nīlakaṇṭha's writing. And they are not limited to just Viṣṇu or Kṛṣṇa:

> *mumūrṣamāṇāsuraśalkavikramaprasaṅgasaṃbhāvanayāpi mūrcchatām /*
> *abhūn na cite nṛpater divaukasām api prasajya pratiṣedhapātratā //*
>
> Although the dwellers in heaven faint at the slightest sign of courage that the moribund demons exhibit, Bhagīratha did not even consider to refrain from asking the gods for help (*GĀ* 3.28).

This verse launches a long description of Bhagīratha's dilemmas in choosing a god capable of absorbing Gaṅgā's force. Unsurprisingly, one after the other, Brahmā, Viṣṇu, and Śiva are disqualified for their demerits: Brahmā is too old and tired, Viṣṇu is too light-headed, and Śiva is not tenacious enough in protecting his devotees (*GĀ* 3.28–42). This audacity in attributing human weaknesses to the gods is not uncommon in Nīlakaṇṭha's writing in general and in *GĀ* in particular. We can observe this feature also in the following segment, which concludes the description of the cold winter, in which Bhagīratha performs his *tapas:*

> *ākṛṣṭayoḥ kumārābhyām aibhavaiyāghracarmaṇoḥ /*
> *saṃbhrāntā patim āvavre savyānāgreṇa pārvatī //*
> *avamucya vataṃsendum avaropyāhibhūṣaṇam /*
> *udghāṭya cākṣi tārtīyam īśenāpi sthitaṃ tadā //*
> *nṛpatis trijagaddāhanidānena tapo'gninā /*
> *hemantaṃ himavantam vā nācintayata cetasā //*

tridaśās tacchirorandhratapognijvālatāpitāḥ /
sasmaruś cākṣuṣaṃ jyotiḥ saṃvarteṣu kapardinaḥ //

> Pāravatī was worried that her husband [might catch cold], because the two sons have pulled the animal-skin blanket completely over to their side. Therefore, she covered [Śiva] with her own garments. Śiva released [from his hair] his crest-moon and snakes-ornaments and ignited the fire of his third eye so they could share its warmth. [In contrast,] the king, who had a fiery *tapas* that could consume all three worlds, did not even consider the cold winter or the snowy mountain. The gods, sensing the fiery heat rising from the aperture of his head, were immediately reminded of the brightest light that was once created by Śiva during the dissolution of the world (*GĀ* 4.30–3).

Consider the reversal of roles in this section: God Śiva, the foremost *tapasvin* (ascetic) of the Puranic literature, is now a householder. His main concern is to survive, together with his family, the cold winter. His iconography (snakes, animal skin, third eye), which traditionally marks his dreadfulness, is transformed here into an artificial outfit which Śiva is happy to put aside when he is back in his home with his family. Indeed, in the seventeen century CE, after almost two millennium of considerable worship, Śiva has transformed from an iconoclast *tapasvin* into an archetypical householder worried about the cold weather. In sharp contrast to Śiva, Bhagīratha is not the least troubled by the cold since *he* is now the foremost *tapasvin*, and accordingly, his inner fire easily consumes all possible discomforts. The implicit reversal of roles between the human and the divine is further supported in this section by the testimony of all the gods, for at the sight of the *tapasvin* Bhagīratha, they are all reminded of Śiva, the skull-bearer, during the *pralaya* (the world's dissolution).

Following this reading, we can now revisit the opening verse of the story: "Once there was a king named Bhagīratha who, much like the sun, was second to none. By whom Śiva appeared in this world and Gaṅgā was brought down to earth" (*GĀ* 1.60). The syntactic reading of Bhagīratha as the agent for Śiva's appearance (in the instrumental case) conveys the implied-but-complete substitution between man and god: It is the human who constitutes and makes tangible the divine, instead of the other way around.

It is important to note that this reversal between the human and the divine is never pronounced explicitly in *GĀ*. In fact, the poem is full of standard and paradigmatic praises to Śiva, Brahmā, Pārvatī, and Gaṅgā.[13] Furthermore, the narrative of this story clearly celebrates the omniscience of Śiva and Gaṅgā. However, all this is true at the explicit register. The implicit register is rather the opposite: By positing the human and the divine closely to one another and redistributing their qualities (the human is divinized and the divine is humanized), Nīlakaṇṭha succeeds in formulating a subversive *vastu dhvani* (suggestive meaning) to the story about the descent of Gaṅgā. This conceptual undercurrent in this work corresponds well with new cultural understandings regarding the position of the human as compared to the divine in the seventeenth-century Nāyaka kingdoms. Although the traditional religious framework is formally preserved, its *symbolic substance* indicates that, now, the human king succeeds the god.[14]

The Goddess of Water

Alongside the reversal in the roles of the human and the divine, there is also a marked change in the role of goddess Gaṅgā. Her behavior is very different compared to the early versions of the story, where she is either completely mute or speaks very succinctly, and, in general, fully cooperates with the task of descending to earth.

The situation in *GĀ* is very different. Although Gaṅgā's enormous hydro-power is still threatening to destroy the entire world, this power has now invaded a new domain—the verbal. Gaṅgā's turbulent, chaotic, and uncontrollable physical power is now accompanied by her vivacious, wild, and unpredictable speeches. They are funny, surprising, manipulative, and most of all brimming with self-confidence and self-esteem. Almost half a chapter is dedicated to the conversation between Gaṅgā and Bhagīratha, and, more than a polite dialog, it is a juicy verbal duel, full of arguments, sarcasm, and mirth. This chapter is titled *Gaṅgāhaṃkāra* ("Gaṅgā's egocentrism"); a title that conveys the autonomous, self-empowered voice of this goddess.

Gaṅgā's speeches and descriptions in *GĀ* are replete of sprinkles, fountains, waves, and breezes; all of them swirling around and submerging everything that comes their way. After reading her speeches, and then the descriptions of her actual descent, the sense of drowning in water becomes utterly real for the reader. For example, when Bahgiratha suggests to Gaṅgā that Śiva will serve as the "shock absorber" of her water's might, she responds thusly:

> *sāvalepanipatan madūrmitāsaṃplavaikakavalīkṛto haraḥ /*
> *saṃgataḥ payasi śaṅkhaśuktibhir nandinā nanu gaveṣayiṣyate //*
>
> Śiva's pride shall crash when he will be swollen by my waves. Then Nandi will look for him buried in my waters under shells and conches (*GĀ* 5.7).

Gaṅgā's irreverence in this verse is repeated again and again throughout the text and is perhaps the most distinct feature of her character in this work, and I discuss below the cultural implications of this central feature. For now, however, we should note that Gaṅgā's power is not merely verbal; her physical might still has the real potential to destroy the world. Her actual descent on earth and her derived convergence with Śiva, located right in the middle of the poem and comprises a complete chapter, is vivid, imaginative, and detailed, and it generates an incredible sense of awe and wonder in the reader toward this goddess. Within this chapter, we find a long and playful passage in which Nīlakaṇṭha depicts Gaṅgā's actual descent through a cavity at the bottom of the heavenly lake Sarasī, from which she arrives at Brahmā's city. Gaṅgā immediately floods the city, ruins Brahmā's palace, and thus irritates Sarasvatī, who is worried that her precious books might get wet. From here, Gaṅgā continues her descent to Indra's city, which she utterly ruins while causing all the celestial beings to flee. Here is a brief passage from this section:

> *saṃbhramopagatacāraśaṃsitasvargasindhupatanaṃ pade pade /*
> *saudhaśṛṅgavalabhīniveśitasvasvamūladhanam apsarojanaiḥ //*
> *mandurodaravimuktavidravatsaindhavānucarasādimaṇḍalam /*
> *diktaṭoccalitajāṅghikāmarasvīkṛtābhrakakulaṃ gṛhe gṛhe //*
> *nirgatatridaśanāthadarśanastabdhavidravadanīkinībhaṭaṃ /*
> *ittham ākulam atarkitāgatā sā cakāra nagaraṃ śacīpateḥ //*

> The city, struck by the auspicious and heavenly river, went under chaos. The divine courtesans quickly seized their earnings and climbed to the palaces' upper chambers. In many places the river's whirlwinds drove the horses outside of the stables, and the gods, seeing them run in all directions, jumped on clouds and fled. At the sight of the heavenly lords fleeing, the army froze in bewilderment. She [Gaṅgā], arriving completely unexpectedly, did this to Indra's city *(GĀ* 5.30-2).

After completing her *tour de force,* Gaṅgā finally gushes down to earth in order to unite with Śiva. Only when she reaches Śiva's head is Gaṅgā finally subdued, for it is only Śiva who can absorb the might of the goddess. Following this meaningful event, Bhagīratha leads Gaṅgā from Śiva's head to Rasātala (the underworld), and then, through the city of Banaras, he guides her into the ocean. Here is where the reader, quite exhausted from all the commotion, reaches the end of the poem.

In order to properly evaluate the cultural implications of Gaṅgā's descent in *GĀ*, whose figure is obviously central for this poet, we need to examine this text against its cultural contexts. For this purpose, we shall briefly turn our view to the wider cultural milieu out of which this work emerged in order to find support for the enhanced centrality of Goddess Gaṅgā as it is depicted in this work. First we should note the general trend of Gaṅgā's presence in everyday life. The story about Gaṅgā's descent, which is the paradigmatic tale of Gaṅgā's penetration into the realm of man, serves as an important cultural signifier for this process. An important key to understanding the importance of Gaṅgā revolves around her quintessential quality of fluidity and her manifestation as a river. These substances—water and rivers—are highly important cultural resources, and Gaṅgā is the foremost agent for representing them. Diana Eck writes: ". . . In every temple and home the Gaṅgā is called to be present in the waters used in ritual, either by mixing those waters with a few drops of Gaṅgā water or by uttering the name and mantras of the Gaṅgā to invoke her presence" (1996: 138). This affinity between the heavenly Gaṅgā and the local water source also penetrates into the semantic sphere. In her study on river worship in the neighboring region of contemporary Maharashtra, Anne Feldhaus states that "my impression is that the term 'Gaṅgā' is commonly used in Marathi in three different senses: as the name of the river in northern India . . . ; as a name of the Godāvarī; and as a word meaning 'river,' which can therefore be used to refer to any river" (1995: 37 fn. 15).

This very general cultural phenomenon is also acutely present in the seventeenth-century world of the Nāyaka kingdoms, which repeatedly suffered from hard famines (Narayana Rao, Shulman, and Subrahmanyam 1992: 112). Considering the abundance of watery descriptions in this poem—as if it is a literary water-park—against the Nāyaka famines, we might conjecture that *GĀ* deliberately served as a wet refresher in times of drought. This speculation can also be pushed further: Given the trans-semantic prestige of Sanskrit and the absolute metaphysical claims attributed to it, we can say that *GĀ* might have served as a literary "rain maker" in a court that its economy was highly dependent on the scarce resource of water.[15]

The fantastic meta-lingual features of Sanskrit poetry are also tightly connected with the esoteric dimension of Gaṅgā's presence. The encounter between Śiva and Gaṅgā in *GĀ*, which is a convergence of the male and female divinities, signifies the metaphysics of the Tantric tradition, in which godhead is perceived as the unity of Śiva and Śakti. Śiva marks a stasis, a passive and observing component, while Śakti represents a continual dynamism, an active and performing component. There is evidence for a connection in the late medieval period between Śakti worship, an often antinomian worship of the goddess, and Gaṅgā. *Gaṅgālaharī*, a short and popular seventeen-century *stotra* dedicated to goddess Gaṅgā, for example, contains at times harsh articulations of iconoclasm and antinomianism.[16] The *stotra Gaṅgālaharī* was composed by a contemporary of Nīlakaṇṭha, the famous scholar Paṇḍitarāja Jagannātha, with whom Nīlakaṇṭha also had scholarly debates. While the theme of these arguments is outside the scope of this paper, it is still important to note the fact that these two figures shared a conceptual world for which Gaṅgā was central, as both dedicated works to her, in Sanskrit. Nīlakaṇṭha was even initiated, at an early stage of his life, into the esoteric Śakti tradition of Śrividyā and also composed a treaty dedicated to the Tantric goddess.[17] Thus, his articulations of Gaṅgā betray a deep conceptual frame dedicated to this goddess; a frame which is not merely mythical, but also tightly connected with ritualistic practices and ancient esoteric traditions. Nīlakaṇṭha's portrayal of Gaṅgā in this work betrays a deep, perhaps even an intimate connection between the adept and his goddess. This portrayal also expresses a longing for a mystical unity that is based on the erasure of all boundaries and distinctions by the powerful streams of the goddess.

Conclusion

This paper explores different aspect of personhood and religiosity as depicted in *GĀ*, a seventeenth-century Sanskrit *mahākāvya* from a specific Nāyaka kingdom. This paper foregrounds the complex relationship between Nīlakaṇṭha and his king

Tirumala and then continues to discuss specific themes in *GĀ* that connect this work to its immediate cultural environment, foremost of these are the restructuring of the dyad king-god during the second millennium and the emergence of the goddess in literary representations.

More generally, and in different ways, we can see how *GĀ* actively engages with its immediate environment. This paper, thus, serves as one example of the rich relationships that abide between poetry and courtly life; between poet and a king; between king and god; and between god and goddess, in the post-Vijayanaraga kingdoms of South-India. An important premise, with runs as a thread throughout this paper, is that Sanskrit poetry *does* maintain meaningful and relevant connections with its cultural environment during the late medieval, and more broadly, that the effort in studying second millennium Sanskrit literature can yield important understandings of the cultural milieu in which it was produced.

NOTES

1. Gaṅgāvatarana was translated by the author of this paper to Hebrew for a Master's thesis titled Man, God, and Goddess in Seventeenth Century South India. The thesis was submitted to The Religious Studies Program of the School of Philosophy, Tel-Aviv University, Israel, in February, 2007. This thesis originated from an oral presentation given at the Regional Sanskrit Literatures Summer Academy, held in Jerusalem, July 2005. I would like to thank my teachers, David Shulman and Yigal Bronner, for their continuous support. And finally, many thanks to HV Nagaraja Rao for his help, infinite knowledge, and wisdom. Notwithstanding their invaluable help in reading this text, its translation in this paper, including possible mistakes, are solely mine.

2. The edition of *GĀ* used in this paper is taken from the Kavyamala Series (Nīlakaṇṭha 1916).

3. These guidelines were laid down by classical sastrin-s (scholars) such as Dandin, Bharata, and Anandavardhana (Vijayavardhana 1970: 89).

4. For a comprehensive study of the literary production in the Nāyaka kingdoms, see Narayana Rao, Shulman, and Subhrahmanyam (1992).

5. Other instances of this story appear in the following Puranas: Bhagavata Purana 9.8–9; Bhrahmavaivarta Purana, Prakrti Khanda 10; Devibhagavata Purana 9.11; Skanda Purana, Kasi Khanda 33.

6. An indication for this popularity is the presence of many medieval stotras that carry the title Gangalahari, one of them was composed in Sanskrit by the famous Panditaraja Jagannatha; a contemporary and intellectual opponent of Nīlakaṇṭha. I return to discuss Jagannatha below.

7. See detailed story in Nīlakaṇṭha (1967: 5).

8. See discussion about the intellectual history of this trend in the Introduction chapter of Bronner (2010).

9. There is a website dedicated to the heritage of Palamadai and its founder Nīlakaṇṭha. See Ganapathy (2006).

10. These descriptions were taken from HV Nagaraja Rao' paper "Nīlakaṇṭha Dīkṣita and His View on Poets and Poetry" (unpublished).

11. This poem was recently translated by Somadeva Vasudeva (Nīlakaṇṭha, Ksemendra,

and Bhallata 2005).

12. This verse actually launches the narrative, since the first fifty-nine verses consist of a meta-poetic prologue.

13. One prominent example for this trend is when Śiva appears in front of Bhagīratha. At that moment Bhagīratha begins to eulogize Śiva and explicitly ridicules the human compared to the godly. See *GĀ* 67–82.

14. The term "symbolic substance" is borrowed from Symbols of Substance : Court and State in Nāyaka Period Tamilnadu (Narayana Rao, Shulman, and Subrahmanyam 1992).

15. See, for example, David Shulman's chapter "How to Bring a Goddess into Being through Visible Sound" (pp. 305-42) in The Poetics of Grammar and the Metaphysics of Sound and Sign (La Porta and Shulman 2007), where he discusses the ability of Sanskrit phonetics to invoke the Srividya goddess Tripurasundari. The Srividya tradition was exceptionally flourishing in the same spatial and temporal spheres in which the *GĀ* was composed, and Nīlakaṇṭha himself was an adept of this goddess, see below.

16. See, for example, verses 34 and 44 (Jagannatha 1999).

17. See Filliozat's introduction in *Oeuvres poétiques de Nīlakaṇṭha Dīkṣita* (Nīlakaṇṭha 1967) and Unni (1995: 16).

WORKS CITED

Bronner, Yigal. 2010. *Extreme Poetry: The South Asian Movement of Simultaneous Narration, South Asia Across the Disciplines.* New York: Columbia University Press.

Eck, Diana L. 1996. The Goddess Ganges in Hindu Scared Geography. In *Devī: Goddesses of India,* edited by JS Hawley and DM Wulff. Berkley: University of California Press.

Feldhaus, Anne. 1995. *Water and Womanhood: Religious Meanings of Rivers in Maharashtra.* New York, NY: Oxford University Press.

Ganapathy, PR. *Palamadai* 2006. Available from http://www.palamadai.net/Welcome.html.

Goldman, Robert P, and Sally J Sutherland Goldman. 1984. *The Rāmāyaṇa of Vālmīki: An Epic of Ancient India.* Princeton Library of Asian Translations. Princeton, NJ: Princeton University Press.

Jagannātha, Paṇḍitarāja. 1999. *Gaṅgālaharī* (with the Commentary by Śrī Sadāśiva and English Translation). Delhi: Nag Publishers.

La Porta, S, and David Dean Shulman. 2007. *The Poetics of Grammar and the Metaphysics of Sound and Sign.* Leiden; Boston: Brill.

Nagaraja Rao, HV. Unpublished. Nīlakaṇṭha Dīkṣita and His View on Poets and Poetry.

Narayana Rao, Velcheru, David Dean Shulman, and Sanjay Subrahmanyam. 1992. *Symbols of Substance: Court and State in Nāyaka Period Tamilnadu.* Delhi; Oxford: Oxford University Press.

Nīlakaṇṭha, Dīkṣita. Gaṅgāvatarana. 1916. In *Kāvyamālā Series,* edited by TS Kuppuswāmiśāstrī. Bombay: Nirnaya Sagar Press.

———. 1967. *Oeuvres poétiques de Nīlakaṇṭha Dīkṣita, Publications de l'Institut français d'indologie; 36.* Pondichéry, France: Institut Francais d'Indologie.

Nīlakaṇṭha, Dīkṣita, Ksemendra, and Bhallata. 2005. *Three Satires.* 1st ed. New York: New York University Press: JJC Foundation.

Pollock, Sheldon I. 2003. *Literary Cultures In History: Reconstructions From South Asia.* Berkeley: University of California Press.

Unni, NP. 1995. Nīlakaṇṭha Dīkṣita *Makers of Indian Literature.* New Delhi: Sahitya Akademi.

Vijayavardhana, G. 1970. *Outlines of Sanskrit Poetics.* 1st ed. Varanasi: The Chowkhamba Sanskrit Series Office.

"Hey, Girl! Dance the *Kummi* Called '*Moṭcam*'!": The Sufi Poetics of Iḷaiyāṉkuṭi Kaccippiḷḷaiyammāḷ[1]

SUSAN SCHOMBURG

Introduction

Since women typically are defined in male-authored normative discourses across world religious traditions as "other" vis-à-vis the "human", scholars might reasonably ask how women have made sense of their own lives in light of this marginal status. South Asian culture, generally, and Tamil culture, specifically, offer avenues for empowerment through emphasis on piety and spiritual quest, a kind of "cultural capital" available to all marginalized folk, including men, but particularly important for women. In Tamil culture, histories of accomplished female saints, strong traditions of veneration of the Goddess, as well as valorization of femininity in a variety of gendered literary genres and female-specific ritual traditions add to this cultural capital in unique ways. In Islamic culture, too, tradition-specific resources encourage women's sense of self-worth, agency, and autonomy—and again, as in the Tamil case, these resources are closely tied to religious values. As Leila Ahmed points out in her ground-breaking historical study, *Women and Gender in Islam,* Muslim women have always "tuned into" the egalitarian message of the Qur'an, that whatever differences exist between the sexes, and whatever the sexist traditions of their local societies, men and women are equals before God. Both are capable of error, of straying from God's path, both are capable of piety, righteousness, and wisdom. In contrast to other strands of Islamic tradition, Muslim women have relied on common sense and a synthetic Qur'anic understanding to live in the confidence that ultimately, human value is sex- and gender-neutral. Historically, in part because of exclusion from male domains of normative Islamic culture, unique Muslim women's ritual traditions have developed as well, engendering avenues for self-expression, group solidarity, and female religious achievement and authority.

This writing presents a preliminary exploration of the poetic corpus of an extraordinary Tamil Muslim woman, Iḷaiyāṉkuṭi Kaccippiḷḷaiyammāḷ, whose work represents a confluence of Islamic and Tamil cultural traditions and who exemplifies not only extraordinary female, but extraordinary human achievement in the terms of both realms.[2] The study represents a first foray into a new research project, an exploration of the lives and literary production of several female Sufis (Muslim mystics) in Tamil Nadu, including Kaccippiḷḷaiyammāḷ of Ilaiyankudi, Sayyida Asiya Umma of Kilakkarai, and Rasul Bivi Amma of Tenkasi.[3] Aside from the interest of their individual writings, a comparison of their work should be instructive: Islamic Tamil literature manifests a spectrum from a more Arabic–Islamic, normative tradition-centered linguistic, literary, and cultural character to a more Tamil, local traditions-based character. Kaccippiḷḷaiyammāḷ's work is situated at the more local pole of the spectrum, rooted within a specifically Saivite *cittar* tradition *(cittars* are yogi-mystics), while Sayyida Asiya Umma's poetry is situated more on the Arabic-Islamic normative tradition pole of the spectrum. Kaccippiḷḷaiyammāḷ wrote in Tamil; Sayyida Asiya Umma wrote in Arwi, which is Tamil written in a modified Arabic script (although lately some of her work has been published in Tamil script, as well). The ancestry, social location, and life histories of these women help explain their distinctive creativities, and will be explored in future writing.

This paper begins to explore the Sufi poetry of Iḷaiyāṉkuṭi Kaccippiḷḷaiyammāḷ — the four poems which comprise her sole published work, the *Ilāhi Meyññāṉa Mālai,* "The Garland of Divine Spiritual Wisdom". For the sake of brevity, the paper will discuss the first poem of the *Ilāhi Meyññāṉa Mālai* in greater detail, summarizing and presenting selected highlights only of the others.

The very title of the work, *Ilāhi Meyññāṉa Mālai,* is instructive, and gives a hint of Kaccippiḷḷaiyammāḷ's agenda, and accomplishment, in the work. The *Ilāhi,* translated here as "divine", is an Arabic term[4] grammatically related to the more familiar Arabic term, *Allāh* ("the God"). *Ilāh* is the Arabic generic term, "god" or "deity". Any South Asian Muslim religious thinker in contact with normative Islamic expectations as well as majority culture religious beliefs and practices must somehow negotiate competing theological claims of Hindu and Islamic traditions, and indeed, this seems to be one of Kaccippiḷḷaiyammāḷ's purposes in this work, aside from describing her extraordinary visionary experiences. This is no generic "*Meyññāṉa Mālai*", but rather, one concerned with divine realities—divinity inflected in the Arabic, so to speak. In South Asia, broadly speaking, one cultural and religious location in which this kind of theological negotiation has proceeded most productively is in the yogic realms—in the Tamil context, among the *cittars,* yogis practicing esoteric spiritual, physical, and *materia medica* traditions and often living in spiritual retreat on the fringes of society. Indeed, Tamil Islamic tradition records eighteen Tamil Muslim *cittars,* among whom several are well-known across Tamil Nadu, such as Kunaṇkuṭi Mastāṉ Sāhib. On a core theological and mystical level, the "distance" between Islamic Sufi and *cittar* traditions is slight—differences may be understood on the level of culture and linguistic convention. While this paper takes the position that Iḷaiyāṉkuṭi Kaccippiḷḷaiyammāḷ does, in fact, assert the primacy of an Islamic theology and worldview, she also readily uses Tamil Saivite *cittar* vocabulary throughout her work, and presents an integrated vision in which the highest realms of both "Hindu" and Sufi theological understanding affirm Godhead beyond form, beyond gender, beyond conventional human understanding.

The Tamil *cittar* tradition is almost an exclusively male domain, with a certain "macho" ethos since these are spiritual athletes par excellence, superheroes of mystical quest, understood to have extraordinary physical powers. Both her writing and her biography indicate that Iḷaiyāṉkuṭi Kaccippiḷḷaiyammāḷ was in close touch with these traditions, and in fact, participates in them, at least on a mental and literary level. In doing so, she is exceptional among her female Muslim peers. While a fuller understanding of Iḷaiyāṉkuṭi Kaccippiḷḷaiyammāḷ's work requires a more extensive study of local influences—Saivite devotional, *cittar,* and Muslim *cittar*—the question of influences and literary parallels may safely be ignored for the purposes of this preliminary presentation. (It will not be surprising to find antecedents in the works of Tirumular, Kunaṇkuṭi Mastāṉ Sāhib or Takkalai Pir Muhammad Appa, for example.) It is clear that whatever cultural material she is working with, Iḷaiyāṉkuṭi Kaccippiḷḷaiyammāḷ had unique visionary experiences and presents a poetic formulation of religious truths in her *Ilāhi Meyññāṉa Mālai* that her peers deemed valuable. In exploring the nature of spiritual truth through a description of her visionary experiences, she certainly negotiates the basic Hindu–Muslim theological dilemma (that is, an affirmation of polytheistic understanding versus an assertion of exclusive monotheistic truth) with skill, in a characteristically *cittar,* and feminine key. Ultimately, Iḷaiyāṉkuṭi Kaccippiḷḷaiyammāḷ does give Islamic claims precedence, while incorporating and affirming both Hindu and Muslim vocabulary, concepts, and cosmologies.

The visionary experiences that inspire Kaccippiḷḷaiyammāḷ's poetry and the specifically *cittar* yogic elements of this work, including symbolic vocabulary and esoteric body–cosmos correlations, create difficulties in understanding the poetry. It is somewhat reassuring, if frustrating, to observe that even the most learned Tamil Muslim scholars have apparently found her work daunting—their discussions of the *Meyññāṉa Mālai* tend to be brief and atomistic, lifting up particular verses of her work, but avoiding synthetic discussion. This isn't surprising; many verses defy easy interpretation.[5]

The secondary literature is also frustratingly terse in its presentation of the biography of Kaccippiḷḷaiyammāḷ. This presents an example of the eternal challenge faced by scholars who would include women's experience for a complete historical account of "being human" (in any cultural or historical realm). In the case of studies of Islamic culture, the difficulties are compounded by traditions of Muslim gender segregation, male delicacy when referring to females generally, but especially females outside of the family circle, and male privilege in terms of access to educational opportunities. Islamic Tamil scholarship is an overwhelmingly male domain. This is not to deride that scholarly tradition—its service in the realm of cultural preservation alone is outstanding—but merely to point out its gendered character, and the "blind spots" that such gendered traditions tend to reproduce.

So, what do we know about Kaccippiḷḷaiyammāḷ from the information available to us?

Biography

A 19th-century native of the Muslim-majority town of Iḷaiyāṉkuṭi, in today's Sivaganga district, just north of the main Ramanathapuram–Madurai road, our sources[6] tell us that Kaccippiḷḷaiyammāḷ was the daughter of a Lukkumāṉ Hakkīm Rāvuttar and sister of Muhammad Mīṟaṉ Mastāṉ Sāhib. (We do not receive information about her mother or other siblings, or Kaccippiḷḷaiyammāḷ's exact life dates.) It is an interesting item of social–historical information that while both her father and brother bear recognizably Muslim names, Kaccippiḷḷaiyammāḷ does not—in fact, her name elicits associations with a Saivite devotional context. From his name, we learn that her father belonged to the subgroup of Tamil Muslims known as Ravuttars (Tamil, *irāvuttar*, "cavalier, horseman, trooper") who may trace their ancestry to Urdu martial cadres who entered the Tamil region from the 14th century and settled, and presumably married local women. The Ravuttars traditionally served local Tamil rulers in a martial capacity and/or supplied the horses that were imported through the Ramnad region for the local rulers' cavalry, and Iḷaiyāṉkuṭi will have been a Muslim trading depot town important for this group. In his *South India and Her Muhammad Invaders,* S Krishnaswami Aiyangar documents a much older, well-established Saivite history in the town: a Shiva temple here contains eleventh century inscriptions, and local traditions refer to Shiva revealing Himself in a "blaze of light" here, on behalf of a local devotee, Iḷaiyāṉkuṭi Māraṉār.[7] "Hakkīm" (from the Arabic, *hakīm,* a pan-Islamic term,) indicates that Kaccippiḷḷaiyammāḷ's father was an authority in traditional Islamic medicine. "Lukkumān" (from the Arabic, "Luqmān") is a traditional male Muslim name, commemorating a Qur'anic hero—a saintly man of the pre-Islamic era understood to have been a God-fearing African, favored by God with extraordinary wisdom after turning down the option of a prophetic career. Professor Bayly discusses the close associations that exist in Tamil history between the Ravuttars, the local hakims, and local Sufi saints: the healers traditionally traveled with the warrior troops and drew on spiritual, supernatural, as well as natural resources in administering their services.[8] Local saints are typically known for their healing powers (whether in life or after death, through the emanation of spiritual grace). It is relevant to note, as well, that Luqmān, the Qur'anic hero, is understood to have had unique qualities of perception and understanding of the natural world, its plants, and animals. Taken together, the father's appellations suggest a respectable lineage of some local status, and a family environment in which the healing profession, local *material medica* wisdom, and Islamic learning and identity are prized. At the same time, a Tamil identity, a history of conversion to Islam, a certain distance from the locally most-esteemed Islamic social status, and from the core learned religious traditions of Islam are implied by the sociological designation, "Ravuttar" and the associations (of "wisdom" over prophecy, of dark-skinned African/Tamil versus light-skinned Arab) of "Luqman".[9]

This sense of a distinctive local inflection of Islamic tradition is supported by reports about Kaccippiḷḷaiyammāḷ's brother, Muhammad Mīṟaṉ Mastāṉ Sāhib, who was apparently a devotee of the Muslim warrior saint Sikandar Badshah enshrined at the top of Tirupparankunram Hill near Madurai and who is said to have composed many "*meyññāṉa*" (mystical) songs.[10] The "*Mastāṉ*" of his name, from the Urdu, indicates that the brother was an "intoxicated" Sufi, associated with the local Muslim *cittar* tradition. Several of the Tamil Muslim *cittars,* including 19th century Kuṇaṅkuṭi Mastāṉ Sāhib, come from the Ramnad region and are known to have practiced austerities at the hills surrounding Madurai, including Tirupparankunram Hill.[11] No doubt her father and brother had an important influence on Kaccippiḷḷaiyammāḷ's worldview, and it should be interesting to compare Kaccippiḷḷaiyammāḷ's poetry with her brother's, at some point. Unfortunately, we do not have much information about her education, at this point, nor about her life situation when she composed the poems. In verse 15 of the *Meyññāṉak Kummi* poem, discussed below, Kaccippiḷḷaiyammāḷ refers to herself as "uneducated *(kalviyaṟiyāta),* presumably referring to formal education and perhaps to literacy, here. How old was she? Was she married? Had she given birth to children? Did she and the women in her family observe seclusion? How did she encounter and participate in Tamil poetic and religious traditions? Her statement in verse 35 of the *Meyññāṉak Kuṟam* (discussed below), indicating that she had tried a variety of spiritual techniques *("mantra, tantra* and *maya,* all of them") leads this reader to suppose that she composed this poetry in her maturity, a supposition supported by the confidence of her poetic voice. Further research may shed more light on these issues.

Nel, the collection of Iḷaiyāṉkuṭi poets' works in which Kaccippiḷḷaiyammāḷ's poetry appears and which I have consulted, was published in 1980 in Iḷaiyāṉkuṭi. That text reproduces the original 1918 Sivaganga publication of Kaccippiḷḷaiyammāḷ's poetry (in chapbook form, available then for two annas).[12] Kaccippiḷḷaiyammāḷ is the only female of the five poets who appear in the 1980 volume. In an appendix at the end of the book that lists sixteen poets of Iḷaiyāṉkuṭi in the last 150 years, she is one of two females mentioned, the other being one Rajammal.

Let us turn now to the poetry itself.

The Ilāhi Meyññāṉa Mālai

A four-line *kappu* verse introduces the collection of four poems that make up the

Meyññāṉa Mālai—in it, God, "whom the entire universe praises", is invoked and explicitly identified as "*Allāhū*", and recitation of the "sword-like" poem is prescribed to "sunder and dispel vicious spiritual ignorance and illusion". Although Kaccippiḷḷaiyammāḷ later makes clear that her poetry flows from the divine realm as a kind of revelation (and in this sense, she is not the true "author", but more of a "transmitter" of wisdom), the image of the "sword-like" poem elicits associations with Devi, the Hindu goddess in her fierce aspect—and an association of the poet with the Goddess arises naturally here. In the Tamil Hindu context, human ability to manifest divinity and serve its purposes is a common cultural assumption, and in South Asian iconography, the sword of the Goddess is typically interpreted as a weapon used to slay both literal and metaphorical demons, including ignorance and illusion. We will see evidence in her poetry that Kaccippiḷḷaiyammāḷ does, in fact, understand herself to be in intimate relationship with divine (or at least celestial) female figures, who may be understood to be forms of the Goddess, or, more metaphorically, manifestations of Supreme Wisdom.[13] Less obvious, perhaps, to many readers may be another historically plausible association of a sword-wielding woman for our poet: early in the 19th century, Kuññumūcu Leppai Kāji Ālim Pulavar penned a Tamil *kāppiyam*-style[14] *paṭaippōr* (defensive war ballad) work of more than 2000 verses that relates the history of an early Islamic battle, and features a champion female warrior, Calkā. Calkā begins as a non-Muslim opponent of the Muslim forces in battle, but over the course of the story converts to Islam and fights heroically with the Muslim forces from that time, together working to banish the "ignorance and illusion" of pre-Islamic Arabia.[15] There is good reason to believe that the work would have been widely distributed in Tamil-speaking areas from the 19th century, and as with many works of Islamic Tamil literature that feature female characters, it is likely that one aim of the work was didactic, intended to educate local Muslim women, specifically, about Islamic values and practices. In any case, we may suppose that Kaccippiḷḷaiyammāḷ knew this work, oral versions of it, or similar tales of early Islamic martial heroines. In this sense, the opening strong sword-wielding female image of the *Ilāhi Meyññāṉa Mālai* is multivalent – and the associations informing it are culturally and religiously quite distinct. How Kaccippiḷḷaiyammāḷ intended the image, or how it "worked" for her, psychologically, is of course the important question—and the answer necessarily eludes us.

The Meyññāṉak Kuṟam

The content of this poem, composed in 36 verses of two lines each, is, in summary, a presentation of a series of visionary experiences, a critique of particular contemporary religious practices, an assertion of the spiritual authority of the poet, and an exhortation to the listener to understand the mystical wisdom of the recital and strive for true knowledge.

Before discussing the poem proper, however, a word about genre is relevant here. While the other three poems in the *Ilāhi Meyññāṉa Mālai* are true to type, fulfilling the conventional expectations of *kuṟavañci, uñcal,* and *kummi* genres, the *Meyññāṉak Kuṟam,* at first glance, at least, appears to be atypical. It is neither a "story of the mountain lass reading the palm of a virgin in love"[16] "in which a hill maid foretells the future of love"[17] or "a theme in *kalampakam* . . . representing the speech of a Kuṟavaṉ (inhabitant of the hilly tract or desert tract . . . member of a caste of fowlers, snake-catchers, basket-makers, and fortune tellers").[18] These are the prominent understandings of "*kuṟam*". But this genre appears, historically, to have been rather fluid, and "*kuṟam*" may also refer to a *kuṟatti* maiden's speech, as she surveys her lovely mountain landscape home.[19] In his discussion of Kaccippiḷḷaiyammāḷ's *Meyññāṉak Kuṟam,* Professor Uwise[20] suggests that "*kuṟam*", in this case, does not refer to the Tamil minor poetic genre at all, but rather is based on the Arabic root, *k-r-m,* having associations of nobility, generosity, and elevated status. This is a strained interpretation, since this particular derivation of the Arabic root is not common. Nor can the Tamil genre name be so readily dismissed, given its natural fit in this *mālai* context, and given the fact that natural companion genres, the *kuṟavañci, uñcal* and *kummi* poems, follow. It would seem that Professor Uwise may not have been aware of the expanded definition of "*kuṟam*", because the *Meyññāṉak Kuṟam* certainly is in a female voice and certainly does highlight mountain imagery and themes of love.

This is clearly a didactic Sufi work: the mountains have mystical significance, and the love is love for the divine. After declaring in the first verse that the purpose of the poem is to enable those born into the world to achieve true *ñāṉam (jnana,* spiritual wisdom) Kaccippiḷḷaiyammāḷ clearly identifies herself as female in the second verse of the poem: "*kanmaniyāyulakilvanta kaccipillai* . . .". Although much of the poem is in impersonal narrative mode, many of the lines include the first person singular verb form. Kaccippiḷḷaiyammāḷ, a woman, speaks of her own experience here, and it is a visionary experience.

Feminine associations resonate in the second line of the second verse as the poet exhorts her reader to learn the lesson of the "womb-like" *ñāṉam:* "*karukkulīyiṉ ñāṉamitaṉ karuttai yaṟivīrē*".

In the third verse of the poem, Kaccippiḷḷaiyammāḷ launches into the first of her visionary experiences, beginning prosaically enough: "Someone closed up shop one day, and set out to see *kāntmalai.*" Is Kaccippiḷḷaiyammāḷ speaking of a journey of her own to the famous hill of Tirupparankunram near Madurai, one of the major pilgrimage centers for Hindu Lord Murugan/*Kanta,* where the shrine to Muslim saint Sikandar Badshah crowns the hill? Or is she, perhaps, contrasting her own (in this cultural context Muslim female-appropriate, home-bound) experience to that of her brother, setting out on an outing to the hill, a popular resort of his *cittar* peers?

The second line of the verse lets us know that "someone" *("oṉṟu",* the poet, clearly, from context) sought the *kaṉaka malai*, that is, Mt Meru or the golden mountain—an allusion to an inner, yogic geography. Given the parallel construction of the lines, and the implied comparison, as well as the critical remarks that follow, I think we can detect a reference to Kaccippiḷḷaiyammāḷ's brother, and perhaps some sibling rivalry, here. Just as the famous 10th century Sufi saint, al-Hallaj, declared the validity of an inner pilgrimage trumping the orthopractic ritual pilgrimage to Mecca, and just as the *ñānis* of South Asia and religious renegades, worldwide, have made the same move, challenging religious authority and "empty ritual", so it would seem that Kaccippiḷḷaiyammāḷ might be contrasting her own more inwardly focussed religious experience with others' here, and asserting the superiority of her own religious way.

In the fourth verse we learn that there is a light-filled spiritual retreat on the top of that golden mountain, and that the great ascetic Muhyiuddin dwells, or has left traces there.[21] Here "*makkām*" for the Arabic "*maqām*" is used; the word means station or stopping place, but is typically used of the places of spiritual retreat of the Sufi saints. The *makkām* is the gem of heaven (using the Tamil "*corkkam*"); it is also compared to "gem-like" Mecca—the center of the earth and the place most proximate to heaven in the Islamic imagination. Next, in deeply resonant images, the poet describes the growth in the gateway to that *maqām* of a "*natām*" (sacred primal "seed" sound, ovum, germ cell).[22] To the discerning intellect, the poet tells us, the *natām* takes the form of a person, "in [the shape of] a letter with the value of 31". After nine months have passed, it emerges as that mystical knowledge (*meyññāṉam*) that has been omitted from the hundred wise scriptures:

> *makkāmatiṉ vāyililē vaḷarum nātam peruki*
> *matikku muppattoṉreḻuttil māntaruruvaki*
>
> *oṉpatumātaṅkaṭantē ulakilvantu nūṟu*
> *ōtiya vētatti ṉuḷḷē yoḻittatu meññāṉam* (vss.6-7)

Here, in images that evoke female fertility and draw on traditions of Sufi letter symbolism, Kaccippiḷḷaiyammāḷ not only declares that she has had a powerful dream vision, but also that she has received what is tantamount to divine revelation, a revelation cast in the uniquely authoritative form of the written word. In both Sufism and Tamil Hinduism, individual letters of the alphabet are conventionally used as numerals, and in appropriate context, may have mystical significance. Here, Kaccippiḷḷaiyammāḷ seems to have a very specific alphabetic image and set of religious-symbolic associations in mind. In Islamic culture, letters of the alphabet are assigned numerical values, in a well-known set of equivalencies known as the *abjad* system. To write the numeral 31, one writes the letters "lam" and "alif" (with values 30 and 1) in combination to form the Arabic word, "*lā*". The meaning of word is that of negation, "there is no", and in fact, this word is the first word of the Islamic testimony of faith, "There is no god but God, and Muhammad is the Prophet of God." As a part of the primary doctrinal statement of Islam, the word features prominently in both orthoprax and Sufi contexts, in the ritual of conversion to Islam (in which the *shahadah* is recited before witnesses), in the call to prayer, the ablution ritual, the five times daily prayers, and, intensively, in mystical ritual *(dhikr)* recitation practices. Further, in the calligraphic traditions of Islam, the written word, "*lā*" is taken to represent the figure of a man in the bowing position which begins the ritual prayer, as well as an image of the famed two-headed sword of the heroic warrior Ali, son-in-law of the Prophet and first Imam of the Shi`a. (Recall the sword imagery evoked at the beginning of Kaccippiḷḷaiyammāḷ's poem; there we commented on the resonance of the image with South India Goddess traditions and early Islamic martial heroine themes; here its resonance with Islamic martial traditions becomes explicit—at least for those familiar with Arabic-Islamic Sufi *abjad* conventions.)[23] In the next several verses of the poem (vss. 8–10) Kaccippiḷḷaiyammāḷ appears to criticize specific yogic techniques such as standing on one foot, manipulating the tongue while gazing upwards and focusing the mind, as useless, perverse—people call whatever they find fitting, "liberation", she asserts. One senses that Kaccippiḷḷaiyammāḷ is arguing against specific practices she has encountered, most likely among Muslim *cittar* peers including her brother. She has declared the superiority of the specifically Islamic way.

Changing topic, the poet moves on to her second vision (vs. 11), that of a six-cornered house, the locus of true liberation, she tells us. Around a lofty platform are nine stone fortresses, with flags all around. Kaccippiḷḷaiyammāḷ declares that she entered the fort in order to see it, and among many posts and pillars she encountered a golden pot in which many flower blossoms were glowing. She saw ladies occupied with worshipping *Aṉṉai* (Mother, elder sister, Hindu goddess Parvati). Seeing this Divine Being, Kaccippiḷḷaiyammāḷ relates that she was captivated, stood with mind awhirl, received blessings, and was overcome with inner joy. Kaccippiḷḷaiyammāḷ further relates that seeing a man in ecstasy, she went out to investigate on all sides. Crossing the threshold with wisdom, she circumambulated the place.

Kaccippiḷḷaiyammāḷ next describes entering another place, the place of two "*kalimās*" (vs.20).

The Arabic "*kalimā*" means "word", but refers in an Islamic religious context to any of several formulas of faith. The first is the well known *shahādah,* or testimony of faith, *Lā ilāha illā Allāh, Muhammadur Rasūl Allāh,* "There is no god but God and Muhammad is the messenger of God". Another (the third *kalimā,* known as the "*kalimā* of glorification"), is: *Subhāna—llāhi, wa-l-hamdu li-llāhi, wa lā ilāha illā-il-lāhu, wa—llāhu akbar. Wa la hawla wa la quwwata illā bi-illāhi-l-aliyyi-l-lazīm* ("Glory be to God and praise be to God, and there is no is no god but God, and God is greatest. And there is no might nor power except with God, the Exalted, the Mighty"). In Islamic culture, including Tamil Islamic culture, the *kalimās* are vital formulations of faith; as mentioned above, the repetition of the *shahādah* in front of witnesses in fact constitutes the act of conversion to Islam. These formulae are spoken each day in the context of prayers. But beyond this, they are ubiquitous in Sufi ritual and Islamic visual culture, in calligraphy, as adornment of architectural features such as the prayer niche in the mosque, and on gateways of mosques and homes. Kaccippiḷḷaiyammāḷ does not specify the two *kalimās* she has seen, but the general sense is clear. She is speaking of a heavenly manifestation, in visual form, of the fundamental doctrines of Islamic faith, and inviting her audience to enter into an explicitly Islamic divine scene. At the same time, the scene appears to be theologically inclusive; the encounter with the worshipping women and *Aṉṉai* (Mother, Hindu goddess Parvati) deeply affects our poet, as well.

Kaccippiḷḷaiyammāḷ says that there are two *mūṭi*s (lids, covers, seals) for the two *kalimās*, an upper and a lower, each representing seven levels of the cosmos. Here our poet is drawing on traditional Islamic cosmology in which both heaven and hell have seven levels. She then goes on to describe a vision of the heavenly throne, using Tamil versions of the Arabic terms, *arsh* and *kursi* (for "throne") (vs. 23), and no doubt drawing on local versions of the ubiquitous and ever-popular story of the Prophet Muhammad's *mi`raj* journey in which he traveled from Mecca to Jerusalem by night, led by the angel Gabriel, then onward up through the various levels of heaven, seeing marvelous sights along the way, until he finally entered God's presence. The throne, according to Kaccippiḷḷaiyammāḷ's *Meyññāṉak Kuṟam*, and following Sufi convention, is the locus of *hakkīkattu*, or truth, again using the Tamil version of the Arabic term *(haqīqat)*. Across the Islamic world, the Sufi quest is represented as progression through four major stages of awareness and action— from *shari`ah* (living in full accordance with Islamic law) to *tariqah* (embarking on the Sufi path with its extra spiritual exercises and disciplines) to *haqiqah* (understanding divine truths) to *marifah* (realizing union with/closest proximity to the Divine/"gnosis"). Kaccippiḷḷaiyammāḷ's dream vision is true to type—an allegory for the Sufi's "pilgrim's progress", modeled on the Prophet's *mi`raj* journey. Exactly what Kaccippiḷḷaiyammāḷ intends (in vss. 23–28) when she refers to the four feet of the throne, the 500 nails in the construction of the platform of *hakkkatu*, the seven souls, the 51 letters of the alphabet found there—and the remaining enumerations from this part of the poem including an 8-cornered boat and 72 gateways—is a topic for further investigation. Kaccippiḷḷaiyammāḷ states clearly that the place is filled with holiness (again using Tamil versions of the Arabic terms, *ruḥ* and *ruḥāni);* it is at the center of all lands, it resembles the famous mosque of Mecca. Whatever its specific references, this part of the poem clearly draws on normative Islamic teachings, as well as popular Sufi tales and pedagogies and esoteric *cittar* visions and vocabularies. For the Sufi *kuru*, each corner of the boat, each gateway, each nail in the platform of *haqīqat* is a teaching point, so to speak.[24]

Whatever questions we might have about the exact content of Kaccippiḷḷaiyammāḷ's account of her mystical visions, or the symbolic references here,[25] she leaves no room for doubt about her overall accomplishments and their value as she closes the poem. She again mentions herself by name (vs. 30), and says that she has investigated all of the fundamental causes and entities, has seen God as both male and female in the four *mūlams*[26]—*nāyaṉaiyunācciyaiyum nālmūlattiṟ kaṇṭēn* (vs. 32)—a reference, surely, to the four bases of the Supreme Heavenly throne. The poem concludes:

(33) *Uccivaṭṭantiṟantiṭavē uyarākācamāṉeṉ*
Unmaiyutan antarattil urukkamutan ninren

I revealed [encountered] the loftiest realm, I became the highest ethereal realm
I stood, with truth, with a melting heart, in empty space

(34) *Purusanillap penpol rentupillaikalaip perren*
Piriyamuṭaṉāleḻuttup pērntuveliaccu

Like a woman without a husband [?], I got two children
They came out as letters because of love

(35) *Mantiramun tantiramu māyamelām ceytēṉ*
Vaiyakattumantiraṉkal poyyenavē kantēn

I've done *mantra, tantra* and *maya,* all of them
I saw that the mantras of the world are lies

(36) *Intamattum potun connen ivvulakattorkku*
Ittanaiyumarintavarkal muttiperuvare

I say this to one of this world: this alone suffices—
For those who understand this much—they will indeed achieve liberation!

As she proclaims the ultimate reality of "empty space", the ethereal realm spatially located above the gender differentiation of the deities supporting the throne of Ultimate Truth, Kaccippiḷḷaiyammāḷ obliquely addresses a fundamental theological tension between Hindu and Islamic worldviews. And Kaccippiḷḷaiyammāḷ adopts a respectable philosophical move to resolve the dilemma: the divine may indeed appear as form, as gendered, as multifarious to the average person, but these appearances are of a lower order of reality than that of the ultimate, transcendent Truth.

While translation difficulties persist, many aspects of the *Meyññāṉak Kuṟam* remain puzzling, and further study of the poem is required, we may suggest several conclusions here. In the Islamic tradition—in which religious authority is in some ways more constrained than in Hindu ("holy person") traditions because of the doctrines of God's transcendence, the prophets' unique missions, and the perfection and finality of divine revelation in the Qur'an—dream visions have played an important role as an alternate source of religious knowledge from the time of the

Prophet Muhammad on. In fact, the Prophet himself provides the exemplary model for visionary experience, in his nighttime *mi`raj* journey (which Muslims interpret variously as a real bodily experience or a dream vision). For all, but especially for the Sufis, visionary experience is one critical path by means of which the boundaries of divine revelation may be expanded and spiritual authority claimed. As a cultural resource, the authority conferred by visionary experience may be especially important for those on the boundaries of the normative tradition—for the non-literate, for women. Given this background, we may best understand the *Meyññāṉak Kuṟam* as Kaccippiḷḷaiyammāḷ's account of her personal *mi`raj* experience—a unique visionary experience, one deeply informed by Tamil and *cittar* cultural background, but one that is also clearly modeled on the tales of the heavenly ascent of the Prophet, which Kaccippiḷḷaiyammāḷ will have encountered in various entertaining Tamil versions. The Prophet's *mi`raj* is structured by a series of discrete visions as he ascends through the seven levels of heaven and observes the torments of the seven levels of hell, and we note that, although much less detailed, Kaccippiḷḷaiyammāḷ's account is similarly structured. One commonly-related experience in Prophetic *mi`raj* accounts is his greeting of a female, a heroine of early Islam, in her celestial palace, where she is attended by celestial damsels. Depending on how we interpret "*Aṉṉai*", we might regard Kaccippiḷḷaiyammāḷ's account of her vision of celestial females (vs. 15) as an encounter with the Goddess (Parvati, a logical association in the Saivite *cittar* mileau and symbol of Supreme Wisdom), or simply as a lady in heaven, a heroine of early Islam who deserves her heavenly palace and the homage of her celestial attendants. Other interpretive possibilities exist, as well. After surveying divine wonders, the Prophet approaches the realm of God; the culmination of his journey is achievement of the highest realm, which defies description or depiction, and represents, for Muslim mystics, the achievement of ma`rifah, the highest stage of mystical awareness. Kaccippiḷḷaiyammāḷ's account presents a close parallel on these points, and incorporates Arabic vocabulary for the throne scene. In any case, the point is that as an account based at least in part on the model of the Prophet's *mi`raj* journey, the *Meyññāṉak Kuṟam* participates in a long-standing, specifically Islamic tradition of establishing spiritual authority for its author. Of course, it accomplishes this on non-Islamic Tamil terms, as well.[27]

Although the revelatory scenes Kaccippiḷḷaiyammāḷ encounters on her visionary journey seem to take on both familiar "Hindu" Tamil as well as Islamic forms, Kaccippiḷḷaiyammāḷ seems ultimately to privilege distinctively Islamic images, signs, icons and cosmology, and the strict monotheism they imply, as the most efficacious tools for spiritual liberation, as the essential keys to the highest realm of religious experience. Finally, however, for Kaccippiḷḷaiyammāḷ as for her Tamil *cittar* and Sufi peers across the Islamic ages, that realm of Ultimate Truth is beyond all imagery, language, mundane experience and thought-ways. Indeed, in the presence of the Ultimate, the self itself vanishes.

The Meyññāṉak Kuṟavañci

The second of the poems of the *Ilāhi Meyññāṉa Mālai* is the *Meyññāṉak Kuṟavañci* of 22 two-line verses. Here, Kaccippiḷḷaiyammāḷ gives us a fast-paced dialogue between Ciṅkā and Ciṅki, a man and woman of a hill-dwelling fowler caste and traditional characters in the *kuṟavañci* genre. The content of the poem is philosophical and didactic, with Ciṅkā a kind of "straw man" posing a question in the first line of each verse, and Ciṅki answering him in the second line. (In the Tamil, the last word of the first line is the first word of Ciṅki's answer). The humor of the genre, traditionally, lies in the bold woman's upstaging of her simple-minded husband. This is hardly a poem intended to entertain, however, unless we think of it as entertainment for philosophers; the content is abstruse, the intent, didactic.

As in the *Meyññāṉak Kuṟam,* aspects of the poem, if philosophical, are fairly straightforward, as in the opening line, when Ciṅkā asks Ciṅki to explain the nature of the "subtle essence of material form" *(tūlamuruvāṉa sūṭsumaṉ collatī siṅki).* Other verses use mystical vocabulary to reveal—in veiled form—the secrets of Reality: Ciṅkā asks (vs. 9), whether Ciṅki has seen "the three aspects which arise from the original cause", and she replies that that is the place where silence arises.

(10) *mulaittitumo nattalattai ni collati cinki atu*
muccatti vitiyin paksam arivaye cinka

Tell about that silence-arising place, Ciṅki
Know that idea of the conjunction of three streets, Ciṅkā

(11) *muccanti vitiyilutta porulenna cinki rentu*
muttolivakiya kinnamirukkume cinka

What is the meaning in the "conjunction of 3 streets", Ciṅki?
That is a small metal cup concealing two pearls, Ciṅkā

(12) *kinnattolivile yenna kantayati cinki anta*
kinnattukkulle kilippillai rentata cinka

What did you see in the cup hiding place, Ciṅki?
In the cup were two baby parrots, Ciṅkā

(13) *intak kilippillai kantu centralenna cinki anke*
elakan palattiri natakkalam cinka

What then, after you saw the baby parrots, Ciṅki?
There a forehead with seven eyes may arise, Ciṅkā

Unpacking the meaning of these kinds of lines will have to await further research into *cittar* terminology and symbolism. In an ensuing line of the poem, Kaccippiḷḷaiyammāḷ seems to return to the world of concrete, everyday reality, when Ciṅkā asks about the result of traveling the earth, and she replies that one may see Prophet Adam's footprint, referring to the Muslim pilgrimage tradition of traveling to Adam's Peak in Sri Lanka.[28] She returns immediately to the realm of the cosmological however, as Ciṅkā asks where Adam's place is, and she replies (vs. 15) that he rules within the cosmic egg. The poem wraps up with Ciṅkā's trenchant questions about the nature of reality beyond that egg, and Ciṅki's responses (vss. 16-22): "A formless king dwells in an ethereal palace there." Ciṅkā doubts, "Will the reigning great king really be there, Ciṅki?",

"He is God most high there and everywhere, Ciṅkā"
"The one which is called God most high of all places, what is that, Ciṅki?"
"That is the quality of eternal light, Ciṅkā"
"What is the report of its nature, Ciṅki?"
"That stands absolutely alone, complete as Supreme Lord, Ciṅkā"
"When one sees that Lord, what is outside, Ciṅki?"

"Beyond that Excellence there is nothing, Ciṅkā!" and finally Ciṅkā poses a clever question in the closing verse, which, like the preceding *kuṟam* poem, raises a fundamental theological dilemma, that of divine omnipresence versus divine transcendence: "But not everyone is in that place, Ciṅki?" and Ciṅki's enigmatic answer, the punchline of the poem. Here Kaccippiḷḷaiyammāḷ takes up the nature of Ultimate Reality and what is the most pressing philosophical/theological problem to occupy Muslim minds since Ibn al-Arabi (the 12th century Sufi scholar mystic whose complex writings about the nature of Divine Reality incurred charges of pantheism). She not only brings the poem to a philosophical climax, as it were, but also a poetic one, closing with a line that is comprised almost exclusively of the letters, *t*, *n*, and *ṉ*—a rhythmic brain-teaser. Here is the closing verse of the poem:

ānāloruvarumavviṭatillaiyō cinki aṅku
tāṉātaṉātantaṉātāntanātamē ciṅkā!

If we take a few liberties with the Tamil (following Kaccippiḷḷaiyammāḷ's Cinki's colloquial speech), the line may be translated:

But not everyone is in that place, Ciṅki?
There, indeed! That is why they say the [cosmic] egg [primal seed-sound/germ of all being] is Father Adam's, Ciṅkā![29]

What does this mean? The Qur'an and pan-Islamic cosmological accounts relate how, in pre-eternity, God drew humanity out from the loins of Adam, their progenitor, and required them to testify to His lordship, which all did. (This establishes God's authority and the responsibility/nature of all to submit to Him.) The mythic scenario condenses creation, as it were, enabling God and humanity to occupy the "same place", and simultaneously maintains God's uniqueness, omnipotence, and transcendence of His creation. Thus, through evoking the image of "Father Adam's" presence in/identity with the primal source of all being (the *nātam* as, here, cosmic egg), the poetic riddle and the theological dilemma are solved!

The Meyññāṉa Ūñcal

The *ūñcal* (var., *ūcal)* is a song sung while swinging—rocking to and fro on a swing. The swinging subject might be a girl, a deity, or a bridal pair. In this twenty-stanza poem, Kaccippiḷḷaiyammāḷ combines description of a visionary experience involving a heavenly swing with lessons about Ultimate Reality. Throughout, as in any swinging song, the words are addressed to a female friend. The familiar term of address for a girl or woman, *a,,ti,* appears within each second and third line of the three-line stanzas, and another term of female address, "*amma,ni*" ends each second line, creating a catchy, rhythmic refrain, suitable for singing while playing on a swing. As in the preceding Ciṅkā–Ciṅki *kuṟavañci* exchange, the folksy simplicity is deceptive. As is common in Tamil Sufi literature, the poet uses veiled language within a folk literary genre format to discuss profound ideas. Here are just a few of the more accessible verses; the first stanza of the poem sets the lilting, swinging movement:

akasamanatile oru
accutakkutamati ammani
accutakkutamati

In the ethereal realm there is an
imperishable hall *ati ammani*
An imperishable hall

Each verse is linked to the next through a key word or idea, an effective mnemonic device. The second stanza is linked through the repetition of "*accutakkutam*", "imperishable hall" but more information is added:

accutakkutattile oru
uccita uncalati ammani
uccita uncalati

In the imperishable hall there is
An excellent/transcendent swing, *ati ammani*
An excellent swing

Kaccippiḷḷaiyammāḷ next describes her vision of a *valāi,* a young maiden, in the swing—an excellent, sublime maiden praised by all the earth. While Kaccippiḷḷaiyammāḷ describes her own mystical experience, that of joining the divine girl on the transcendent swing, the tone of the poem is hortatory, she is encouraging her audience to see and join the maiden on the swing. In verse 9:

cittirakkūṭattilē vantu
cērntataippāraṭi nī ammani
cērntataippāraṭi nī

In verse 12, the poet describes how the maiden pours milk "without spilling", and in verse 13, how with abundant sweet delight, the two seated on the swing relish their solitude. The poem's swing image resonates on multiple levels: girls swing on swings for play; a bride pours milk for her husband on the wedding night, and doing so flawlessly is of course auspicious; brides and grooms swing on swings, literally and metaphorically, in the sweet joy of union; images of deities are united on the swing, in temple ritual, with attendant theological implications. Swings imply passage to dizzying heights; cool comfort in the stirring breeze; enhanced vision of the mundane world; intimate proximity to the friend or beloved; the single-minded focus of intense play or, on a more metaphorical level, of sexual union. Here, our poet brings these pleasant, pleasurable, verging-on-ecstatic associations to bear on an explicitly transcendent religious experience: if the maiden represents Supreme Wisdom, then all of these associations communicate the bliss of realizing true awareness, the paradigmatic quest of the yogi. Next, Kaccippiḷḷaiyammāḷ encourages her audience to see/try the swinging dance/movement, which she compares to the dance of Chidambaram. In the closing three verses of the poem (18–20), Kaccippiḷḷaiyammāḷ exhorts her audience to dance the subtle dance of love that traverses the entire universe, and promises that liberation *(mutti)* exists for those who have seen and rejoice:

naṭpuṭaṉē yiruntē āṭum
naṭaṉattaippāraṭi nī ammani
naṭaṉattaippāraṭi nī

antapinntamunkatan tatum
akacakkuttamati ammani
akacakkuttamati
kantukalittavarkke mutti
untenrarivayati ammani
untenrarivayati

The Meyññāṉak Kummi

The *kummi* genre is a girl's circle dance song. In Kaccippiḷḷaiyammāḷ's *Meyññāṉak Kummi* of 16 five-line verses, the poet begins with straightforward Islamic exhortations, but continues almost immediately with veiled mystical language. In each verse, a pleasing rhythmic refrain is created with the repetition of the command to "dance the *kummi!*" ("*kummiyaṭi*") and the combination of the command with the rhyming expression, "*-uṅka,ṭi*". The first verse sets the pace:

kummiyati penkal kummiyati enkal
huppana penkale kummiyati
sammatamennanak kummiyin patalaic
carrik kummiyatiyunkati nitam
porrik kummiyatiyunkati

Dance the *kummi,* girls, dance the *kummi!* My
Dear girls dance the *kummi!*
Sing the song of the esteemed spiritual wisdom
Dance the *kummi* Hey, girl, daily
Praise [God] and dance the *kummi!*

The second verse:

atimutalonranai ninaitu nitam
aintorkuttun tolute pukalntu
otimukammatu patam anutinam
ukantu kummiyatiyunkati mika
makilntu kummiyatiyunkati

Meditate on the Original Supreme Being daily
Pray five times and praise
Ascend wise Muhammad's path daily
Hey, girl, joyfully dance the *kummi!*

With the third verse of the poem we enter the world of veiled language, of symbolic reference. Kaccippiḷḷaiyammāḷ tells us in one of the closing verses of the poem that she, the unlearned girl, has had a spiritual vision and then sang this *kummi* song—the content of the poem seems to be arranged according to the *cittar* yogic visualization of progression through a series of (typically 16) mystical energy centers in the body, correlated with cosmic and/or divine phenomena. Kaccippiḷḷaiyammāḷ mentions a miraculous fortress and 32 letters, along with a dancing prostitute who is expelled through silence and aspiration. In verse 5, the "*ciṟuvācal*" (little hole, entry) is equated with the *kalima,* the Islamic formula of faith, and the "womb" (*karukkuḻi*), is equated with the Arabic term for life, *hayyāt:*

aṭiciṟuvācaṟ kalimāvām hayat
taṅkēmulaitta karukkuliyam
utalumuyirumulaittatuvamitil
ulm‹ulamanatu monramati ninkal
ukantukummi yatiyunkati

The small gateway at the foundation is said to be the *kalima*
Life is said to be a womb arising there
The arising of body and life are said to be in that
That and the inner source are said to be one, Hey, girl, you
Rise up and dance the *kummi!*

Over the course of the poem, we meet the treacherous five senses, baby parrots, Saint Muhyiuddin, and a palace of many paintings, where the audience of imagined girls is instructed to dance the *kummi.* In verse 9, along with mentioning prayer, recitation of the *Fatiha* (the opening chapter of the Qur'an, a common recitation), and *du`a* in that place (the Arabic term for individual, petitionary prayer), Kaccippiḷḷaiyammāḷ says, "when one leaves that place and looks up"—"*Paramacivan vītu tōnumaṭi*" ("Siva's abode appears"). In it is the essence of Unity, the poet says—and exhorts her listeners, "Go in there without fear!" Describing her own entrance into the house, which Kaccippiḷḷaiyammāḷ calls "the Mother's (Parvati's) abode of compassion", the poet describes how the female inhabitant poured milk for her into a green cup, and how she (Kaccippiḷḷaiyammāḷ) grew large and traversed the universe.[30] "Seeing the mind, hey, girl, dance the *kummi!*" (vs. 12). This kind of exhortation closes each verse: Hey, girl, dance the *kummi* as the light of the world!" (vs. 13), "Declare that one who prays and seeks compassion receives it, Hey, girl, dance the *kummi!*" (14), "Hey, girl, dance the *kummi* called *mokšam* [spiritual liberation]!" (vs. 15). In the closing verse of the poem, a kind of petitionary eulogy, Kaccippiḷḷaiyammāḷ prays, "God and Prophet, support the mind! Inhabitants of the Vindhya mountains [that is, the ascetic sages], support the mind! All those who have achieved a good station—glory be to you!" and again, she closes with an exhortation:

Hey, girl - seeking, dance the *kummi!*
Searching, dance the *kummi!*

Thus concludes the *Meyññāṉak Kummi,* the last of Kaccippiḷḷaiyammāḷ's four poems presented in the *Nel* volume. The printed version of the *Ilāhi Meyññāṉa Mālai,* the collection as a whole, concludes with an 8-line series of felicitations, probably by the editor, calling blessings upon the entire earth, learned persons, illustrious renunciants, and Kaccippiḷḷaiyammāḷ herself.

Conclusion

Iḷaiyāṉkuṭi Kaccippiḷḷaiyammāḷ contests the terms of limitation that constrain her life experience, on at least two levels. First, like many of her peers, she contests the very limitations of being human through her spiritual quest. She exemplifies *bhakti, cittar,* and Sufi ideals in her project to achieve proximity to the Divine and realize the essence of divine wisdom. Second, she also contests the limitations that constrain her physically and culturally as a woman, and as a Tamil Muslim woman. She must assert her authority to speak of religious truths—a more difficult task for her as a woman than it would be for a man, and a more difficult task for her as a Tamil poet, at some remove from the core normative literate traditions of Islamic culture, than it would be for an Arab-descended, *madrasah*-educated male, working within established, Arabic-Islamic discourses. (Although it is not clear how and to what extent that realm of discourse informed Kaccippiḷḷaiyammāḷ's life, her work clearly demonstrates familiarity with and allegiance to certain normative Islamic teachings.) Kaccippiḷḷaiyammāḷ's Sufi poetics implicitly assert the full humanity of women before a more important divine Reality and do so in a uniquely authoritative way—her authority based on that age-old South Asian criterion of spiritual experience, cast in a uniquely Tamil, *cittar,* and feminine key. We have seen that Kaccippiḷḷaiyammāḷ establishes her authority by asserting the divine-revelatory significance of her visions, and by working with the multiple possibilities of key religious traditions, including Arabic mystical letter symbolism and the paradigmatic model of the Prophet's *mi`raj* journey. But whatever her struggles as a woman, or as Tamil, clearly it is the first of these "contestations", that against the limitations of the mundane human condition that is the more important to Kaccippiḷḷaiyammāḷ. And clearly she feels that she has, in fact, made a quite a breakthrough in this most basic quest, and is confident that her own experience qualifies her to guide others according to the age-old South Asian *kuru* and Sufi master paradigms.

Unfortunately, we have little sense of the performative contexts of Iḷaiyāṉkuṭi Kaccippiḷḷaiyammāḷ's poetic works, or of their reception or influence, except that her peers have praised her, and her work has been preserved in the volume of poetry by Iḷaiyāṉkuṭi natives, and documented in several works of Islamic Tamil scholarship. Many intriguing questions remain and further research should shed light on the poet's life as well as the exact nature of her visionary experiences and intended teachings. While a complete and rigorous English translation presents the immediate scholarly challenge, other interesting analytical puzzles await. For example, given standard practices in the Tamil literary arena, we might expect at least aspects of Kaccippiḷḷaiyammāḷ's work to be closely modeled on those of her male Sufi and cittar peers. If we understand the gendered minor literary genres, including the ones Kaccippiḷḷaiyammāḷ works with here, to be largely male literary appropriations/ romanticizations/making "precious" various folk genres and the real-life play and work songs of women and girls, what are the implications of a female poet then appropriating these male appropriations? What are the implications of a female poet's adoption of gendered images in contexts with metaphorical sexual associations (e.g., union on a celestial swing)? Do the gendered and sexual metaphors popularly employed in the male-dominated *cittar* and Sufi mystical traditions "work" for women? Do they "work" in new ways?

Beyond contesting the terms that limited her own life, Kaccippiḷḷaiyammāḷ's work encourages us to challenge the terms that may limit our scholarship. Her distinctive feminine voice unquestionably enriches Islamic Tamil literature, and suggests the utility of seeking additional women's voices for a fuller account of this particular cultural tradition, as well as histories of religious experience in general. But further, as with much of Islamic Tamil literature, the vocabulary and images of Iḷaiyāṉkuṭi Kaccippiḷḷaiyammāḷ's *Ilāhi Meyññāṉa Mālai* problematize common assumptions of discrete and incompatible Hindu and Muslim identities and cultures. The Tamil Muslim *cittar* tradition, especially, demonstrates that spiritual quest is a shared Tamil project, with a great deal of overlap between Sufi and cittar traditions, if not identity. Siva, the Goddess and Allah, prophets, pearls and parrots, archetypal Hindu and Muslim divine landscapes and journeys, can and do easily coexist and mingle in the mind of Iḷaiyāṉkuṭi Kaccippiḷḷaiyammāḷ. Still, in part through uniquely Islamic metaphor and veiled language, in part through explicit assertion of personal authority achieved through experience, and through explicit critique of extant religious practices, perhaps of her Tamil *cittar* peers, Kaccippiḷḷaiyammāḷ makes clear that entrée to the highest realm is achieved through Islamic portals, with Islamic keys. Her poetry valorizes essential and distinctive Islamic religious formulae and practices—one should utter the testimony of faith in one sole God, one should ascend the path of Muhammad (a prescription with a multitude of practical implications), one should perform the Muslim prayer rite five times daily. But beyond the signs on the gate, so to speak, Ultimate Reality is beyond words for Kaccippiḷḷaiyammāḷ, and is best characterized by neutral images of silence, light and ethereal space. Here, distinctions of "Hindu" and "Muslim" fall away.

Kaccippiḷḷaiyammāḷ clearly believes that having played with the Goddess on her swing, having sipped the milk of Paradise dispensed by the Mother, having achieved wonder and ecstasy in the presence of the Real, she, like the sword-wielding Goddess and the Islamic warrior heroine, is uniquely qualified to wield the instrument of wisdom to cut through the snares of illusion, and thus assist her audience. This is not *bhakti*-style poetry of devotion and easy grace, in either Hindu or Muslim keys, but a more arduous exercise. Kaccippiḷḷaiyammāḷ's constant exhortations to her listeners underline the lesson common to both Islamic Sufi and the Tamil *cittar* wisdom traditions: the listener must him- or herself undertake the correct effort, embark on the journey, seek to understand the truth. Using the Tamil idiom Kaccippiḷḷaiyammāḷ so artfully deploys, the seeker must pursue the vision of the divine landscape, climb up onto the swing, and dance the dance of inner meanings. And although demanding, this is, Kaccippiḷḷaiyammāḷ assures us, a blissful project.

NOTES

1. I am grateful to the anonymous reviewer of the first draft of this article for several helpful suggestions and the information that Takkalai Basheer, scholar of Islamic Tamil

literature, has written on Sayyida Asiya Umma and Tenkasi Rasul Bivi as well as Kaccippiḷḷaiyammāḷ in his *Ñāṉa Ilakkiyaṅkaḷ*. He has apparently also composed an independent work on the *Meyññāṉak Kuṟam*. I have not yet been able to consult these works, but look forward to doing so. (Obviously my comments in this paper about secondary literature on Kaccippiḷḷaiyammāḷ's poetry do not apply to Basheer's work, as I have not yet seen it.)

2. It is problematic to speak of "Islamic" and "Tamil" traditions as separate entities, since Islamic Tamil culture is an integrated whole, and fully Islamic as well as fully Tamil. Here I refer to the historic confluence of non-Tamil Islamic traditions with non-Islamic Tamil traditions, specifically Hindu *bhakti* and *cittar* traditions. I use "confluence" because these traditions are distinct, and not coextensive, historically. As scholars of Islam in South Asia have richly demonstrated, the process of the "Islamization" of South Asian regional cultures demonstrates the negotiation of differences between immigrant Islamic and local cultures over long spans of time, a process that is caught at different historical moments in works of creative literature. See the work of Richard Eaton for more on this topic.

3. For a full bibliography for Islamic Tamil studies topics, please see my 2003 Harvard University dissertation, *'Reviving Religion': The Qadiri Sufi Order, Popular Devotion to Sufi Saint Muhyiuddin `Abdul Qadir al-Gilani and Processes of 'Islamization' in Tamil Nadu and Sri Lanka.* Harvard University Committee on the Study of Religion Ph.D. dissertion, 2003.

4. Kaccippiḷḷaiyammāḷ's poetry contains less Arabic vocabulary than do many of the writings of her Tamil peers, but a number of terms do appear, and are important for an understanding the work. A full understanding of Islamic Tamil literature requires knowledge of Arabic and Islamic studies as well as Tamil and South Asian studies.

5. See Uwise, *Muslim Contribution to Tamil Literature* (Kilakarai, Tamil Nadu: Fifth International Islamic Tamil Literary Conference, 1990), pp. 180–183 (English); Abdur Rahim, *Muslim Tamiḻp Pulavarkaḷ* (Chennai: Universal Publishers, 1957, 1980), pp. 509–512 (Tamil); M Uwise and Ajmal Khan, *Islāmiyat Tamiḻ Ilakkiya Varalāṟu*, 4 (Madurai: Madurai Kamaraj University, 1997), pp. 648–653 (Tamil). Aspects of my own translations are tentative, at this point.

6. See the preceding note.

7. Krishnaswamii Aiyangar, 1991 (orig. pubd. London 1921), *South India and Her Muhammadan Invaders*, Madras, p. 163.

8. Susan Bayly, 1989, *Saints, Goddesses and Kings: Muslims and Christians in South Indian Society 1700-1900*, Cambridge: Cambridge University Press, pp. 98–99.

9. Doctrinally and historically, the Islamic tradition is in many ways the most inclusive, least racist of ideologies – color-blind and explicitly affirming of human diversity, as well as social justice. Yet the tradition also prizes proximity to the golden age and founders of the faith, in a variety of ways, including genealogy. In South Asia, social status varies according to bloodline heritage, and this awareness is sometimes accompanied by a racial awareness (as in the literary trope of the light-skinned Turk and the dark-complected Hindu). In the Tamil context, one can certainly imagine a local (light-complected) high-status, Arab-descended, sea-trading *maraikkayar* merchant patron suggesting the name "Luqman" to a valuable local ally such as a skilled physician; or the local Tamil Muslim choosing the name, with pride, for a child. A close parallel on the racial aspect of the issue is the manner in which many African Americans and Tamils prize the name, "Bilal", the name of the Prophet's close companion of Abyssinian descent.

10. See note 3 above.

11. See Uwise and Ajmal Khan, *Islāmiyat Tamiḻ Ilakkiya Varalāṟu*, Vol. 4, Chapter 3.

12. The original text was published as the *Ilāhi Meyññāṉamālai* in 1918 in Sivaganga by

Sri Kala Press. That text is reproduced (with footnotes added later, I believe) in *Nel ["Paddy" (Rice Plant)]*. Publisher: Cıtakkati Tamilppanik Kalakam, Dr Zakir Hussain College, Iḷaiyāṉkuṭi, 1980. The volume bears the subtitle, *Iḷaiyāṉkuṭi Ilakkiyaṅkal—Tokuti—1* ["Iḷaiyāṉkuṭi Literary Works—Volume 1"].

13. See Uwise, *Muslim Contributions to Tamil Literature*, p. 182.

14. A *kappiyam* (Tamil for the Sanskrit *kavyam)* is a long narrative poem with numerous exacting formal requirements.

15. For more on the *Calkā Paṭaippōr,* also known as the *Iṟavuculkūl Paṭaippōr,* see MM Uwise, 1990, *Islāmiyattamiḻ Ilakkiya Varalāṟu,* vol. 2 (Maturai: Maturai Kāmarācar Palkalaik Kaḻakam), pp. 330-364 and (in English) Uwise, 1990, *Muslim Contribution to Tamil Literature* (Kilakkarai: Fifth International Islamic Tamil Literary Conference), pp. 84-87.

16. A Vellupillai and M Mathialagan, "Introduction to the History of Tamil Literature", in the *Institute of Asian Studies' Encyclopaedia of Tamil Literature,* vol. 1, p. 88.

17. Annie Mrithulakumari Thomas, "Literary Genres in Tamil: A Diachronic Study" in the *Institute of Asian Studies' Encyclopaedia of Tamil Literature,* vol. 1, p.353

18. *Madras University Tamil Lexicon*

19. Professor Buck clarifies this point in the Introduction to his *Kuṟṟālak Kuṟavañci.* David C Buck, 2005, *Melagaram Tirikutarasappa Kavirayar's A Kuṟavanji in Kutrālam* (Chennai: Institute of Asian Studies).

20. Uwise, 1990, *Muslim Contribution to Tamil Literature* (Kilakkarai: Fifth International Islamic Tamil Literary Conference), pp. 180–181.

21. Textual corruption compounds difficulties of translation here. The subject of both lines is "*oṟu*", and it could be that Kaccippiḷḷaiyammāḷ is referring to herself in both journeys. In the case of the second mountain reference, the poet's vision could have some association with an actual site known as Daftar Jailani near Balangoda, Sri Lanka, where the great Sufi saint, Muhyiuddīn Abdul Qadir al-Gilani, is said to have rested on his pilgrimage to Adam's Peak. There is a cave at the site where a miraculous light is supposed to shine. Kaccippiḷḷaiyammāḷ will have been familiar with Muslim shrine sites in both Tamil Nadu and Sri Lanka, through hearsay if not actual visits.

22. But note the alternative meanings and additional resonances of the term: "sound, musical sound and nasal sound represented by a semicircle and used as a mystic symbol, a particular manifestation of Siva", according to the *Madras University Tamil Lexicon.* In *cittar* literature, *nātam* typically refers to the primal sound that plays a central role in the process of generation of the universe, and may further be associated with the lingam, symbol of Siva's procreative power—with undeniable male associations. I am grateful to the anonymous reviewer of the first draft of this article for calling my attention to the prominence of the "sacred sound" associations in *cittar* literature (see also TN Ganapathy and KR Arumugam's *The Yoga of Siddha Tirumular* [Eastman, Quebec, Canada: Babaji's Kriya Yoga Publications, Inc, 2006] on the uses of *nātam* in the *Tirumantiram).* In the context of Kaccippiḷḷaiyammāḷ's poem, her evocation of specifically feminine imagery—the womb and the nine months of gestation, support privileging the less-deployed "egg/embryo" association of *nātam* in this translation. Of course this is non-exclusive imagery in creative interplay with the genderless, generative "primal sound" and written letters/mantra associations.

23. For more on the *abjad* system in Islamic culture generally and Sufism, specifically, see the glossary of the National Library of Medicine Islamic Medical Manuscripts webpage: http://www.nlm.nih.gov/hmd/arabic/glossary.html. (Eastern and western Islamic world variants of the *abjad* system are presented in table form here.) For more on the *abjad* system in Sufism, specifically, see Appendix 1, "Letter Symbolism in Sufi Literature" in Annemarie

Schimmel, 1975, *Mystical Dimensions of Islam* (Chapel Hill, NC: The University of North Carolina Press), pp.411-425, and p.419 on "*lā*", specifically.

24. One is reminded of the blooming yet ordered profusion of 20th century Sri Lankan Sufi saint Bawa Muhyiuddin's colorful poster art, the teaching tool he developed with his community of North American followers in the Bawa Muhyiuddin Fellowship of Philadelphia.

25. These questions will be pursued in the course of future research.

26. A polyvalent Tamil term including the following meanings: root, foot, base, bulb, tuber; origin, source; cause, foundation; agency, means. *(Madras University Tamil Lexicon)*

27. For more on the Prophet's *mi`raj* journey and Sufi interpretations of it, see Annemarie Schimmel's *Mystical Dimensions of Islam* (Chapel Hill, NC: University of North Carolina Press, 1975), John Renard's *Seven Doors to Islam: Spirituality and the Religious Life of Muslims* (Berkeley: University of California Press, 1996) and Renard's *Friends of God: Islamic Images of Piety, Commitment and Servanthood* (Berkeley: University of California Press, 2008). Illustrated manuscripts (conditioning expectations of visionary experience) and Tamil poetic renditions of the Prophet's *mi`raj* journey exist, as well.

28. Adam is understood by Muslims not only to be the first human (or part of the first co-created human pair), but also the first prophet appointed by God to guide humanity. As a prophet, Adam has cosmic significance.

29. After strenuous effort, I reach this interpretation by parsing the line as follows. I will be delighted to be corrected if anyone else can reach a more suitable translation/solution to this brain-teaser:
Aṅku tāṉā [ā = exclamation expressing surprise, wonder] *atāṉā(l)* [elision with preceding final ā; "l" omitted, mimicking colloquial speech] *tantaṉ Ātām ta(ṉ) nātamē, Ciṅkā!* ["a" of *Ātām* (Adam) lengthened for emphasis; elision of final "ṉ" of *taṉ* with initial "n" of *nātam].* I interpret nātam as "egg" because of the "*aṇṭam*" of verse 15, where Prophet Adam is said to rule.

30. Green is the color associated with Paradise in the Islamic tradition, and symbolically implies everlasting life in blissful proximity to the divine.

From Temple to Battlefield: Dance in Jaffna

JANET O'SHEA

On July 11, 2004, an audience of 300 viewers gathered in Veerasingham Hall in the northern Sri Lankan city of Jaffna to watch the bharatanatyam *arangetram* (first public performance) of a thirteen-year-old girl. The dancer presented ten solo items, in itself a clear demonstration of accomplishment. Yet, the ceremony that attended the performance overshadowed the young performer's achievement. The event opened with a *puja* before the large Nataraja on stage. Eminent guests lit ceremonial lamps, each at different stages in the concert. A speech by an esteemed member of the community followed the presentation of every dance item. The speakers included the Vice Chancellor of Jaffna University, a renowned dance teacher, and a *sannyasi* from a local ashram.

Dance, for this subset of Jaffna, was both literally and figuratively centre stage. It was highly visible and valued both as a show of mastery and as a point of convergence for the community. At the same time, ritual and explanation bracketed choreographic practice. On the one hand, there is a certain familiarity to pageantry overshadowing performance at a bharatanatyam arangetram. As Saskia Kersenboom (2004) and Magdalen Gorringe (2001) have pointed out, bharatanatyam arangetrams in India and internationally operate more as social debuts than as the launch to performance careers. The spectacularized arangetram contributes to the amateurization of bharatanatyam,which, according to Amrit Srinivasan (1985), enabled the legitimization of the dance form.

On the other hand, this was not an ordinary setting for a dance debut. Veerasingham Hall sits at the southwest edge of Jaffna town, directly across from an old Dutch fort. The fort lies within the high-security zone controlled by the Sri Lankan police and is, therefore, off limits to civilians. Next to the hall are the ruins of the old Regal Cinema. Pock-marked by bullets and shrapnel, the facade of the old theatre remains, its name still emblazoned in chipping paint, the faded remnants of a film poster visible on the broken cement. Behind the facade, there is only a foundation overgrown by plants. It is the beginning of a stretch of Main Street that was particularly hard hit by two decades of war and is populated only by the inhabitants of the shanties that have sprung up between the shells of bombed-out buildings. Across from the hall stands a memorial for the civilian victims of a 1974 attack by the Sri Lankan Army at the International Conference of Tamil Research.

Jaffna has been under military occupation for decades. Its residents have lived with shortages, curfews, and restrictions on public assemblies. Large group gatherings now appear primarily at temple festivals and performances. A classical dance concert in the midst of this devastation would be striking enough without the dancer having travelled from New Zealand to perform before the friends and family of her emigrant parents. Although Veerasingham Hall is one of Jaffna's few performing arts venues, it has seen numerous arangetrams; dancers performed before crowds of hundreds even during times of active conflict, with dance concerts taking place while buildings outside were hit by shelling. Generators supplied performance lighting when the Sri Lanka government cut off power to the peninsula during the period of the Liberation Tigers of Tamil Eelam control.

Bharatanatyam in Jaffna is a practice that has been maintained in situations of adversity, repression, and deprivation. However, its choreographic interpretations, unlike in India and the Indian diaspora, remain surprisingly uniform. There seems to be little of the choreographic diversity that I have observed and written about in Chennai, London, and Toronto. Much of the research I conducted earlier (2003, 2007a, b) relies on an intersection between new choreographic production and allegiance to the past. Although defining itself as traditional, the bharatanatyam I witnessed in India, North America, and the United Kingdom was anything but uniform. It took on strikingly different forms as its practitioners used it to grapple with the concerns—social, political, and aesthetic—of their surroundings. I have therefore argued that classicism and innovation do not operate at odds but that, instead, a mutually reinforcing relationship exists between tradition and the role of the individual in choreography.

Yet, in Jaffna, a place characterized by conflict, bharatanatyam appeared, if anything, to embody a carefully constructed neutrality—a source of solace through continuity rather than a platform for expressing views. This has encouraged me to explore the reasons for this interest in continuity rather than innovation. It has also led me to question where, exactly, the individual agency that I saw as so central to other articulations of bharatanatyam might lie in this context. In this essay, therefore, I begin with exploring the cultural and historical conditions that encourage this emphasis on continuity before moving on to explore contrasting individual interpretations of bharatanatyam that I encountered in Jaffna.

Jaffna lacks the economic resources to support a dynamic dance milieu. Warfare, shortages, and a 'brain drain' accelerated beyond that of most developing world cities have destroyed whatever surplus may have been available for the arts. The high cost of an arangetram allows only relatively well-off dancers to launch a solo career.

Most dancers do not perform after their debut. Social conservativism encourages those that remain in the field post-debut to quit performance after marriage. For example, I have rarely seen an adult woman performing dance in Jaffna, and then only when the performance was part of a teaching-training certification.

If performance options are limited, training possibilities are anything but. Bharatanatyam developed and maintains itself in northern Sri Lanka through a syllabus-based educational system. Public schools and colleges throughout the Jaffna peninsula offer training in bharatanatyam as do many private organizations. The University of Jaffna's Ramanathan Academy of Fine Arts includes a bharatanatyam degree programme in its curriculum as do many teacher-training colleges. This emphasis on training and its concomitant attention to standardization and certification fosters more a desire for preservation than for experimentation.

This attention to continuity emerges out of political as well as economic concerns. There is a gender politics to the emphasis of classicism over individual expression, one that dovetails with the relative rarity of long-term professional performance in Jaffna. The gendered resonances of the dance emerge out of a history that is specific to Sri Lanka.

Bharatanatyam in Sri Lanka has its roots in Southern India. This line of descent comes not through a single historical connection or even a set of shared sources but rather through a process of continual, intentional, and self-conscious import of dancers and dance. Temples and temple festivals have been the focus of social and cultural life in Jaffna for at least the last two centuries. Throughout the nineteenth- and twentieth centuries, Jaffna residents hired devadasis, who were retired or excluded from Indian performance milieus, to dance at these events. According to choreographer and scholar Krishanti Ravindran, devadasi performance continued up until the 1970s, when Tamil militancy forced a redefinition of Tamil culture. Yet, the city never supported its own devadasi tradition. Devadasi dancers travelled from India, performed, and returned to India. A few settled in Jaffna but did not continue in the dance field as mentors once their performing career ended.

The teaching role was taken up by a group of young men who, in the 1950s, travelled to India to pursue training in bharatanatyam and other Indian classical dance forms. Through their efforts, bharatanatyam in Jaffna underwent a 'revival', as classical dance did in India: performers validated classical dance through reference to religion and to ancient texts, they standardized its pedagogy, and transferred its practice to 'family women'. This group of male dancers founded private dance schools and developed the syllabus system that integrated dance into organizations such as the North Ceylon Music Society.

Sri Lanka, like India, saw a movement to abolish dance by devadasis and in Hindu temples. Known as the Anti-Nautch Movement in India, this campaign foregrounded the status of devadasis as courtesans and decried the erotic content of the dance. Activists maintained that the non-domestic status of dancers debased the dance and, conversely, that the ostensible prurience of the dance corrupted its practitioners.

For example, Tamil cultural revivalist Arumukam Navalar (1822–1879) urged the reform of Hinduism. He condemned dance practice, as well as eroticism in temple sculpture, as part of the debasement of the Hindu religion. The solution proposed, as in India, was the eradication of dance by women in Hindu temples. In Sri Lanka, however, unlike in India, much of the Tamil public ignored this campaign and continued to promote devadasi dance. Thus, an Anti-Nautch style agitation developed in Sri Lanka earlier than in India but its devadasi performance continued for longer. The convergence of these two factors meant that 'family women' avoided the practice of dance until the 1950s.

In Jaffna, then, unlike in Chennai, the newly legitimized dance did not replace the devadasi tradition. Jaffna experienced the three contradictory elements that consolidated classical dance in India—a marginal courtesan tradition, a social reform movement, and a legitimization of dance—but it contended with all of them at once. Seen in this light, amateurization is a strategy that enabled women of a range of classes and backgrounds to enter the dance field, in the presence of an ongoing devadasi tradition, without compromise to 'social respectability'. The contradiction between the popularity of arangetrams and relative rarity of professional dance in Jaffna developed out of the coexistence of stage and temple versions of bharatanatyam.

I have argued elsewhere (2007a) that the symbolic domesticity cultivated by Indian nationalists integrated itself into dance through the re-ritualizing and 'purification' of dance repertoire. By foregrounding such values as spirituality and traditionalism in dance, bharatanatyam performers could move into resolutely public roles without threatening dominant models of gender identity. In Jaffna, even more so than in Chennai, this 'domestication' is partial and, therefore, amateurization validates the previously marginal tradition.

The decades-long ethnic conflict in Sri Lanka also accounts for the importance of preservation of Jaffna's bharatanatyam. The Tamils of Sri Lanka have contended not only with persecution at the hands of Sinhalese militant mobs and Sri Lankan soldiers but also with cultural destruction. Attempts at cultural exclusion included the government's Sinhala-only policy, which pushed Tamils and other minorities out of positions of power and influence. A more localized but equally pernicious strike occurred with the destruction of the Jaffna Library in 1981 by a security unit of the Sri Lankan military. This attack destroyed nearly 100,000 rare books and irreplaceable manuscripts, eliminating one of the largest repositories of ancient and modern Tamil literature.

It is little wonder, then, that Tamils bolster community cohesion through tradition. The decision to support Tamil identity by importing bharatanatyam from India, however, is striking in light of the complex relationship between the two South Asian countries. The intervention of governments of the subcontinent's mainland into the politics of Sri Lanka has a history that spans centuries. For Sinhalese nationalists, the fear of subordination to India has resulted in the development of what Stanley Tambiah (1991) has called a 'majority with a minority complex'. Sinhalese militants perceive Hinduism as a threat to Theravada Buddhism and describe Sri Lanka as the sole source of Sinhalese language and culture. Sinhalese militants accuse Tamils of being spurious Sri Lankans: Indians in disguise. That Tamils have been in Sri Lanka for over five hundred years and that their culture remains distinct from Indian Tamils falls out of this equation.

Thus, any relationship between 'Tamil' and 'Indian' is fraught. The contradictory policies of the Indian government in the late twentieth century complicated this vexed relationship. Indira Gandhi's government funded and trained the Tamil separatists in the 1980s. India then sent 'peace keeping' forces into northern Sri Lanka in the 1987. These soldiers became notorious for terrorizing the Tamil civilians they were called in to protect. Ironically, Tamil and Sinhalese militants came to share a rejection of things Indian; both militant groups have vehemently and, in some cases, violently rejected Indian individuals and cultural products. In Jaffna, under LTTE control, this found form in the prohibition of Indian popular culture: the revolutionaries banned Indian films, periodicals, and music.

And yet, Tamil revolutionaries did not have a problem with importing classical culture. On the contrary, in the 1990s, when the LTTE regained control of Jaffna, they strove to cultivate a Tamil identity through the arts; the revolutionary government sponsored classical dance and music competitions. They also commissioned propaganda dances.

These pieces were not only performed by civilians who supported the LTTE but also by female cadres of the rebel forces. Mahendra, a musician and dance lecturer described such a situation: he choreographed for a group of women soldiers who danced a piece narrating the liberation struggle through the movement vocabulary of bharatanatyam. The guerrilla leader, Prabhakaran, was not only present for the rehearsals but he also contributed to discussion on the sound score and on the use of mridangam instrumentation to mimic the sound of the invading army's helicopters.

In such pieces, and through the movement vocabulary of bharatanatyam, dancers depict the oppression of the Tamils. The pieces deploy bharatanatyam footwork and hand gestures to narrate the struggle of the Tamil people to free themselves from subjugation and to form the separate nation-state of Tamil Eelam. Dancers in fatigues portray invading Sri Lankan troops and the Tamil Tigers' paramilitary soldiers. Choreographers develop new mudras to portray the implements of modern warfare, using articulate and stylized gesture to invoke images of helicopters and machine guns. Some of these dances invoked parallels between older Tamil literary and religious figures and the military struggles of today.

These compositions provide an exception to the rule of classical dance as representing continuity and preservation in Sri Lanka. Towards the end of my stay in Jaffna, I encountered instances of experimentation with choreographic form that offered a more optimistic interpretation of dance's potential. Initially these experiments seemed restricted to dramatic productions, where playwrights and directors created pieces that commented on the current political situation, portraying the horrors of war, or striving to cultivate communal harmony. Shantini Sivanesan, a local dance teacher showed me a video of a dance drama she had directed and staged at Jaffna University. This production depicts an episode from the *Mahabharata* through bharatanatyam choreography, spoken dialogue, and theatrical blocking. Shantini portrays not the moment where Krishna urges Arjuna to fight or the war itself but the episode immediately following the battle. In this section, the characters speak openly of the futility of combat, depicting their anguish, and concluding as an ensemble in mourning gently removes the slain bodies from the stage. Shantini commented openly on the parallel that this piece offered to the present-day situation.

The resonances of this piece are manifold. On the one hand, it depicts the hopelessness induced by war, a radical statement in a region under military occupation where support for the LTTE is still high. That she staged the piece at Jaffna University—a stronghold of separatist sentiment—augments the choreographer's critique. Moreover, the combatants in the epic are relatives. By drawing a parallel between the Mahabharata's battle and the present-day conflict, Shantini's piece unsettles the racialization and polarization of languages in Sri Lanka. On the other hand, in the Mahabharata, war is catastrophic but also inevitable. The Pandavas are heroes although their victory is a melancholic one and they remain morally compromised. This piece therefore constitutes less a straightforward statement against violence than a depiction of its tragic consequences, a portrayal that speaks effectively of and to a populace exhausted by, yet accustomed to, war.

In evoking these examples, I suggest that bharatanatyam in Sri Lanka relies upon an intersection between dance, history, and politics. Bharatanatyam reflects and contributes to a range of social, political, cultural, and economic concerns but also provides a way of negotiating through them. Thus, LTTE cadres dance out their resistance to Sinhalese hegemony. This strategy forms its own orthodoxy as it is part of the fixed ideology of the revolutionary group which, like that of Sinhalese militants, locates the ethnic conflict in binary categories of essential difference. When Tamil choreographers create work that comments on the current political situation, they use choreographic practice to argue back to militants as well as to the Sri Lankan government. Dance fosters competing community affiliations but also problematizes them. As such, bharatanatyam offers alternate ideas of belonging in present-day Sri Lanka.

WORKS CITED

Gorringe, Magdalen. 2001. Arangetram: Performance or Party? Arangetram, Social Conventions, and Artistic Endeavor. http://www.boloji.com/dances/00106.htm. Posted 10 March 2001.

Kersenboom, Saskia. 2004. Mirrors, Frames, Reflections: on the Transformation of Bharata Natyam in the 20th Century. Conference paper presented at *Performing Pasts, Imagining Futures: Nationalism, Globalization and the Performing Arts in Modern South Asia.* Columbia University, New York.

O'Shea, Janet. 2003. At Home in the World? The Bharata Natyam Dancer as Transnational Interpreter. *TDR: The Drama Review* 47(1): 176–186.

O'Shea, Janet. 2007a. *At Home in the World: Bharata Natyam on the Global Stage.* Middletown, Connecticut: Wesleyan University Press.

O'Shea, Janet. 2007b. Dancing through History and Ethnography: An Inquiry into Bharata Natyam's Performance of the Past. In *Dancing from Past to Present: Nation, Cultures, Identities*, edited by Theresa Buckland. Madison, Wisconsin: University of Wisconsin Press.

Srinivasan, Amrit. 1985. Reform and Revival: The Devadasi and her Dance. *Economic and Political Weekly* 20 (44): 1869–1876.

Tambiah, Stanley Jeyarajah. *Sri Lanka: Ethnic Fratricide and the Dismantling of Democracy.* Chicago: University of Chicago Press.

ACKNOWLEDGEMENTS

An earlier version of this paper appeared in *Pulse* magazine. Thanks are due to T Sanathanan, the other members of the art department faculty at Jaffna University and to Professor Emeritus Sivathambi for taking time to discuss the current situation of bharatanatyam in the Tamil-speaking regions of Sri Lanka, to S Vinodhini for research assistance and translation, and to the dancers, teachers, and choreographers of Jaffna.

Brown Masculinities and the Contours of Social Marginality: Implications for Psychological Well-Being

JENNIFER YOUNG YIM AND RAMASWAMI MAHALINGAM

Asian Immigration, Social Marginality and Idealized Cultural Beliefs

The history of Asian-Americans in the United States has been largely shaped by immigration and gendered race relations. These experiences have crafted a depiction of Asian-Americans, particularly South Asians, in the public imagination as a visibly successful, yet socially marginalized community. Individuals' reactions to the complexities of social marginalization can be simultaneously negative and positive, particularly in the context of model minority beliefs. This section will provide a brief overview of general Asian-American history that is relevant to the formation of a feminized model minority context in which Asian-American men negotiate social marginality and idealized cultural beliefs. We will explore the contours of brown masculinities by exploring the complex dimensions of second-generation, Tamil Americans—Indian Americans of Tamil descent in the United States. Using qualitative interviews of male Tamil American college students, our study examined how these men construct, resist, and challenge hegemonic masculinities. We briefly review the Asian-American immigration to the United States and using a social marginality perspective, we will analyze the construction of Tamil masculinities.

Immigration History

Migration from the Indian subcontinent to the United States dates back to 1804 and the major wave of early immigrants to the United States was largely from the Punjab region who worked and owned farms (Leonard, 1992). With the introduction of immigrant quotas in 1946, immigration from India and China was virtually halted until 1965. With immigration reform by Lyndon Johnson, which allowed the migration of professionals from India and China, highly educated and successful men and women engineers, scientists, and doctors migrated to the United States (Bacon, 1996; Mahalingam *et al.*, 2006; Rangaswamy, 2000). According to Prashad

(2000), between 1966 and 1977, 83% of the Indian Americans who entered the United States were professionals and technical workers. A combination of the immigration policy and post-Independent India's emphasis on higher education in science and technology contributed to the migration of highly educated professionals from engineering, science, and medicine. Many thousands of engineers and doctors came to the United States for better education and employment opportunity. Now the Indian diaspora is one of the most economically successful immigrant groups in the United States. For example, a recent report from the American Association of Physicians of Indian Origin indicates that there are approximately 35,000 Indian doctors working in the United States (see Mahalingam *et al.*, 2006). The Indian diaspora which is within the larger umbrella of Asian Americans are seen as a "model minority" because of their economic and academic success in the United States. The perception that Asian Americans as a whole were succeeding as a minority group eventually led to the "model minority myth," such as in a 1982 *Newsweek* article speculating on why Asians were so successful academically and professionally (Chan, 1991; Kasindorf *et al.*, 1982; Prashad, 2000; Takaki, 1998).

A Model Minority

The stereotype of the "model minority" depicts Asian Americans as meek, quiet, studious, and successful, and pits them against other racial minority groups, oftentimes justifying continued oppression or withholding of public assistance in the form of policy programs or affirmative action (Mio *et al.*, 2007; Prashad, 2000). It is commonly assumed that the hard work and success attributed to the model minority stereotype are achieved by sacrificing personal relationships and sexuality (Liu & Chang, 2007). Just as the category "Asian American" originated as an external, socially constructed label appropriated for political purposes for brown and yellow Asians alike, the category of "model minority" has also been widely internalized and cherished as an idealized cultural value by Asian Americans (Bhatia, 2007; Hacking, 1999; Prashad, 2000). This looping effect has resulted in many Asian Americans attributing their "success" in the United States to supposedly Asian cultural ideals such as hard work, discipline, filial piety, and focus (Hacking, 1999; Kim *et al.*, 2006). These model minority values, in fact, often become internalized cultural ideals such that some parents pass onto their children with the hope that they too will succeed as minorities in the United States, ignoring previous social privileges afforded to some in the immigrant generation such as elite education and prestigious professional occupations (Kim Abboud & Kim, 2006; Prashad, 2000). The youth of the 1.5 and second generations may experience intergenerational conflict from parents' expectations to assimilate in ways that encourage educational and professional career successes yet maintain traditional aspects of the home culture, which some joke about with the South Asian American term ABCDs or

American Born Confused Desi (Zia, 2000).

Social marginality. The internalization and perpetuation of a marginalized group identity is characterized by tensions between essentialized stereotypes of the dominant society and the internalized, however artificially created, cultural ideals of positive self-identity (Mahalingam, 2007). For Asian Americans, external stereotypes of the model minority have become so deeply internalized by members of a recently constructed group category that it has become a prevailing cultural narrative across ethnic groups (Hacking, 1999; Prashad, 2000). Although the notion of a model minority is a contested myth, it is also an important cultural narrative to understand how members of a socially marginalized group negotiate power differentials with dominant groups and create a positive group identity as a reflection on the self, especially when negotiating other negative ethnic or racial stereotypes (Mahalingam, 2007). The multi-layered intersection of power differentials and group identities provide insight into the complexity of how endorsing such idealized self and group perceptions may also contribute to the psychological well-being of individuals in socially marginalized groups.

The model minority stereotype applies broad generalizations to all Asian Americans and thus "marginalizes the cultural context of coping ... and ... denies the experience of racism discrimination that Asian Americans face" (Inman & Yeh, 2007, p. 329). While culturally relevant coping strategies outlined by Inman and Yeh (2007) for Asian Americans, such as indigenous healing, family support, religious support, and social support networks are effective in general, Asian American college students may use other strategies to cope with the extreme academic pressures in college, such as the use of anti-depressant drugs, stimulant drug use (i.e. caffeine, energy drinks, amphetamines), and drinking. Judging the effectiveness and the ethics of these coping strategies becomes increasingly complex irrespective of whether they are considered positive (e.g. relying on social support networks) or negative (e.g. binge drinking), because Asian American men may resort to these strategies in order to cope with model minority expectations. However, this possibility is nested within a deficit-model approach to men and masculinity and has not been broadly tested, particularly among South Asian American male college students. This lacuna in the literature leaves open the possibility of unexplored levels of identity-related coping strategies, both negative and positive.

Model Minority and Hegemonic Masculinities

In a review of gender role strain paradigm research, Pleck (1995) notes that empirical research needs to examine the possible positive psychological consequences of not fitting masculinity standards (and thus experiencing gender role strain) because confronting traditional role standards of any kind can lead to psychological maturity and integration. Additionally, because oftentimes the traditional standards of masculinity are themselves dysfunctional (i.e. emotionally distant, engaging in unhealthy, risk-taking behaviors), resisting conformation to dysfunctional gender role ideals, at a pragmatic level, reduces psychological and physical health risks (Courtenay, 2000; Pleck, 1995). For Asian American men, Chen (1999) has described repudiation as a gender strategy that rejects negative views of Chinese masculinity in relation to hegemonic norms and paints a healthier self-image for it. It is possible, too, that the rejection of model minority stereotypes may lead to similar outcomes of physical and psychological health. If the rejection of dysfunctional standards can contribute to increased well-being, then it would be beneficial to identify how Asian American men cope with stress, related both to masculinity and model minority pressures. Additionally, it would be a rich discussion to examine the individual differences in how and why Asian American men cope differently, and to explore whether any particular coping strategies are more effective than others.

Non-deficit Model Approaches

To date, the majority of research and theoretical writing on masculinity has focused on the white European American man as representing the complete embodiment of idealized masculine traits in the United States (Chen, 1999; Goffman, 1963; Liu & Chang, 2007; Pleck, 1995). It is important to recognize, however, that there may be multiple masculine ideals that any one individual man may strive to fit that do not necessarily fit the standard white European American norms, depending on social and political context (Connell, 2005; Levant & Majors, 1995; Liu & Chang, 2007; Pleck, 1995). A relational approach to studying men from any racial group recognizes that masculine ideals are constantly reconfigured in response to symbolic representations of men from other racial groups (Connell & Messerschmidt, 2005; Hacking, 1999). It may therefore be useful to structure a relational or reference group approach when studying men from a racial minority population, especially Asian American men, because there has been a narrow assumption in men's studies that racial minority men have compared themselves only against the norms of white European American male ideals (Lazur & Majors, 1995).

Recent research has shown that ethnic minority men do not necessary hold themselves to a standard held by the ethnic majority group and that individual men may in fact have multiple reference groups and standards to strive toward, depending on the context (Liu & Chang, 2007; Wade, 1998). For example, Lazur & Majors (1995) note in an overview of ethnocultural variations of male gender role strain that Asian American men may experience conflicting pressures to fulfill standards of *both* the traditional white European American male gender role *and* the traditional Asian male gender role, which are at times incongruent (e.g. the traditional Asian male standard of putting family obligations first contradicts the traditional white European American male standard of acting as more of an independent individual).

Therefore, in order to capture a more holistic view of the multiple standards of masculinity that individual men within ethnic minority groups may hold themselves to, non-deficit, relational approaches and within-group variation must be considered.

According to Mahalingam (2007), individuals in socially marginalized groups construct essentialist beliefs about their group identity in four different ways: *resistance, transcendence, disidentification,* or *internalization.* In *resistance,* marginalized persons can resist biological essentialist accounts of group identity and, in turn, adopt social essentialist strategies to combat the biological essentialist assumptions of the dominant group. Participating in resistance can lead to increased resilience in the form of self-esteem and success. *Transcendence* refers to marginalized individuals seeing a united human race that shares "the same essence and the same predicaments, regardless of the sociocultural context" (Mahalingam, 2007; p. 49). Using a transcendental worldview can also help a socially marginalized individual to combat negative stereotypes and discrimination. *Disidentification* refers to individuals disconnecting their self-worth from essentialist group representations, thus protecting their self-image from outside evaluation, and *internalization* refers to a heightened awareness of "stigmatized essentialist representations" that could lead to a sense of helplessness and negative psychological outcomes such as depression and self-defeating behaviors (Mahalingam, 2007, p. 49).

It is apparent that within the social-marginality perspective, individuals in socially marginalized positions are not only affected by negative stereotypes that the dominant society holds about a particular group, they are affected by the various reactions of other individuals within the same group as well (Mahalingam, 2007). The relational interplay between dominant and marginalized groups is important in understanding the complex intersection of group identities, including gender and masculinity. Therefore, any examination of a socially marginalized social group requires the simultaneous examination of what is considered dominant or hegemonic and how individuals of the socially marginalized group relate to hegemonic ideals, all of which are situated in a socio-political context.

Most of the research on Asian American masculinities focused on Japanese, Chinese and Korean Americans. Very few qualitative studies examined how Tamil Americans negotiate the pressures of model minority myth and hegemonic masculinities. In this study, using an in-depth life history interviews we examined Tamil Americans' construction of masculinities with a specific focus on model minority myth and hegemony of white masculinities.

Present Study

For the present study, four South Asian American male undergraduate college students who identified as Tamil and were raised primarily in the United States were recruited using convenience sampling at a large mid-western university to participate in one-on-one semi-structured interviews. Participants were invited to talk about their experiences as being Tamil men on a college campus and were compensated $20 on iTunes or a donation to charity for their time. Interviews lasted approximately 40 to 90 minutes, were audio taped and later transcribed and identifying information such as names were changed to protect confidentiality. Four participants completed the interviews, all of whom were of Indian Tamil background, preferred to self-identify as Indian or South Asian American, and had brothers (none had sisters).

Participants

Arun was a sophomore music major who was passionate about the performing arts and had a background in Bharathanatyam. Though Arun was a music major, he planned to apply for medical school after college. In fact, he had researched what medical school admissions prefer in their candidates and, having been told that they preferred candidates who had majored in areas they were passionate about, chose the music major over a science major. Overall, Arun was a driven student who tenaciously worked toward his goals and overcame adversity when his goals were not met. His perspectives on culture were influenced by the years he spent in India attending high school and he consistently strove to meet and exceed the standards set by his older brother.

Bala was a graduating senior who majored in neuroscience and minored in economics. He was set to attend graduate school for public health and hoped to one day attend medical school and eventually work in a developing country to treat persons with HIV/AIDS. Bala also had a background in music and dance, and he met a number of friends through his involvement in a campus performing group. He had frequent contact with his family who lived nearby and noted that though he saw his family about once a week, the experience of moving out to attend college made them miss one another and thus strengthened their family relationships.

Kannan was also a graduating senior and majored in Cellular and Molecular Biology. He was involved in South Asian student groups, musical performing and dance groups, as well as community service volunteering. He described himself as not brilliant per se, but as a hard-worker who maintains above-average grades. Kannan, who expressed a love of biology that he had had since childhood, was enrolled to begin medical school the following Fall.

Krishna was a sophomore public policy major who was considering a double major in math. He had considered majoring in math first in order to go into business in order to make a large income, but felt a desire to do something meaningful and therefore enrolled in the public policy program. Krishna had a "study hard play hard" mentality who had a brother and noted that if he had a sister, his parents' rules would have been different for her. Overall, Krishna was a self-described high-achieving student and had occasionally experienced stress in college, particularly during a relationship breakup. Krishna also had plans to attend medical school and emphasized his intent to be involved with community work in whatever he could throughout his life.

All participants reported themselves to be good students and noted that their families never intervened with school unless it was to correct undesirable behaviors, such as getting a lower than expected grade. In one example, the bad grade was a "B" in grade school and the intervention consisted of a lecture on how the son needed to work harder. No families were reported to teaching specific study skills or giving particular academic advice. Yet, these college students were academically high-achieving and successful. This emphasis on education may reflect the high levels of education that their parents had as well as an internalized model minority message that academic excellence is central to success as an individual in the United States.

Additionally, the lack of advice regarding how exactly to do well in school (i.e. tips on how to organize homework, take notes, etc.) is most likely a reflection of the different, exam-driven Indian school system that the parents were brought up in as opposed to an American school system of which they may know little. And while some participants speculated that their grandmothers or aunties might have talked to them about more specific socialization, such as how to be a good man, their relatives were mainly in India and thus there was little opportunity for those conversations to arise. This distance from extended family indicates the great importance of parental socialization in immigrant communities, since there are not as many extended family connections nearby to influence a young male child.

Major Themes

From these interviews, four interrelated themes emerge: (a) masculinity is moderation; (b) reference groups are defined within ethnicity, not just in relation to whites, in a large university context; (c) parental socialization is unspoken, yet understood; (d) Tamil identity is still practiced, yet unnamed and merged into a larger Indian identity. In this section, we discuss how these emergent themes are embedded within a context of brown masculinities and social marginality. Then we reflect on how the gender experience of living as a young racial minority may simultaneously positively and negatively impact mental and physical health for college students.

Masculinity is Moderation. The next emergent theme is one of masculinity being defined as moderation or balance. While the bulk of available masculinity literature talks about masculinity as risk-taking and aggressive behavior, these Tamil male participants prided themselves on moderation. For example, when asked to describe what an ideal man is like, one participant responded, "You know, not getting too excited about things, knowing how to be in control" (Bala). The emphasis here on control is typical of masculine traits, but in the context of being a racial minority in the United States may symbolize a subconscious feeling of being a representative of one's family, ethnicity, and race.

> "Well I kind of wanted to do something that had meaning like I just didn't want to, like I could have done the math major and gone into business and made a lot of money but I kind of wanted to do something that had a meaning. That's kind of corny ... I think I'm well rounded. I do a little bit of everything. Ah study hard, play hard. That kind of mentality .... Uh I mean I try to get my work done. I'm also pre-med. I want to get into med school so I stay on top of my work because that's important. That's always been important to me. I try to have a good time. Even in high school I always found time to hang out to go out have a good time with friends because that's important too." (Krishna)

It is possible, however, that this feeling of being a "racial representative" increases the self-awareness of behavior and consequently an individual imposes a policy of moderation in order to avoid actions that might not only embarrass themselves, but their families and racial peers as well. Participants emphasized balance in their responses about everyday activities and made a point to regularly engage in exercise and healthy socializing, such as playing basketball with friends several times a week. Also, participants noted that while they worked very hard in school, they still knew how to have fun and socialized quite a bit, either formally through extracurricular activities or informally by hanging out with friends they met in the dormitories or through student groups. While some students occasionally drank alcohol, it was in moderation, never going overboard to the point of embarrassment or losing control, and some did not even consume substances like caffeine.

> If you don't drink its sad but if you don't drink too much you get made fun of, not that I was I'm just saying people in general will just get made fun of which pushes you to drink more, which is the dumbest idea, but once you start drinking you're like "oh" because that's a good idea. So, which is I've seen people do that and it's just it's just stupid and that's pushing your limits and that's when you get to places you don't want to go [laughs]. (Kannan)

This quote suggests that by exercising moderation in the practices that are commonly associated with hyper masculinity, these men avoid the threat of bringing shame to their families, peers and communities by their excesses in college yet also try to assert that they can have fun and also be academically successful unlike other "Indian Geeks." Seeking moderation in response to typical risk-taking masculine behavior has been a major theme of their narrative account of their enactment of their masculinities.

Referent Groups of Masculinity

Participants noted that they were not like the Indian students who were imbalanced to the point of only studying that "They're constantly threatened that if they don't study every day they're going to end up on the street" (Arun). In the subsequent section of the interview he says:

> I mean drinking is probably the best example of like um because then we're taught like I mean obviously at our spiritual center its just kind of assumed that you don't drink and do all that stuff um and so coming here was different and like getting to like understand how to like relate with people that were so Indian because I, I had this mindset of like oh, you need people that are just like me but then realizing that maybe they're not you know maybe they come from a very different background and stuff like that so um that's been very interesting and um learning to deal with that but it's also been really cool because like you're not usually it's like the happy medium between you're very little like me you're totally like me so I can find people that are like part of it who I have common interests with but then some things we disagree on too which is fine its just been interesting you know? (Arun)

This was also distinct from those "repressed" Indian students whose parents were too hard on them in high school and went wild with partying in college to the point that they either had to take time off or transfer to a college closer to home.

Instead of trying to have distinct within-group identity that is in opposition to the "bad" Indians, Krishna talked about consciously building a multicultural peer group.

> It is easy to get sucked up into the Indian crowd and it kind of becomes a cult, so I try not to do that. And being from Edison [New Jersey] ... Edison has a large Indian population. So most of my friends back home are Indian, not because I planned it like that, that's just because of the way things turned out. So here like I try to keep a very diverse group of friends and stuff so I don't get suck for that frame of mind. (Krishna)

> I guess I consider myself not your typical Tamil male [laugh].... I think I do a pretty good job of being able to balance both worlds. I kind of see who I am and what I like in culture here and I try to incorporate as much of both as I can while trying to be myself.... I think sometimes people fall too easily in one or the other because I think it is important to be able to relate to both.... In American I'd say the typical Tamil man probably falls into the typical college things and I think, I obviously hate to generalize there, I think the typical Tamil man that I see knows all these values and stuff that he's been taught but sometimes maybe would rather ... I think one of the biggest things I saw that they've been so suppressed their whole lives that they get to college and they go extra nuts, they go extra crazy because they've been sheltered for so long like 'don't do this, don't do that, do drink' blah blah blah, they come to college and there's no rules and they just got nuts...like partying, sex, all that stuff. (Arun)

The implicit message of within-group comparison here is that in order to define themselves as balanced and moderate, extremes that are of a less desirable lifestyle have to be identified and then distanced. The assumption is also that those of a moderate nature do not associate with those on the extremes.

Parental Socialization

In the interviews, participants were asked if anyone in their family ever talked to them about how to be a good son, man, or student. Across all four interviews, participants shared that working hard was a value that their parents particularly emphasized, but had difficulty thinking of more specific examples related to fulfilling certain social roles (student, son, man). One participant, speaking in reference to how he and his brother knew how to be good sons shared that, "It's just always been an expectation, and we've kind of made it an expectation for ourselves.... It's just kind of always been an underling expectation references from the community to talk about [it]." (Arun). There are instances where parents either explicitly or implicitly used positive and successful men in their immediate ethnic network as an example of being a good son. Interestingly, this does not seem to have negative consequences for one of our participants.

> Like sometimes I know there's patterns of like being compared so much that you just get sick of it. But I've always looked up to my brothers, but I've never seen myself as inadequate or unable to achieve what he is. And if anything, he's always been like a milestone that I reach and then go past, that kind of thing. So that's always the way I've seen it and he's definitely my guide and my parents tell me to use him as my guide a lot because we're so close in age so it's easier to relate. Um, and yeah, to other kids outside of the family, definitely. We get, my parents compare us to, well, other parents compare their kids to us too, so that's the good part. And then sometimes my mom will be like, "You should be more like so and so" and stuff like that. Um, yeah, it's always like, they're always just trying to, it's never been 'you are inadequate, you need to be more like so and so' kind of thing, it's always been like 'they're great kids, they're doing these things, you guys should try to emulate that,' sort of thing. I've never seen it as something as abrasive or hurtful. (Arun)

This excerpt demonstrates the emergent theme that though participants could not recall any specific conversations or life lessons about how to fulfill parental expectations of behavior, they implicitly knew what to do and consequently internalized a set of values and behaviors. Some speculated that they learned by example in a way that was so subtle, they were consciously thinking about it for the first time during the interview.

Another within-ethnic group that was identified in order to distance themselves from were those of competitive parents. When asked if their parents compared them to other children in the Indian community growing up (i.e. SAT scores, grades), respondents made it clear that while there are many Indian parents who pressure their children to an extreme and compare them with others, their own parents were nothing of the like. Rather, respondents described their parents as supportive and pushing them in a way that they appreciated. When ask if his parents ever compared him to other family members, or community members, Kannan responds: "I was lucky enough not to be compared to my brothers .... But there is always a tendency for people to be like, 'oh look at X, he got an A+ in this class and look at you' [laughter]. Not to bring you down but just to keep you aware of what other people are doing, maybe spark something...." So while there indeed is a comparison between children, it is seen as a form of encouragement so that participants can be inspired and motivated to strive for higher goals.

Krishna's response to this same question was, "They never did that, but they'd ask me like 'oh so and so took this test, [do] you know what they got?'.... They would never, they would never compare me to anybody." Thus, even in explaining the respect they had for their parents' child-rearing styles, there is an implicit identification of more extreme or "harsh" Indian parents to distance their own parents from. This identification of comparison groups within ethnicity indicates a need for us to more closely examine the complexity with which individual Asian Americans, such as Tamil male college students, see themselves in reference to others.

Identity

One of the complexities of within-ethnicity reference groups involves the transition of self-identification across generations. When asked how their parents identified their race/ethnicity, all participants said "Tamil," but they themselves, the second generation, responded more in this way: "I don't really identify as Tamil, I identify as Indian or South Asian." While on the surface it could be perceived that participants were denying their Tamil identity, in practice most were deeply rooted in Tamil practices and pride in a way evidence by their activities in cultural arts like barathanatyam and taking Tamil language class in college. For example, Arun shared that

> [What] my parents really drove home was that they really wanted to preserve the culture, preserve Indian culture and we'd heard many stories of people coming here and like kids forgetting about who they are and like kind of blending in with their being here. And so they always made a big deal that we learn Tamil at home. So my parents always spoke Tamil at home and never English. Even today we speak Tamil at home." (Arun).

These responses indicate that while these young men may not self-identify as Tamil outwardly, their Tamil identities become implicit in practice. This shift in self-identification allows the young men to capitalize upon the benefits of labeling themselves as Indian or South Asian, which include joining South Asian or Indian student groups in which they can meet a number of friends and engage in extracurricular activities. One student even founded his own South Asian acapella group. If the reach of these organizations were just to Tamils, then their social circles would be much smaller. In fact, then, shifting self-identification in this context is a useful coping mechanism that allows them access to empowering activities and an impressive number of friends and acquaintances, thereby increasing the strength of their social network and diminishing their risk for negative psychological outcomes during college. However, by living out a Tamil identity in practice through cultural arts and language, the participants simultaneously are able to hold onto their parents' values and Tamil identity. For example, Bala took singing lessons growing up and while in college continues to commute with a friend one hour every week to attend classes. And Krishna, who was taking Tamil language class in college, shared:

> I play an instrument called the mridungum. It's a classical Indian instrument and I, there's a group called Indian classical music and dance so I play in that group just to get practice because I don't want to lose touch. (Krishna)

We can see here that these students make it a point to stay connected with their respective cultural arts that their parents encouraged them to begin as children and as a result they meet other students of a broader pan-Indian background with similar interests. These connections offer positive experiences and helpful social networks. For example, when asked if there was any one person who had a particularly positive impact on him in college, Bala responds:

> I've felt like I've made a lot of friends in college. They're people that I'll stay in touch with for the rest of my life so definitely I've learned things from them. I've learned about myself and in general just interacting with people exposed me to new ways of thinking, seeing things, [I am] definitely glad to have that. (Bala)

So it seems in this series of interviews, the letting go of an outward Tamil identity label in favor of a pan-Indian identity label, but holding onto cultural practices such as music and language study, allows students to bond with others and create strong social networks that allow them to have positive and growing experiences while in college.

General Discussion

Moderation in expressing masculine behavior is one of the major themes that emerged from these narratives. We suspect that hyper masculinity is associated with a person who is more physical and less intellectual and someone who does not self regulate or control impulses. In general, African American are seen as a physical threat whereas Asian American men are seen a threat to professional jobs and for contributing an intensely competitive academic environment, such as "throwing" or "skewing" the grade curve (Lazur & Majors, 1995; Majors & Billson, 1993). We contend that ethnic minority men in the United States have to be extra cautious about expressing their masculinity and they need to contest these implicit expectations associated with these stereotypes. It seems they are pressured to project a masculinity that is in control of impulses and does not seem to be a threat to the dominant masculinities. Our participants constructed a narrative of their masculinities where they tried hard to strike a balance between being seen as either "out of control" or geeks.

The construction of masculinity as moderation, however, involves identifying the two ends of what represents the extremes; without these extremes, there is no middle path for an individual to place himself within. In this study, one extreme represented those who took their studies too seriously to the point of fearing any kind of failure, while the other extreme was described as those who came to college and "went wild" with partying to the point of completely shirking their studies. Thus Tamil masculinities may be triangulated within these two extremes and the invisible yet insidious hegemony of "white" masculinities. Within the larger context, the construction of Asian American masculinities need to contest, negotiate and transcend the stereotypical expectations of what it takes to be an Asian or South Asian man.

It is interesting that while in men's studies on race, Asian American men have been depicted as creating reference groups in relations to hegemonic white males (i.e. seeing themselves as more responsible or family-oriented than whites), in this study the reference groups were other Indian college students. This in-group comparison suggests the significance of reference group theory within masculinity studies and may offer some further insight into the complex nature of how individual Asian Americans negotiate the model minority stereotype, and these men seem to have multiple referents for their representations of masculinities. They were aware of some of these referents and were not fully aware of others, such as White masculinities, in their construction as well as resistance to representations of ideal manhood.

Parental socialization of masculinity seems to be implicit. Unlike the stereotypes about competitive and perfectionist parents, our participants were happy about the higher standards their parents set for them. In some cases, they internalized those expectations to the point that they have high personal standards for academic excellence. They viewed their parents as sources of inspiration and motivation to excel. In turn, these students were genuinely and intrinsically motivated to succeed in school and not just to please their parents. This is in contrast to many studies or ethnographic accounts of Asian immigrant families. Our participants' self worth is contingent upon the standards they set for themselves to work hard. All participants also have lot of respect for their fathers and viewed them as role models. We did not see any feelings of emotional distance with their fathers. This is in contrast to findings on American men's interaction with their fathers. In the absence of extended family network, close parental interactions were instrumental in transmitting ideal expectations of what it takes to be a man.

We were interested in how intersections of ethnicity and gender in a displaced context shaped the masculinity construction of these men. Interestingly although these men spoke Tamil at home and strongly identified with Tamil culture, such enactments of "being" Tamil did not necessarily map on to self labeling their identity as Tamil. Although these men have very close Tamil-speaking friends, they identified themselves as Indian Americans not as Tamils. This is consistent with research on generational differences in using ethnic labels. Research shows that first-generation immigrants typically use their national or sub-ethnic identity to label themselves. By contrast, later generation immigrants use broader pan ethnic labels (e.g. Asian-American, Hispanic) to talk about their identity. The immigrant context and the greater interaction with other ethnic groups from South Asia might have facilitated the process of identity formation of these men. They also talked about their efforts to build coalitions with other ethnic groups to broaden their circle of friends. This dynamic may not apply to other immigrant contexts where a sizable immigrant population can provide many cultural affordances to maintain a unique ethnic identity. For example, second-generation Sri Lankan Tamil men who grew up in Scarborough could maintain their Tamil identity because of the larger social context where maintaining a Tamil identity may be more feasible than our participants who did not grew up in a predominantly Tamil ethnic community. Our studies show that in addition to transmitting the language and practices, larger social context also shapes the identity development of second-generation Tamils. In-group referencing to identify extremes that distinguished themselves from other Indian students inadvertently creates categories of different kinds of Indians within the larger group.

Conclusion

The larger themes found in this qualitative study on second-generation Tamil American male college students indicate that there are a number of possibilities for future studies on Asian American men of various ethnic identities that take a non-deficit model approach to socially marginalized masculinities. It is apparent in this study that the participants were for the most part satisfied with life and as eager to engage socially in the arts and community development as they were to push themselves toward academic and eventual career achievement. Taken at face values, these students could be classified as falling within the parameters of the model minority stereotype, yet who simultaneously negotiate these parameters by exploring the holistic potential of themselves as campus community members. Additionally, their individual choices to self-identify as Indian or South Asian, combined with their interests in the arts, led to their involvement in pan-South Asian performing arts groups and they thus gained all the associated social and mental health benefits of having a reliable social network.

Despite the interesting emergent themes that came forth in this qualitative study, there are a number of caveats to observe. First, the size of this sample is particularly small and future studies would benefit from having a larger pool of participants to sample from. Second, the participants who were interviewed were drawn from a student sample at a prestigious and large Midwestern university. The results may have been different if students were drawn from a campus that was not as prestigious and had a lower median student household income. Additionally, the numerous cultural student resources on the large campus seemed to have accounted for much of the participants' social network support, which may differ from the experiences of Tamil students at universities where they are in the racial minority and do not have the same chances to be involved in cultural student organizations.

Third, the Tamil students sampled for this study were all of Indian origin. The negotiation of South Asian and Tamil self-identification would surely look different if students had come from a Sri Lankan Tamil background. Further study could perhaps sample from the Sri Lankan Tamil community in the Toronto area in order to explore the variance in self-identity. Last, none of these participants had sisters, and one even commented that he probably would have seen a different side of his parents if he had a sister. Since there was no variance in gendered parental socialization to experience while growing up, and for the most part a lack of extended family socialization as well, it should be assumed that the participants in this study have a fairly male-sided perspective when it comes to reports on parental socialization.

However, the possibility of non-deficit model approaches to the study of South Asian men, such as second-generation Indian Tamil male college students, has potential for expanding the perspectives on socially marginalized categories within the masculinity literature. The context of immigration is prominent in this category, especially if parental socialization becomes a primary form of family influence in instances where the extended family is far away. And contrary to some existing discourse on the expression of young masculinity, this study indicates that the parameters of model minority stereotypes and the pervasive standards of white hegemonic masculinity may not be explicit, but can still be negotiated by maintaining a conscious balance of masculinity as moderation. The implicit naming of extremes between which to place themselves as moderates may happen within a social identity, in this case among South Asians, and thus has community implications for whom these students are distancing themselves from in the process of developing independent self-identities as moderate, well-rounded young South Asian men.

WORKS CITED

Chan, S. 1991. *Asian Americans: An Interpretive History.* New York, NY: Twayne Publishers.

Chen, A. 1999. Lives at the Center of the Periphery, Lives at the Periphery of the Center: Chinese American Masculinities and Bargaining with Hegemony. *Gender and Society* 13: 584–607.

Cheng, C. 1999. Marginalized masculinities and hegemonic masculinity: An introduction. *The Journal of Men's Studies,* 7: 295–316.

Connell, RW. 2005. *Masculinities,* 2nd ed. CA: University of California Press.

Connell, RW, and Messerschmidt, JW. 2005. Hegemonic Masculinity: Rethinking the Concept. *Gender and Society,* 19: 829–859.

Courtenay, WH. 2000. Constructions of Masculinity and Their Influence on Men's Well-

Being: A Theory of Gender and Health. *Social Science and Medicine,* 50: 1385–1401.

Goffman, E. 1963. *Stigma: Notes on the Management of Spoiled Identity.* Englewood Cliffs, NJ: Prentice-Hall.

Hacking, I. 1999. *The Social Construction of What?* Cambridge, MA: Harvard University Press.

Inman, AG, and Yeh, CJ. 2007. Asian American Stress and Coping. In *Handbook of Asian American Psychology,* 2nd ed., edited by FTL Leong, AG Inman, A Ebreo, LH Yang, L Kinoshita, and M Fu. Thousand Oaks, CA: Sage Publications.

Kasindorf, M, P Chin, D Weathers, K Foltz, D Shapiro, and D Junkin. 1982. Asian Americans: A 'model minority.' *Newsweek* (6 December): 39.

Kibria, N. 2002. *Becoming Asian American: Second-generation Chinese and Korean American Identities.* Baltimore, MD: The Johns Hopkins University Press.

Kim Abboud, S, and J Kim. 2006. *Top of the Class: How Asian Parents Raise High Achievers—and How You Can Too.* New York: The Berkeley Publishing Group.

Lazur, RF, and R Majors. 1995. Men of Color: Ethnocultural Variations of Male Gender Role Strain. In *A New Psychology of Men,* edited by RF Levant and WS Pollack. New York, NY: Basic Books. 337–358.

Lee, SJ. 1993. *Unraveling the "Model Minority" Stereotype: Listening to Asian American Youth.* New York, NY: Teachers College Press.

Liu, WM, and T Chang. 2007. Asian American Masculinities. In *Handbook of Asian American Psychology,* 2nd ed., edited by FTL Leong, AG Inman, L Ebreo, H Yang, L Kinoshita, and M Fu. Thousand Oaks, CA: Sage Publications.

Liu, WM, and DK Iwamoto. 2006. Asian American Men's Gender Role Conflict: The Role of Asian Values, Self-Esteem, and Psychological Distress. *Psychology of Men and Masculinity* 7: 153–164.

Liu, WM, and DK Iwamoto. 2007. Conformity to Masculine Norms, Asian Values, Coping Strategies, Peer Group Influences and Substance Use Among Asian American Men. *Psychology of Men and Masculinity* 8: 25–39.

Mahalingam, R. 2007. Essentialism and Cultural Narratives: A Social-Marginality Perspective. In *Contesting Stereotypes and Creating Identities: Social Categories, Social Identities, and Educational Participation,* edited by AJ Fuligni. New York: Russell Sage Foundation. 42–65.

Mahalingam, R, C Philip, and S Balan. 2006. Cultural Psychology and Marginality: An Explorative Study of Indian Diaspora. In *Cultural Psychology of Immigrants,* edited by R Mahalingam. Mahwah, NJ: Lawrence Erlbaum.

Majors, R JM Billson. 1993. *Cool Pose: The Dilemmas of Black Manhood in America.* New York, NY: Touchstone Books/Simon & Schuster.

Pleck, JH. 1995. *The Gender Role Strain Paradigm: An Update.* In *A New Psychology of Men,* edited by RF Levant and WS Pollack. New York, NY: Basic Books. 337–358.

Prashad, V. 2000. *The Karma of Brown Folk.* Minneapolis, MN: University of Minnesota Press.

Takaki, R. 1998. *Strangers from a Different Shore: A History of Asian Americans.* Boston, MA: Back Bay Books.

Wade, JC. 1998. Male Reference Group Identity Dependence: A Theory of Male Identity. *Counseling Psychologist* 26: 349–383.

Situating Adivasi Identity: Contested Resources Among Castes and Tribes of the Palni Hills in Tamil Nadu, South India

CHRISTER NORSTRÖM

To be 'indigenous' in general and to have 'indigenous knowledge' in particular have become intensively debated in recent years (Kuper 2003; Saugestad 2001). In India, this discussion has often been focused on questions related to the rights of local people, most often confined to the so-called Scheduled Tribes, versus the State, especially highlighted through national or state-run projects such as the construction of dams and the management of forest and protected areas (Béteille 1998; Karlsson 2003; Roy Burman 1996; Xaxa 1999). One of the reasons behind this controversy is that the concept has become heavily politicised and the claim of being indigenous, or the Indian equivalent *adivasi,* is often used as an argument for enhancing the negotiating force of some groups in relation to other groups. In other words, the identity as indigenous has a significant capacity of boundary creation, promoting a view of those who 'have' and those who 'have not' rights in relation to political and economic issues.

In 1994, the Tamil Nadu Government declared about one third of the Palni Hills in Tamil Nadu as a sanctuary (Tamil Nadu Forest Department 1994). Although not yet implemented in practice, the eventual sanctuary and its socio-economic consequences have brought in new views of land use, thereby making room for new lines of arguments and strategies in the ongoing negotiation over resources in the area. While the primary aim of a sanctuary is to protect the flora and fauna for various ecological reasons all aiming at 'future use', local people inevitably feel that they are deprived of something of a more 'immediate use.'. Often local people view notification of national parks and sanctuaries as a continuation of a state policy begun in colonial times with the declaration of state-controlled forest areas. However, sanctuaries in contrast to national parks, give room for limited and controlled use by local people of certain resources within the boundaries of the protected area, opening up a space for negotiation between local people and the state. In the last decade a discussion promoted by certain environmentalists in India has started with the aim of widening this negotiation space further, introducing the idea of Joint

Protected Area Management (JPAM), including the possibility of making local people part of the management of national parks (Kothari *et al.* 1996); Saberwal *et al.* 2001).

In light of this discussion and the increasing use of an identity as 'indigenous' as part of negotiations over resources in India, I will place this debate at the local arena of the Palni Hills, an area I have been following closely since the beginning of the 1990s.[1] By situating the notion of indigenous/*adivasi* locally my aim is twofold. The first is to provide a more sensitive account of the way local people view their relation to the physical environment, views that to a significant extent influence the political processes concerning their relation to each other, to the government and state policies, as well as to non-governmental organisations working in the area. Second, by placing the local perspective in the forefront my suggestion is that some of the controversies concerning the otherwise often internationally laden use of the notion 'indigenous', with its tendency of increasing competition in political processes, may be avoided.

The strong boundary-creating capacity of the concept 'indigenous peoples' and the linked notion of 'indigenous knowledge' have given me reasons to focus on two important interrelated aspects. First, and one of particular interest concerning discussions about national parks and sanctuaries, is the content and distribution of indigenous knowledge. Second, by looking at the relation between claims of *adivasi* status and its relation to actual forest use, discuss the implications of government forestry policies. Before taking these aspects into consideration it is necessary to give a short description of the local area in question, the Palni Hills of Tamil Nadu.

The Palni Hills and its People

The Palni Hills is an eastern offshoot of the Western Ghats, the great mountain chain running along the border between Kerala and Tamil Nadu, the southernmost states of India. These mountains dramatically turn the vast dry plains stretching out from the Bay of Bengal in the east into moist tropical forests and steep hills in the west, with peaks reaching more than 2500 msl. People have inhabited these hills as far back as we know, but they have also attracted the immigration of caste people from the plains, both for refuge and labour. In addition to this, the forests have been exploited of their resources by other outsiders, and been an important divider in the formation of political structures in South India.

The combination of inaccessibility and marginality in relation to colonial and modern Tamil politics and at the same time its attraction as a place of material, cultural, as well as aesthetic value, have made the Palni Hills a highly contested arena of knowledge, ideas and preconceptions. Nevertheless its remoteness has protected large parts of the hills from the most destructive measurers of forest exploitation. This geographical fact saved the flora and fauna of the Palni Hills to such an extent that during recent times when 'environmentalism' became a powerful political catchword, the Palni hills received tremendous support for environmental protection. The remoteness also saved many of the forest people from central social engineering, and a majority of them still collect and hunt traditional forest foods. Parallel to this development the area has been, since the nineteenth century, an object of commercial forestry and plantation agriculture, the last including cardamom and coffee, and later on, among others, silk, cotton and lime. Not only did the new economy pull new caste groups as labourers into the hills, the increased attraction of hill stations as holiday and tourist spots for Indians has, since the 1970s, made tourism a flourishing economic industry. More than one million visitors reach Kodaikanal, the hill station of these hills, each year, and Palni is today outnumbered only by the most popular Hindu pilgrim temples in South India.

The flora of the forests exhibits a considerable variation due to the wide range of microclimate, peculiar physiography, topographic features and altitudinal and biotic influences, which has contributed to the presence of almost all important forest types of south India in the Palni Hills. These forests are also the home of the wild relatives to a number of economically important plants such as banana, pepper and cardamom. The wildlife is still plentiful, including elephant, gaur, leopard and occasional spotting of tiger, although several of the bigger mammals have had to face a dramatically shrinking habitat. We can also find endemic species such as the Giant Grizzled Squirrel and the Nilgiri Thar.

The people of the Palni Hills and their economy have always been directly based on this physical environment. It still applies whether we talk about hunting and gathering, animal husbandry, agriculture, forestry or the contemporary tourism industry. While these diverse economic activities have all been governed by the notion of 'environment exploitation,' apart maybe from hunting and gathering, the declaration of a Palni Hills Sanctuary in 1994 introduced the contrasting view of 'environment conservation'.

Only two groups of the people populating the Palni Hills today claim descent from the area, the Paliyans and the Puliyans, respectively. Later immigrants confirm this, as well as early British records (Nelson 1989). The Puliyans were once the agriculturalists of these hills, cultivating dry grains like *tennai* and *ragi* for their own subsistence. During the sixteenth and seventeenth century they were overrun by people from the plains, escaping from violence, famine and epidemic diseases during the wars between state-building forces in the plains (Nambiar 1966: 8).

Protected Areas and Indigenous Knowledge

In the discourse around conservation and protected areas such as national parks and sanctuaries and the idea of participatory conservation in contrast to an exclusionist policy (Saberwal *et al.* 2001), indigenous knowledge and especially what is often called 'traditional ecological knowledge' is held in high regard (Grenier 1998). Knowledge of this nature is supposed to be localised to specific geographical areas and its core objects the local flora and fauna. If this were the main criterion for defining a group of people as 'indigenous' to the Palni Hills, the obvious candidate would be the Paliyans. Classified as 'hunter-gatherers' in the anthropological literature (Gardner 1993; 2000; Norström 2003), they collect more than 60 edible plants and many more of medical purposes, where the staple food has been different species of wild yam *(Diascorea)* found from the foothills up to the *sholas* (high elevation moist evergreen forest) at around 2000 msl. They hunt game such as deer, wild boar, monkey, squirrel and lizards, catch fish and crabs in the small mountain rivers, and collect honey from several bee species (Gardner 2000: 33–61; Norström 2003: 20–26). When asked, they refer to this kind of subsistence with the words 'We eat wild yam, honey and monitor lizards', referring to the most valuable and relished items of forest foods. Many Paliyans have been able to turn this knowledge into an important economic asset in relation to outsiders by collecting non-timber forest produce for the regional markets in the surrounding plains. This pursuit dominates the economy for some Paliyan groups (Norström 2003: 62–70; Schmidt 1997). While most Paliyans have, since many decades, been involved in wage labour; their hunting and gathering is still a vital and an ongoing practice. Out of the about 40 Paliyan groups in the Palni Hills (a population of about 4000 individuals), only two groups claimed in the 1990s that they do not use forest resources any more. Their closeness to the forests is also manifested in their settlement practice and migration pattern. In spite of a tendency of 'moving out' of the forests due to the increasing commercialisation of forest areas, no Paliyan families have shifted into urban areas or moved into the surrounding plains (Norström 2003).

To what extent is this knowledge and interaction with the environment only confined to the Paliyans in the Palni Hills? The Puliyans (about 15,000), the other group who descends from these hills, in spite of their former identity as swidden cultivators and today's identity as farm hands and farmers, often claim extensive knowledge and interaction with the forests. In my fieldwork in the 1990s, many Puliyans have given me extensive descriptions and demonstrations of plant species used as forest foods, including both tubers, greens, mushrooms, fruits, berries and plants for medical purposes. They can easily find and dig up wild yam on request, and say that they sometime turn to this source as a food complement. Hunting was common earlier, but due to government restrictions they claim they avoid it today. In some areas they are also involved in the collecting of non-timber forest produce, although it plays a minor role in their economy as compared to that of the Paliyans. Another reason for the Puliyans to emphasise their closeness to the forests can be traced to their myth of origin. This myth states that in olden days, the Puliyans were also hunters and gatherers, as the Puliyans and the Paliyans are one and the same people, born of the same mother, as big and little brother. This myth is also acknowledged by some Paliyans, and especially so among those Paliyans living as neighbours to the Puliyans (in the area of Lower Palnis). While the Paliyans and the Puliyans both consider the Palni Hills as their place of origin, it is a different matter with the hill castes who today dominate the rural areas of the hills. They all claim descent from the plains, but nevertheless have strong relations to the forests since their arrival to the area several hundreds of years ago and also because their villages and cultivations are often surrounded by forests without road connections. The only means of transportation are by foot or the use of donkeys and horses. The history and lives of these groups, including the Puliyans, is yet to be written, and therefore my information is very scanty, and only confined to the Mannadiars, in number the largest hill caste of the area.

Narajanan, a middle-aged man from Vellagavi, a Mannadiar village situated in an isolated area on a ridge on the southern slopes, whom I worked very closely with during my fieldwork with the Paliyans, disqualified the otherwise common Tamil caste idea of the border between the village as 'the controllable' and the vulnerable periphery (where the guardian deity attacks those who cross it in darkness), in this case the forest, 'the uncontrollable' (see Daniel 1987: 61–79), with the following words:

> For us in the hills it is different. We sometimes collect greens and herbal plants from the surrounding forest. We even worship trees and our Gods are in the forests as well, which they protect. We are not afraid of the forest because we are depending on it. From there we get fruits like *ambla* and *kadukai* and *sambiram* (incense). Actually it was our Gods who told us to settle down in this forest area. When we ran away from the wars in the plains our Gods and Goddesses directed us to these places, showed us the streams in the forest for water and where we should place our temples and houses for protection. That is why you find our places high up on the ridges and inside the forests today.

The Mannadiars used to have herbal specialists within their communities, using their knowledge for treating their own people. Narajanan's mother is a good example. Narajanan himself has inherited this knowledge from her, and combines it with ayurvedic medicine and other forms of healing, today treating people from all over Tamil Nadu.

The above examples, although only briefly described, indicate that there is no absolute divide between 'tribes' and 'castes' when it comes to the knowledge of the flora and fauna, or their respective relation to the forests over time in the Palni Hills, although the content and distribution within each group may vary. In what way then are relations to the forests claimed and recognised?

Forests and Identity

When the British in the nineteenth century made the distinction between Reserved Forest Land and Revenue Land, they created a clear demarcation between those peoples supposed to fall within the forests and those outside its periphery. The Puliyans at that time, who worked as farmhands and even serfs for the Mannadiars and other hill castes, were simply identified with cultivation and therefore instructed to live outside the Reserved Forest boundary, in the same manner expected of the Mannadiars and other hill castes. Their interaction with the forests was basically ignored. This fact, as part of the argument, later changed the notification of the Puliyans from Scheduled Tribe to Scheduled Caste by the Tamil Nadu Government in the 1970s. The forest boundary implemented by the government was no major obstacle in the early days as the 'forest border' at that time was very difficult to uphold. At the same time the government adjusted to their main objective for controlled cultivation by notifying areas around the caste settlements as Revenue Land open for cultivation. The same boundaries are in use today; though, with an increase of population and changing cropping patterns there is strong pressure from the local people to adjust these boundaries. Encroachments (cultivation) inside the forests are rather common, though seldom permanent, and claims to build roads through the forest are strongly advocated by the isolated villages to break their relative isolation from the local markets. The last comes in direct conflict with the authorities' ideas of forest-land use as these roads by necessity need to be built through large tracts of forests, and will inevitably open up the areas for further encroachments. This is why the government still hesitates to build roads to villages such as Vellagavi, Periyur and Chinnur, although some new minor roads have been constructed, the latest in the 1990s to Adukkam and Ahagamalai.

In spite of these boundaries, the Puliyans have always kept a certain attachment to the forests. Because most of them are landless they have often turned to cultivation within the Reserved Forests, often coming in sharp conflict with government regulations. This conflict culminated in 1997 when many Puliyan settlements and cultivations were attacked by the Forest Department with hired men (totally more than 500). Houses were set on fire, rifle butts were used to beat up people and 17 men were arrested (IWGIA 1998: 282). These conflicts prompted many Puliyans to organise themselves into the Palni Hills Liberation Movement, linking up to the nationwide Indian Conference of Indigenous and Tribal Peoples. The Puliyans in the Palni Hills have taken part in rallies to Chennai (the capital of Tamil Nadu) and Dindigul (the district headquarters) to highlight their issues together with other Scheduled Tribes over the last 15 years. They are demanding to be re-notified as Scheduled Tribe and have even voiced 'self-rule' for tribal areas. Although the Puliyans as well as the Paliyans are generally identified by outsiders as *adivasi* in the Palni Hills, the imposed meaning of *adivasi* is here used to demarcate a stigma of inferiority in relation to the surrounding caste groups. However, the increasing politicisation of the Puliyans have become a way for them to re-formulate this ascription, and to be an *adivasi* today has become 'an important mark of identity and consciousness of the people, an identity that evokes a sense of self-esteem and pride rather than a sense of lowly and inferior society that often goes with terms like tribe or tribal' (Xaxa 1999).

Another event that demonstrated that the Puliyans do not agree with outsiders' definition of their relation to the forests took place in the valley of Siruvattukadu in 1995. In this valley the Palni Hills Conservation Council (PHCC), the major environmental organisation in the Palni Hills, , discussed with the local Paliyans, as part of their increasing social involvement, the possibility of starting a non-timber forest produce co-operative. The PHCC board had two reasons for pushing this issue: First they wanted to regulate this kind of collecting, as it was thought to be done in a non-sustainable way under the ordinary Forest Department's contract system. Second, they wanted to secure this asset solely for the Paliyans, as the latter were the economically disadvantaged group in the valley and in the board's view was qualified as an 'indigenous people' with their history as hunters and gatherers. Therefore, the Paliyans had the traditional rights to the forests. This was strongly rejected by the Puliyans in the valley, who in the eyes of the PHCC did not qualify as an 'indigenous people' because of their history as farmers and their notification as a scheduled caste. The Puliyans had, however also been involved in the collecting of non-timber forest produce under the contractual system since its introduction in the 1960s and could not watch this important asset drift away. They claimed their rights to these resources and demanded to be included in the co-operative. The Paliyans hesitated to accept such cooperation, as the Puliyans were politically dominant the valley (here many Puliyans have their own land since the 1960s). As a result of this conflict the government contractual system is still in work and the trial of co-operative failed.

While the relation between caste groups and the forests of the Palni Hills were regulated by the government, in 1882 with the introduction of the Madras Forest Act declaring large forest tracts as Reserved Forests, the situation for the Paliyans has been significantly different from the earlier unregulated regimes. The British classified from the outset the Paliyans as a forest people, where 'the forest[s] have been their home from time immemorial (Thurston 1909: 463), in contrast to the Puliyans who 'have always been the praedial slaves of the Kunuvans (Mannadiars)' (Ibid: 464).

In the earliest written account of the Paliyans in the Palni Hills, Jesuit Fr Dahmen, running the St. Michael's Estate at the turn of the nineteenth century, captures well the outside view of the Paliyans:

> [T]hey avail themselves of the first opportunity to slip back into the jungle and enjoy once more the free and hazardous life in the woods. From those that remain all that has been obtained so far in the way of labour is to work about two or three days in the week, the other days being generally spent roaming idly through the forest or lazily reclining in their huts. The almighty rupee, that powerful incentive to the industrious Tamilian's activity, is no allurement to them; coercion is no avail either, as the safe retreat of the woods is near at hand. (1908: 20)

The introduction of forest regulations did never affect the Paliyans in any direct sense. Their staple food was wild yam, and their hunting was mainly small game, forest resources of little or no concern for others. The Paliyans' use of trees for hut construction, food extraction and household implements were restricted to small trees. Their low number, semi-nomadic life-style, and the habit of staying in the more inaccessible tracts of the hills, made them fall outside state concern, leaving them with a high degree of autonomy. This autonomy however, was not the result of any regulation between the Paliyans and the government. It was a relation based on what James Woodburn calls 'autonomy by default' (1979: 248), where the administration, for their own convenience, did not bother too much about the Paliyans as long as they did not come into conflict with government objectives. This situation has prevailed up to today. While the Forest Department staff could anyway harass the Paliyans, many of them usually avoided outsiders by hiding. In an interview with Kappan in 1993, an older Paliyan man from the northern slopes, he referred back to his younger days in the 1940s:

> In that period we did not get these matchboxes (showing a matchbox). Our group of people made fire with the help of *vengakallu* (flint stone) and cotton from the forest (the floss from the wild silkcotton tree, *Bombax malabaricum),* which was ignited. We lived like that in the older period. We disappeared when we met strangers, because of fear. If you had come in that period, we would have run away, one after the other. It is only now that we are talking to people like you. Earlier you could not find anyone. Not even I could find other Paliyans if they were hiding and the Forest Department for sure could not find us.

The authorities 'default' attitude against the Paliyans prevailed after Independence and is still common. This has become especially clear over the last decades, when many Paliyans have changed their ambitions and strategies. The most obvious change among the Paliyans is a shift from semi-permanent settlements to permanent villages of their own, or in some cases mixed villages together with caste groups. Usually such a shift among groups of hunter-gatherers in India has been pushed by state-run settlement schemes. However, in the Palni Hills no such centralised scheme has been introduced. This fact has given room for a high degree of local initiatives and variation. In this process though, intermediators in the form of local caste leaders, benevolent landowners, non-governmental organisations, or individual local government officials, have been instrumental in pushing the authorities to oblige the Paliyans' ambitions of creating villages of their own. The last village established in this way was at Manjalar Dam, at the southern side of the hills in 2003, but still many Paliyans live in small sibling groups dispersed in the forest areas.

The Changing Notion of Adivasi*: Some Concluding Remarks*

While the notion of *adivasi* has been applied in India since at least the early twentieth century, mainly to describe the tribal groups in contrast to the dominant society, with the internationalisation of the term 'indigenous peoples' during the 1990s, the notion of *adivasi* has been filled with a new content, thereby becoming highly contested and questioned in India (Bétielle 1998). Adopted by the UN in the ILO convention No. 107 and revised in 1989 (No. 169) the definition of indigenous peoples has been focused on the idea of 'original inhabitants' of certain areas. While this can be rather easily applied in the so-called 'settler colonies', as the Americas, Australia and New Zeeland, with their recent history of conquest, immigration and colonisation, the discussion in India has pointed out a much more complex historical process of population movements, and where it is not, in many cases, easy to identify the original inhabitants. Even the case of the Palni Hills indicates this fact, as all the above-mentioned groups have for several hundreds of years been living in the region. Another argument used against the international way of using the indigenous identity is by referring to the significant difference in culture and social system among 'indigenous peoples' and the dominant society. While this is more obvious in the recent colonised societies, the people of India have shared more or less the same territory for a very long time, where the groups we today identify as tribes and castes, respectively, have to a great extent been constituted in relation to each other, and where the boundary between them has changed over time and from one region to the other. As we have seen, this is also the case in the Palni Hills, where, for example, during the twentieth century the Puliyans were first classified as a tribe and then later as a caste, and today want to be re-classified as tribe.

Does this way of reasoning disqualify the claims of those promoting an indigenous/*adivasi* identity? I would not like to think so. The more the notion of indigenous becomes politicised, the more we need to look into the content and reasons behind such claims. A paradox here is the fact that the strong 'son-of-the-soil' theory applied by the dominant regional communities in India, most prominently manifested in the linguistically defined states, creating a strong feeling of a particular homeland, as Tamil Nadu, meaning 'the Land of the Tamilians', is often denied the tribals. The failure to recognise such rights and privileges and the absence of power to promote these issues give tribal groups reason to form new identities (Xaxa 1999). In the case of the Puliyans, their history of being serfs to landowning caste people and their landless situation even 60 years after the independence of India have given them ample reasons to turn to the nearby forests to be able to live a decent life.

The Paliyans are still more or less ignorant of the new kind of *adivasi* identity growing since the 1990s among tribal groups all over India. The main reason has probably been that they still have been able to use forest resources without the intervention of outsiders, including the authorities. Further, an *adivasi* identity is based on the underlying principle of group identity and this is still very weak among the Paliyans because the relation between a hunting and gathering economy and social relations do not need an organisation above the family level.

Forest resources are collectively owned and individually procured, leaving room for an extremely high degree of individual autonomy (Norström 2003), described by anthropologists as the lowest level of social integration (Steward 1963: 101), with a fluid condition (Misra 1969: 201), a fragmentary nature of group structure (Morris 1982: 102), and permeated by an individual autonomy syndrome (Gardner 1991). Denigrating authorities and solving conflicts through fission (voting with their feet) have created a lot of frustration among landowners, non-governmental organisations and local authorities. The Paliyan elusiveness, 'they come and go as they want,' as farmers use to formulate it; 'we do not like unnecessary words,' as the Paliyans formulate it, results in the fact that the temporary group of Paliyans cooperating with outsiders slowly fragments, one leaving after the other. The main prerequisite for these actions among the Paliyans is the possibility to still be able to procure forest food without negotiation with others. However, with the increase of Paliyan villages, wage labour, and farmland of their own, they are now on the way to change these strategies. In this rather new situation they often made to feel ignorance from those in power, making many of the Paliyans inclined to join the spreading *adivasi* movement in the hills.

When (if) the Palni Hills Sanctuary becomes implemented, with the planned area of 900 sq km (a third of the total area of the Palni Hills), it will change the circumstances for all the people in the region. After all, so far the notification of protected areas in India has had the increased power of the state as one of its major effects. If the authorities and environmentalists do not recognise the different claims the local people have on the same area, drawing from their self-identification mentioned above, the authorities and environmentalists invite an even stronger adherence to *adivasi* identity and boundary creation than otherwise may be called for. Even caste groups such as the Mannadiars will not be silent as their villages and farms will also be circumscribed by the sanctuary boundaries.

NOTES

1. An extended anthropological fieldwork was conducted in several periods, totalling about two years, mainly between 1993 and 1995, with revisits up to 2003. The focus was on the Paliyans, the hunter-gatherers of the Palni Hills and their interaction with plantation owners, the state and non-governmental organisations. SAREC (Swedish Agency for Research Cooperation with Developing Countries) and several smaller grants from NIAS (Nordic Institute of Asian Studies) funded the research.

WORKS CITED

Béteille, A. 1998. The idea if indigenous people. *Current Anthropology* 39 , 2.

Dahmen, F. Rev. 1908. The Paliyans, a hill-tribe of the Palni Hills (South India). *Anthropos* 3: 19–31.

Daniel, EV. 1987 (1984). *Fluid Signs: Being a Person the Tamil Way.* Berkley: The University of California Press.

Gardner, PM. 1991. Pragmatic Meanings of Possession in Paliyan Shamanism. *Anthropos* 86: 367–384.

Gardner, PM. 1993. Dimensions of Subsistence Foraging in South India. *Ethnology* 32: 109–144.

Gardner, PM. 2000. *Bicultural Versatility as a Frontier Adaptation Among the Paliyan Foragers of South India.* Lewiston, New York: The Edwin Mellen Press.

Grenier, L. 1998. *Working with Indigenous Knowledge: A Guide for Researchers.* Ottawa: International Development Research Centre.

IWGIA 1998. International Working Group for Indigenous Affairs (IWGIA), Yearbook 1998. Copenhagen.

Karlsson, BG. 2003. Anthropology and the 'Indigenous Slot': Claims and Debates About Indigenous Peoples' Status in India. *Critique of Anthropology* 23, 4: 403–423.

Kothari, A, N Singh, and N Suri, eds. 1996. *People and Protected Areas: Towards a Participatory Conservation in India.* New Delhi: Sage Publications.

Misra, PK. 1969. The Jenu Kuruba. *Bulletin of the Anthropological Survey of India* 28, 3: 183–246.

Morris, B. 1982. The Family, Group Structuring, and Trade Among South Indian Hunter-Gatherers. In *Politics and History in Band Societies,* edited by E Leacock and RB Lee. Cambridge: Cambridge University Press. 171–188.

Nambiar, PK. 1964. Vilpatti Survey Monographs 5. Madras: Census of India, IX.

Nelson, JH. 1989 (1868). *The Madura Country: A Manual.* New Delhi: Asian Educational Services.

Norström, C. 2001. Autonomy By Default Versus Popular Participation: The Paliyans of South India and the Proposed Palni Hills Sanctuary. In *Identity and Gender in Hunting and Gathering Societies. Senri Ethnological Studies 56,* edited by I Keen and T Yamada. Osaka: National Museum of Ethnology. 27–51.

Norström, C. 2003. *'They Call for Us': Strategies for Securing Autonomy among the Paliyans, Hunter-Gatherers of the Palni Hills, South India. Stockholm Studies in Social Anthropology 53.* Stockholm: Almqvist & Wiksell International.

Roy Burman, BK. 1996. The indigenous peoples and the problem of Human Rights. In *Perspectives of Human Rights,* edited by VK Gupta. New Delhi: Vikas Publishing House.

Saberwal, V, M Rangarajan, and A Kothari. 2001. *People, Parks, & Wildlife: Towards Coexistence.* New Delhi: Orient Longman.

Schmidt, T. 1997. Biological versus Cultural Diversity. The Paliyans, Hunters and Gatherers of the Palni Hills and a Proposed Sanctuary. Unpublished Report from a Minor Field Study. Department of Cultural Anthropology: Uppsala University.

Steward, J. 1963. *Theory of Cultural Change.* Urbana, IL: University of Illinois Press.

Tamil Nadu Forest Department. 1994. Report of the Committee on the Formation of a Wildlife Sanctuary at Kodaikanal. Madras.

Thurston, E. 1909. *Castes and Tribes of Southern India.* V Madras: Government Press.

Woodburn, J. 1979. Minimal Politics: The Political Organization of the Hadza of North Tanzania. In *Politics and Leadership: A Comparative Perspective,* edited by WA Stack and PS Cohn. Oxford Clarendon Press. 244–266.

Xaxa, V. 1999. Tribes as Indigenous People of India. *Economic and Political Weekly* 34, 51: 3589–3595.

Suffering and Celebration: Older Tamils in a Multicultural Toronto

GLYNIS GEORGE

Introduction

The expansion of the "Diaspora" to include a wide range of migrating actors has complicated our analysis of diasporic cultural identities (Reis, 2004; Abdelhady, 2005; Brettell, 2006; Cheran, 2007). Specifically, this approach to the diaspora begs a more fluid and plural approach to the cultural referents which mark the passage of diasporic personhood (Agnew, 2005; Cheran, 2006). One doesn't speak of a diasporic self, marked by longing and displacement, but of plural selves embedded in complex social ties and hybrid spaces. Diasporas are then, both "ghostly places" and sites of cultural creation (Agnew, 2005:12), a productive tension that can decentre normative assumptions of "culture".

Sri Lankan Tamils certainly exemplify the narrow definition of Diaspora as a forcibly dispersed social group (Reis, 2004; Cheran, 2006). But the conceptual opening of diaspora directs us to situate the Tamil diaspora in more complex cultural relations. A diasporic lens foregrounds the way social identities are forged and refashioned to query cultural production and the depiction of Tamils in multicultural nations such as Canada. Although Tamils are a fairly recent immigrant group, there are well over 100,000 in the Greater Toronto Area, and according to recent Census reports, Tamil is reported as the second most common mother tongue amongst recent immigrant groups[1]. Now, more than 20 years after the first wave of Tamil immigrants, Tamils are well settled in business, media, and a range of employment. Hence, it is important to capture diversity within, to foreground living within, the "DiasporCity" (Cheran, 2007: 159) that Toronto has become.

In this paper I take an actor-centred approach (Ortner, 2005) to explore the way older Tamils in particular make sense of changing cultural practices and in so doing, work through the sense of suffering that marks their lives in the past and present. I focus on their participation at Harmony Hall, a community centre in Toronto's east end which provides culturally integrated and culturally specific services and programming for Tamil-, English- and Chinese-speaking residents over the age of 55. A multicultural space, it emphasizes active living for older adults who, in spite of aches, chronic illness and loss, are relatively mobile and interested in creative, leisure and educational pursuits.

In this culturally diverse space, Tamils figure as a group who require more in services and support than the other cultural groups. This reflects the barriers that inform their experiences with respect to health issues, for example (Beiser, 2003; Chandrakanthan, 2007, cf Grønseth, 2006). The purpose of this paper, however, is not to foreground this vulnerability. Rather I seek to enhance it, to complicate their depiction. Older immigrants are frequently viewed as a "traditional bag of needs", as one informant put it, a characterization that may inadvertently marginalize them as cultural creators. I consider older Tamils as cultural agents who convey their suffering and celebration in a process of becoming and overcoming loss, aging and social isolation.

To situate older Tamils at the crossroads of suffering and celebration, I examine the cultural discourses that members draw on to make sense of their lives. This is exemplified in the way family forms a site of struggle and support to frame the way suffering is conveyed and to mark the social identities of women and men as mothers, fathers, grandparents and siblings. On the surface, their reference to family appears to support a traditional cultural script; it certainly marks the way older Tamils interpret current living conditions and disruptions in the past which spurred their immigration. To foreground the traditional script, however, would be to support the notion of Tamil culture as a fixed entity, and older immigrants as mere bearers of Tamil cultural tradition. A diasporic lens points us to the dynamic features of living and being neither here nor there.

Moreover, as I argue, the cultural discourse of family is only one template which frames the "shifting suffering of migrants" (Quayson, 2005: 344). Their mobilities subject them to an embodied suffering that is plurally marked and narrated—in memories of the past—and interpretations of the present. This emphasis on mulitiplicity, in suffering and in the diaspora more generally, serves to decentre reified notions of culture. By way of conclusion, I suggest that the analysis—this glimpse of loss and living amongst older Tamils, has implications for "multiculturalism", a template that does not necessarily foster the intelligibility of collective suffering.

To foreground the expression of suffering and celebration, this paper takes an ethnographic approach as a way of entering the diasporic space[2]. In the case of Harmony Hall, diasporic space is marked by time—the one-day-a-week devoted to Tamil programming. Every Tuesday, Tamil members congregate for English and computer classes, yoga and dance lessons, luncheons and cultural events which mark the Tamil year. The analysis I offer here draws on participant observation, personal narratives and focus groups both at Harmony Hall and in the Tamil diaspora community in Toronto.

My weekly participation in Tamil Tuesdays includes everyday conversations at lunch, and a discussion group I conduct with ten "ladies" who choose weekly topics to practice their English. It was during these discussion groups that I noticed the importance of family to Tamil members, and that a particular model of family life was preferred—a model that was disrupted by conflict in Sri Lanka and by living arrangements in Canada. As I show below, family forms one template in a diversifying set of arrangements. Older Tamil members do not cling to its traditional associations; rather, they draw upon it in the creation of a social imaginary (Strauss, 2006).

I use imaginary here, not only as code for culture, but as an actor-centred process of imaging that is "situational" (Strauss, 2006: 338). In this sense, "imagining" refers to expectations—of what could and should be, but in a way that acknowledges the already contested and dynamic nature of Sri Lankan Tamil "culture" (cf Schrijvers, 1999; Fugerland, 2001). A social imaginary in this sense expresses complex notions of Tamil identity that are gendered, diasporic and actually quite contemporary.

In the next section I offer a brief overview of the older Tamils who frequent Harmony Hall and the emotional and social disruptions they have experienced. I then explore specific struggles in family life. In particular, I draw attention to financial hardships because they point to a reconfiguration of gender roles in family arrangements and highlight the material and emotional aspects of social suffering. Family, however, is also a metaphor for relations of community within the Tamil diaspora, and Harmony Hall offers a space from which to examine this social imaginary as an expression of diasporic identity, diversity and interconnection.

Cultural Templates, Disruptions and Diasporic Trajectories

One Tuesday morning during our conversation group, Gayatri, a regular participant, asked, "Madame, how can we live happily in Canada? Next week can we talk about this topic?" I nodded that we could and brought handouts the following week to aid our conversation. My handouts were admittedly pathetic—magazine pieces on the importance of "balance", good eating, wellness and exercise. I am no self-help expert. While the ladies did enjoy the excerpts, what they preferred was a more robust conversation—one that begins in Toronto and invariably, no matter the topic, ends in Sri Lanka. But on that occasion, first they needed to talk about what made them unhappy before they could figure out how to live happily. Their comments and disagreements with each other drew largely on family life—financial problems, family conflicts and the way many, but not all of them feel—ignored, disrespected, bored and isolated. While these feelings are commonplace amongst the members, they are also gendered and reflect historical and current gender relations that are rooted in both familial norms and changing social relations.

If you ask Tamil-speaking members as I did, to elaborate on their idea of family, replies point to the importance of extended "relations"; a good family is one where there is at least one boy, where "proposal" marriages are arranged by parents to fit with one's "community"; where parental responsibility includes a strong emphasis on education, particularly for boys, who in return take care of their elderly parents.

This ideal of familial reciprocity and relations of respect are, however, gendered. Women in particular emphasize that Tamil women are "passive" and their husbands, the family leaders, a perception they connect to male "earning" power in Sri Lanka, as well as to cultural values. But motherhood is highly valued by women and men alike reflected, as the ladies put it, in the notion that "you can buy many things, but never your mother." Such gendered relations are also reflected in the life histories I have conducted so far where women largely engaged in household labour while men worked as farmers, in factories and in the civil service. Several women, however, were teachers, a role that gave them economic and social status.

The disruption of this somewhat generic model, however, marks the lives of most Tamil members whose narratives so far also recount moments of "communal" conflict, discrimination in employment and state oppression in Sri Lanka. Conditions where bombing, harassment and, in several cases, deaths displaced families, terminated employment and disturbed education. These breaks in cultural practice were further breached by subsequent departures: a migration trajectory where children left Sri Lanka, one by one. Older Tamils, were either the last to leave, or arrived on their sons and daughters doorsteps with their youngest, unmarried children in tow. The association of women with domesticity and men as wage earners is then, cross-cut by these disruptions and separations, the chains of migration and the reconfigurations of family and gender roles which living in Toronto entails.

Most of the 140 Tamil members at Harmony Hall arrived in Canada between 1990 up to the present. They were sponsored by their sons, most (not all) of whom were themselves refugees or, in some cases, by daughters whose marriages had been arranged with males who became permanent residents or Canadian citizens. While a few members did earn an income in Toronto, and a few still do paid work, most of them, having arrived in their 50s or later, are financially dependent on their sons and daughters. Although Toronto is a key residence for the children of these older adults, most members have family including sons and daughters, scattered in the US, the UK, Germany, Switzerland, Denmark, Australia and Sri Lanka. The predominant and preferred living arrangement is for Tamil members to reside with a son or a daughter and their grandchildren. Several members however, either live alone or separately with their spouses, some by choice, others, by necessity.

This pattern of immigration, along with changing cultural expectations, language barriers and the rules of sponsorship which govern Canadian immigration generates loneliness, ambivalence and social isolation. These emotions are further fuelled by financial hardship, health issues, and limited mobility. For example, studies point to the way their experience of mental health and physical well being are shaped by these wider social experiences and of suffering in the past and present (Beiser, 2003;

Sadavoy, 2004; cf. Grønseth, 2006). As newcomers, they make sense of Canadian norms, including western medical approaches to wellness, illness and age from an unequal position of power.

In this context, family emerges as a significant source of emotional, social and economic support. However, combined with current working and living patterns in Toronto, including the increased education and earning power of Tamil women, family emerges as a shifting and contest terrain. It forms a social imaginary and a significant site of conflict, ambivalence and support that impacts on women and men in relation to their position as daughters, sons, parents, in-laws and grandparents. Individuals occupy complex social roles and identities which may be mutually congruent or conflicting; older Tamils are in-laws, parents and grandparents, sisters and brothers to their extended family in Canada, Sri Lanka and elsewhere. In other words, they bear a heavy social weight of suffering and the possibilities of celebration that comprises these changing family arrangements.

I turn to a closer glimpse of family dynamics to draw out the way emotional, social and material aspects of suffering are shaped by changing familial roles. This sense of suffering is, as Quayson (2005) argues, a marker of personhood inflected in the case of migration, by displacement, normative assumptions about gender and social and collective expectations. Differences within the Tamil diaspora are reflected, as I discuss, in the different ways older men and women perceive and experience financial hardships for example. Moreover, there are wealth disparities at play here which do not neatly correspond to Sri Lankan class relations, but are emergent and rooted in the paid work possibilities of older Tamils and their children. As a social imaginary, however, 'family' is also a metaphor of support and struggle that these members experience as Tamils, as newcomers, as Canadians and Sri Lankans, discursive constructions which also inflect familial social identities.

Suffering Through the Lens of Family

At Harmony Hall financial hardships were frequently mentioned as a barrier that inhibited Tamils as a whole from participating in programming and fieldtrips. This difference reinforced the notion that Tamil members were more vulnerable than English and Chinese speakers, who are generally more diverse in their socio-economic circumstances and migration histories. Financial hardship was significant enough to prompt Harmony Hall to provide additional subsidies to Tamil members for transportation and social events, which they do not provide for the other cultural groups. Unable to collect Canadian pensions until they have reached 10-years' residence, most seniors are without funds, except for the small pensions some have received from Sri Lanka. For those who do live with children, the most common difficulty is their reluctance to ask their children for money, "to bother them" given their own financial hardships, the high costs of real estate, education and raising a family in Toronto.

Men stress this problem slightly more and more often, in ways that draw on their own sense of value and identity as family providers. For example, several mentioned that they tried or did gain some paid work when they arrived in Canada as security officers or in temporary service work. A few have queried how they can gain more financial support. Ravi for example, wondered if he could "break" his sponsorship agreement, to apply for separate government moneys. His son was having financial difficulties, and Ravi didn't like to ask him for money. He knew, however, that a sponsorship break would reflect badly on his son and prevent him from making further sponsorships, so he was reluctant to do this.

In a second example, Lakshmi does not have her own source of income. As I came to learn, she now lives with her daughter. Her husband had lived here but found it too lonely and difficult to ask his son for money. He returned to Jaffna where he now lives with their other daughter. Couples who do live separately from their children indicate that money is one of their primary burdens. After rent, food, television and transportation there is very little money left. While some couples who have resided here for several years live in subsidized housing, there is a long waiting list.

Financial hardships are also related to unemployment, particularly when adult children or their spouses are unable to work—due to depression, disability or their inability to transfer their Sri Lankan training into decent employment. One couple, for example, moved out of their son's house because it was no longer feasible to share living expenses and financial constraints caused considerable conflict. Some members have found themselves alone and make more creative living arrangements (a few live as roommates). These arrangements can have their own difficulties, as in the case of Parvathy, who expressed these living arrangements as a form of daily suffering.

Parvathy is a single woman of 66, who arrived here in the early 1990s. While she had emotional and financial support from her brother and another relation, she was not able to sustain these connections over time. For a few years she lived with a young family and in return for a room and lower rent, cared for the children overnight while this couple both worked. "But I suffer so much," she told me; "they don't treat me well—they don't care about me. I am vegetarian and I cannot make my meals easily." Later Parvathy told me that she had decided to move in spite of the high rent she would pay. "They were trying to control me, they wanted to know when I would go out; where I was going, and I am no longer happy there." She now lives in a one bedroom apartment and will be eligible for a subsidy after one year. I can make it for this year she says, but it is very hard.

Financial hardships, the material basis of suffering, is of course embodied, and understood, in terms of past and present expectations, the perceived success and strength of social relationships. Sons who have not fared well in terms of employment, marital problems, the threat of divorce, are all signs of failure, of expectations gone terribly wrong. Parvathy draws on the notion of suffering to express these discontents and also when she isn't feeling well, as if the one, life experiences, informs the other, her sense of wellness.

In fact I found the expression of suffering to be common at Harmony Hall, although more marked publicly by women than men at least to me: "I am suffering now, or I suffer was so common that I asked staff and members to explain their use of this word. Is this a particular translation you are offering me? Is there a special word in Tamil I asked? "I just say it; it is the way we talk," said Sita, a staff member. "We *have* suffered," says Vani; "Sri Lankans have suffered. We say it because we have suffered"—as if no linguistic explanation or translation was required. This expression of suffering may be framed by religious belief,[3] a sense of fate that shapes Hindu notions of existence; yet it was also conveyed by Christians who are a minority in numbers at Harmony Hall.

In the case of Tamil members, moreover, suffering is personal and yet cannot be separated from the wider political struggles that many members have experienced and reflect upon in the present. In life stories, men and women recount their suffering as parents, particularly when their sons and daughters were threatened.

For example, Lakshmi recalls that she never thought she would end up in Canada, and she recounts the final years that led to the departure of her sons as an extremely difficult time. This is reflected in the way she draws out particular events as illustrations of this fear and hardship.

> Armies came to our house. Indian army. The Sri Lankan army. Nine soldiers came at different times. When they came I told my sons to go outside into the paddy fields. It was so wet. "Where [are] your children?", the men asked me. "My sons are out," I said. They asked about the bicycles—"whose are these? Why did your sons go out? Do they support the Tigers?" I know a little Sinhalese and I said I was alone. They were talking to all the mothers, looking for guns inside the mattresses. They went to one house, then another house. They took two boys; they asked me about two more boys and I said, "they are innocent". They asked "what type of woman is she (the mother of the boys)?" "She is innocent," I said. The Indian army came too—I was ill and my daughter was there. She was 13. My daughter is beautiful. She is beautiful. We were afraid of molestation so I told her to look ugly. I messed up her hair (she laughs, gestures with her hands)—I dirtied her face—and they left her alone.

For Teresa, the most difficult period began when her husband could no longer work in the army and from that point was always sporadically employed. Teresa finds it difficult to talk about this period, as if she could not sufficiently render in words the difficulty she experiences.

> We had financial problems. So many problems, so many problems (her hands gesture upwards). We were not well off. My husband was not always working. We had no land—we rented. And I had seven children. I cannot talk about these times; I cannot even explain how hard it was for us. I worked for the priest—made some money for

> our family. Then my children left—they got married—one by one and I felt OK; slowly, the weight was lifted.

In some cases suffering is both embodied, the past disrupting the present, feeding into current experiences and difficulties (cf Grønseth, 2006).

Consider Nila, a 60-year-old mother of three children, one who still lives in Colombo. One day, during lunch, Nila came up to me, and rubbed her neck in pain, to explain that she wasn't well enough to talk much on that day. As I nodded, Nila continued, "I am suffering right now. The pain is in my neck. I have suffered a lot" She reminded me that her daughter was blind and although now married, was a constant source of worry; she said, "my husband, he has also suffered." Nila went on to explain that he had been taken and tortured some years ago by the Sri Lankan army, and has never recovered from the slashes to his legs. "He was almost dead", she said, "they thought he was dead at the hospital." Nila did not dwell so much on this event but focused more on how difficult it was for her during his 10 days in captivity, unaware of where he was, and whether he would return. "He was gone for 10 days, and I didn't know what happened, where he had gone. He still suffers from the pain," she explained.

Nila has turned more than once to the pain in her neck and linked it to other sources of anxiety, such as her sister's motorcycle accident in Colombo and her concern that her daughter has not yet produced a child. In this sense, she was similar to other women who connected their physical pain to social and political conditions in the past or present. Her suffering is informed by her role as wife, as sister and mother. She makes regular phone calls. The distance does not seem to sever her relationships and may even sharpen her worry.

Social suffering is also publicly marked and its expression at Harmony Hall reflects the way Tamil members participate as cultural agents to enact social identities in which familial idioms take on wider social and political expression.

Harmony Hall: The Penetration of Diasporic Space

It is important to note that Harmony Hall provides a space where older Tamils interact as both family members, and as peers, with other older Tamils. The suffering they convey is rarely expressed as passive because it is often informed by narratives in which they centre themselves as agents, witnesses, observers, thinkers and judges in particular situations. For example, they actively worry about their children, those living in Sri Lanka, Canada, or in the case of Theresa, India, where her daughter recently "escaped" to seek refugee status. Worries also circulate in lunchtime conversations at Harmony Hall as members note the busy lives of adult children, or the marriage possibilities of their youngest.

At times, personal suffering has been politicized and given structured, collective expression at Harmony Hall. I draw attention to this because it demonstrates the way Tamil members intervene in the performance of selected traditions and construct family as an expression of Tamil identity.

For example, the public character of suffering was apparent this past November, when the celebration of Deepavali was cancelled (as elsewhere in Toronto) at Harmony Hall to acknowledge the assassination in Sri Lanka of Thamilchelvam, a prominent LTTE peace negotiator. Instead of lanterns, dances and a special luncheon, members gathered to mourn the loss of a "favourite son" and the loss of peace opportunities. On that afternoon, Meena, a 58-year-old widow whose husband was shot in a "squirmish" [sic] by the Sri Lankan army, took me aside. "I am always thinking of Sri Lanka", she said. "I was able to flee, but I think of my neighbours and relatives, and I wonder how I can help them, what I can do for them. They suffer so much. When I'm feeling good about myself here then my mind turns to Sri Lanka and I worry." Meena, who arrived here in 2003, went on to explain how her own son was rounded up by the Sri Lankan army, taken along with other boys and interrogated, beaten. "My son was released and others were killed" she said. "I do not know why they released my son."

Later, Maria, a 70-year old widow empathized with Thamilchelvam's mother, who lives in Toronto, and whom she said was not permitted to return to Sri Lanka for the funeral. "I know how that feels because my own son died at 41 years and I know that you need to see the body for satisfaction, for closure. She was denied this."

Deepawali typifies the selected traditions that are celebrated at Harmony Hall along with *Pongol,* and Tamil New Year, as are events for and with other cultural groups. The cancellation of *Deepawali* exemplifies the interruption of the present, the contemporaneity of cultural expression, modified here to mourn instead of celebrate. It is this contemporary quality I want to draw out to elaborate on the creative capacities of older Tamils. I contrast the cancellation of *Deepawali* with the play that was performed at Tamil New Year, a celebration which drew both English and Chinese speakers and which was recorded by the Tamil television network.

The play centred on the story of a man who had been "corrupted" by cultural trappings. Self-indulgence, alcohol, familial neglect and hobnobbing with his ne'er-do- well friends somehow led to the pregnancy of his daughter. Two, "ladies", regular members—were cast as the ne'er-do-wells. Sporting flannel shirts and baseball caps, they strode across the stage, bellowing and swilling a bottle of whiskey with the main character.

The crossing-dressing quality of the play produced a lot of laughter and translated well across the linguistic barriers, to create a space of intelligibility, co-evalness in humour perhaps for all members of the audience. It signified a rare moment, the interpenetration of the diaspora into the multicultural mainstream.

But I do not want to root the creative capacities of older Tamil in public performance alone. Rather, cultural engagement also means a rethinking of social relations and the refashioning of social identities in diasporic space. The insight of the diaspora is the way it foregrounds the creation of new strategies, new social relations that are not reducible to home or host, Sri Lanka, or Canada. This kind of reconfiguration was illustrated in the way different Tamil members debated and made sense of marriage: love marriages, proposal marriages and mixed marriages. For example, in life histories, proposal marriages themselves figure as a traditional ideal, and a migration strategy. This implies that older Tamils as parents had visions of a future, however unwanted, that moved outside of Sri Lanka long before they left. These visions came to embrace a good marriage as a transnational process.

Moreover, while most members view divorce as very uncharacteristic of Sri Lankan norms, (and a practice they do not favour), they do reflect and disagree on the issue of marriage choices. There is considerable debate over the preference of love or proposal marriages (some had love marriages themselves) and the importance of marrying other Tamils. While several members are currently active in the arrangement of their child's marriage, others say that they will leave it up to the choice of their child. In other cases, they are resigned to the notion that their child will exercise more choice, a position that reflects their preference for the ideal. What emerges in conversation in fact is the notion that an ideal, when entertained in dialogue, is situational. The ideal in the mind of a parent depends on where one is located; what is ideal in a marriage may differ for husbands and wives. Normative discourses then are not only historically contested but actively reflected upon.

As for "mixed marriages", Janani for example, explains how she struggled when her daughter decided to marry a Chinese boy. "What could I do?" she asked. "I was miserable; I would not accept. I was so depressed and I cried so much. Then one day my son-in-law saw me crying; he came to and told me that I shouldn't worry that he would take care of me too—and slowly, slowly I started to accept. Now I accept and I like him. I really do." In another case, a couple are quite happy with their in-law, a Euro-Canadian from northern Ontario, although it did take time to adjust to their child's marriage decision.

In sum, while a Sri Lankan, Tamil model of family life emerges, it is important to note that members reflect on these norms as situational and changing. This exemplifies the contested and dynamic character of "Tamil" cultural practices reshaped by their diasporic character. The examples also suggest that Harmony Hall provides a context for members to both sustain and re-think these cultural practices, a trend that is reflected not only in celebrations, but in the peer support that it fosters. Many members did not know each other prior to attending Harmony Hall. Now, they visit each other in hospital, arrange drives to doctors, and provide mutual support. There are more affluent members (particularly those who arrived over a decade ago) and there is a public ethos of sensitivity to the vulnerabilities of newcomers.

This public, collective character is also displayed in the expression of a political identity which is both here and there, in Canada and Sri Lanka. Members would like better health care, like vision care, in Canada; they call for better terms in sponsorships and a shorter time before financial support kicks in. They discuss the conflict in Sri Lanka passionately, dispelling the notion that "the Tigers" (the LTTE) are terrorists, hoping for peace and attending many more political events in the greater Tamil "community". Yet, few of them see themselves as returning. These notions position them in a globalized space where ideas about citizenship might be contested.

Conclusion

I return to Gayatri's question about happiness. While older Tamils express the personal and collective character of their social suffering in the past and present, it does not stop them from reflecting on happiness, on the possibilities of a better future. This future is imagined as a state of living and ageing in Canada, of maintaining wellness, of learning wherever possible and of engaging. Harmony Hall, as a multicultural space, fosters cultural creation, so that norms are both affirmed and re-configured, but not in a codified way.

Moreover, the expression of Tamil identity within this space provokes reflection on multicultural policy more broadly insofar as Harmony Hall bears the imprint of its policies. Its funding arrangements are influenced by the way service delivery is organized to meet targeted groups, a trend that renders Tamil members, at this point in time, beneficiaries. These infrastructural arrangements can lead to tensions, perceptions of unfairness within the larger membership, all of which Harmony Hall works to address. As a community centre that serves different language groups, it seeks to balance the needs of Tamils in relation to English and Chinese speakers. Culturally integrated events are designed to encourage mutual recognition, with multiple translations that generate both grumbles and appreciation.

It is, however, difficult to communicate the complex experiences of these different groups, to disrupt boundaries of difference; to foreground diversity within and to expose social suffering as it bears upon the aging body requires talk and translation. Veena Das (2002) points to the way cultural boundary-marking can undermine attempts at mutual intelligibility, the communication necessary to render cultural differences and collective suffering commensurable.

By capturing the dynamics of cultural practice, the parameters of suffering and celebration, I use the diasporic lens to foreground the fluidity within the "Tamil" membership. I suggest that Tamil social identities are shifting and draw out the way older Tamils as an example draw on cultural templates while they negotiate and interpret disruptions and change. Harmony Hall provides a context where they can socialize amongst their peers, a perspective I suggest which permits more complex scripts than one which identifies them as grandparents or seniors. This analysis, of course, begs a much fuller mapping: of the diversity of Tamil identities in the Toronto diaspora, of Harmony Hall and of multiculturalism. The diasporic lens can also foreground the extent to which multiculturalism frames lived experience, to enable or foreclose on the expression of social identity as an ongoing, multiply situated process.

NOTES

1. See Release for the 2006 Census on Language, Immigration, Citizenship, Mobility/Migration, http://www.toronto.ca/demographics/pdf/2006_lang_imm_citizenship_mobility_backgrounder.pdf, p. 8. Retrieved July 25, 2008.

2. The research is based on a pilot project that was undertaken from May 2007-June 2008. It lays the groundwork for an expanded project on the Tamil diaspora and multicultural policy that will follow. All names used here are pseudonyms.

3. I thank Mark Whittaker for his insights on the relationship between suffering and Hindu beliefs.

WORKS CITED

Abdelhady, Dalia. 2005. Beyond Home/Host Networks: Forms of Solidarity among Lebanese Immigrants in a Global Era. *Identities* 13, 3: 427–453.

Agnew, Vijay. 2005. Introduction. In *Diaspora, Memory and Identity: A Search for Home,* edited by Vijay Agnew. Toronto: University of Toronto Press.

Beiser, Morton, Laura Simich, and Nalimi Pandalangat. 2003. Communities in Distress: Mental Health Needs and Help Seeking in the Tamil Community in Toronto. *International Migration* 41, 5: 233–245.

Brettell, Caroline B. 2005. Introduction: Global Spaces/Local Places: Transnational Diaspora and the Meaning of Home. *Identities* 13, 3: 327–334.

Chandrakanthan, Joseph. 2007. When Two Cultures Collide at the Bedside: Religio-Cultural Value Conflicts and Medico-Ethical Decision-Making among the Tamil Community in Canada. In *History and Imagination: Tamil Culture in the Global Context,* edited by R Cheran, Darshan Ambalavanar, and Chelva Kanaganayakam. Toronto: TSAR Publications. 138–149.

Cheran, R. 2006. Multiple Homes and Parallel Civil Societies: Refugee Diaspora and Transnationalism. *Refuge* 23, 2: 1–6.

———. 2007. Citizens of Many Worlds: Theorizing Tamil DiasporiCity. In *History and Imagination: Tamil Culture in the Global Context,* edited by R Cheran, Darshan Ambalavanar, and Chelva Kanaganayakam. Toronto: TSAR Publications. 150–168.

Das, Veena. 2002. Violence and Translation. *Anthropological Quarterly* 75, 1: 105–112.

Fugerland, Ovind. 2001. Time and Space in the Sri-Lankan–Tamil Diaspora. *Nations and Nationalism* 7, 2: 195–213.

Grønseth, Anna Sigfrid. 2006. Experiences of Tensions in Re-orienting Selves: Tamil Refugees in Northern Norway Seeking Medical Advice. *Anthropology and Medicine* 13, 1: 77–98.

Ortner, Sherry B. 2005. Subjectivity and Cultural Critique. *Anthropological Theory* 5, 1: 31–52.

Quayson, Valentina. 2005. Social Suffering and Embodied States of Male Transnational Migrants in San Francisco, California. *Identities* 12, 3: 335–362.

Reis, Michele. 2004. Theorizing Diaspora: Perspectives on Classical and Contemporary Diaspora. *International Migration* 42, 2: 41–60.

Sadavoy, J Meier, and Anoy Uuk Mui Ong. 2004. Barriers to Access to Mental Health Services for Ethnic Seniors: The Toronto Study. *Canadian Journal of Psychiatry* 49, 3: 192–199.
Schrijvers, Joke. 1999. Fighters, Victims and Survivors: Constructions of Ethnic, Gender and Refugeeness Among Tamils in Sri Lanka. *Journal of Refugee Studies* 12, 3: 307–333.
Strauss, Claudia. 2006. The Imaginary. *Anthropological Theory* 6, 3: 322–344.

"Madrasi" Identity in Guyana

PAUL YOUNGER

In the groundbreaking book *Imagined Communities* (1983)[1] Benedict Anderson opened up the wide-ranging question of how human communities are formed. His specific concern was with the formation of "nations" during the last three centuries, but he discussed the way in which issues of race, language or religion sometimes hovered in the background, even though national identity was seldom aligned with any, let alone all, of those group characteristics. As he sees the history of this period, nationalism arose because of the widespread migration of population and the spread of print capitalism. Because of these two developments, groups of people, first in the Americas, then in Europe and eventually in Asia and Africa were able to discuss their identity and "imagine" themselves as a human community.

Since Anderson's book was published, he has been attacked from two different directions. Some social scientists attack him because they think his use of the word "imagination" still leaves too much room for primordial forms of loyalty in the formation of groups and nations. Martha Kaplan and John Kelly set forth their version of this critique in the form of a book entitled *Represented Communities* (2001)[2] in which they argued that history is determined by the specific actions of persons and that it is the "representations" made on behalf of groups of persons that we should concentrate on in explaining the rise of nations. From the opposite direction, Anderson's explanations have been challenged by a fairly large number of groups who are proud to claim that their current identity is indeed rooted in loyalties that long predate the representation those loyalties now receive in the discussions of nationhood. In South Asia alone, the struggles of the Muslims, Sikhs and Tamils have all appealed to this deeper basis for explaining their present need for a national identity. Nationalist theory has yet to properly understand these appeals to deeper bases of group identity, and a good first step would be to trace some of these groups back historically and see how their group identity was expressed in different historical situations.

Tamil Identity in Guyana

I realize that issues associated with Tamil identity are being played out in many different places in the world, and that the issues associated with Tamil identity in Guyana are not among those that people would initially think of as central to an understanding of what constitutes Tamil identity. I chose to study Guyana, however, precisely because its Tamil community is not in the midst of a political crisis, and we might be able to learn from that situation what some of the more traditional issues were in the constitution of a sense of Tamil identity. During periods of time, such as we have now in Sri Lanka, when a community is vigorously "represented" by a political movement, the leaders of the movement have a near monopoly in the defining of the community's identity. In such a situation, the natural evolution of the culture in terms of art, religion, social interaction and language use is distorted and made to serve the urgent needs of the political initiative. When that happens, our primary access to understanding the community is, of course, through its "representation".

Communities of immigrants are, by contrast, in a very different kind of special situation. While they are both socially and intellectually disrupted by the experience of immigration, they have almost no political representation, and are, in fact, to an unusual degree at the mercy of other forces in the political environment. They are what Anderson would call "imagined" communities in that they are trying to determine what it is in their memory that they want to carry forward as they try to find their place in a new social environment. While recent Tamils immigrants to Canada and other places constitute one of the most interesting examples of new immigrants trying to find their identity, those stories are complicated in a variety of ways, and, because they are still unfolding, it will probably be some time before the social patterns involved can be clearly explained. By turning our attention to the story of Guyana I hope we will be able to show what some of the issues in Tamil identity were when they were dealt with by the immigrants there almost two centuries ago.

History of Guyana

In 1838, ships began arriving in Guyana from Calcutta and Madras with loads of indentured or "contract" workers for the prosperous sugar plantations of the coastal areas. For a century or more the work on those plantations had been carried on by slaves from West Africa, but with the abolition of the slave trade in 1807 a labour shortage had developed, and, with the end of slavery in 1834, a whole new arrangement had to be put in place.[3] The slaves had no alternative employment available, so they moved off the plantations to settlements at the end of each plantation and continued to work on the plantations. The Indians were for the time being housed in the old slave quarters on the plantations, but each new generation was encouraged to also move into the settlement with their African fellow workers, and by the end of indentureship in 1917 most of the workers were living together in the crowded settlements.[4] In 1966 Guyana became an independent "nation" with Indo-Guyanese constituting a bit over half of the population.[5]

Detailed studies of the records of the shiploads of indentured workers have yet to be conducted, but it seems that during the first twenty or more years there were roughly equal numbers brought from Calcutta and Madras,[6] and they were assigned to the hundreds of plantations a few at a time as needed. Among those on the Madras ships there appear to be roughly equal numbers from Tamil-speaking areas and from Telegu-speaking areas, and a surprising number on some ships that are described as from "Malabar". After 1860, Madras ships started going primarily to South Africa, and the percentage of South Indians in Guyana and Trinidad dropped. By the turn of the century, however, the much larger steamships began to, once again, bring significant numbers of workers from South India to Guyana and Trinidad. By the end of indentureship in 1917, the estimates are that about 25 percent of the Indian workers to Guyana had come on ships from Madras.

People of both North Indian and South Indian background in Guyana even today love to use the term "Madrasi" to describe both the people and the religious institutions of those who arrived on ships from Madras. Part of this usage they are quick to tell you involves nostalgia in that it reminds everyone of the "early days" when the bonding that took place on ships, and the family-like status of the "ship-brother", was important to all concerned. The use of the term also seems to indicate that a general differentiation between North and South Indians did continue within the plantation housing, even though plantations themselves were not differentiated in that way.[7] The use of the term also indicates that a differentiation between Tamil-speakers and Telegu-speakers did not continue—as it did, for instance, among the indentured workers of Mauritius. Today this lack of differentiation between Tamil and Telegu speakers is so strong that many persons asked me if their name came from a Tamil-speaking or Telegu-speaking family. What we can probably assume is that, in general, language did not provide a long-term basis for group differentiation in Guyana because the workers were introduced to the work site by the Creole-speaking Afro-Guyanese, and that by the time everyone had moved to the settlements Creole and English were the day-to-day languages for everyone. People with North Indian backgrounds still sing in Hindi in temple settings and people with South Indian backgrounds also use Tamil songs in their own temple settings, but neither language is used in day-to-day settings. Our first tentative conclusion therefore might be that "Madrasi" identity in Guyana is not significantly based on the use of the language.

Race

To what extent is the term "Madrasi" as used in Guyana a racial term? In the 1850s, the planters' association approached the colonial government and complained that the "Madrasis" were dirty and not good at their work,[8] and asked that no more ships be brought from Madras. At much the same time, numerous missionary reports on social conditions in Guyana made the same argument, and used detailed descriptions to emphasize how small and dark those from Madras were.[9] I was only able to realize how deep the 19th century racial divide was among the Indians when I was copying down the names on an old settlement graveyard and discovered that the settlement actually had two graveyards. In one the Madrasis were buried with the Afro-Guyanese and in the other the North Indian Hindus were buried with the Muslims. In 1860, the colonial government heeded the request of the planters and temporarily stopped bringing in workers from Madras. This aggravated the "Madrasi's" situation even further as their numbers dropped and they became a distinct minority among the Indian workers. By the turn of the century, the big steamships once again began bringing in large numbers of "Madrasis", and in the new atmosphere many family groups were included, and government reports describe the new arrivals as "hard workers".

What we need to recall is that Guyana was a backwater location in a vast colonial empire in the 1850s, and the attitudes of the planters, missionaries and government officials in that location echoed in a crude way those of the leaders of the empire. One of the most colourful intellectual figures in Britain at the time was Frederick Max Muller, a German, who had learned Sanskrit as a teenager and was brought to England to help the imported Indian pundits with the publication of the four volumes of the *Rig Veda.*[10] Although he was bitter about never being appointed professor of Sanskrit at Oxford, he remained an important intellectual figure In Britain throughout the century and is the one who insisted that the racial term "Aryan" be used to describe the people who composed the hymns of the *Rig Veda.* He is the one who developed the now very controversial theory called the "Aryan Invasion Theory" (AIT) and argued (although he never visited India) that many North Indians (and Singhala speakers in Sri Lanka) were racially "Aryan" because their languages were taught to them by invading Aryans and were linked with European languages, such as his native German. Once Max Muller's theories swept through colonial thinking, it was not long before the racial/linguistic typology was completed by designating the various South Indian languages as "non Aryan" by using another racially charged term or "Dravidian".

The links between colonial activity and race are tangled. Missionaries tried to continue to bring their message of light to the darkened humanity, but North Indian Brahmans (and Buddhist monks in Sri Lanka) were quick to pick up on the link they supposedly had with Aryans, and they developed their own form of colonialism. Not only did they use the reputation their ancient texts had brought them to bolster the confidence of their people in their religious traditions, but they also mounted missionary-like movements and argued that only the Aryan part of their traditions should be preserved. In Guyana this borrowed colonial racism led to a major increase in "Brahman" names among the North Indian workers, and the development of a Protestant-like *mandir* worship tradition that borrowed heavily from the worship traditions of the colonial masters. These North Indian *mandirs* had little traditional Indian ritual content, and, like the Protestant churches nearby, centered on "sermons" from the Brahman *pundits* on ethical responsibility and loyalty to one's religious community. Even though more Madrasis than North Indians became practising Christians in Guyana, in the racial logic of the 19th century it was the North Indian claim to have an "Aryan" link, and a Brahman name, that placed them closer to the Europeans.

In South India and Sri Lanka, those who felt cut asunder from this "Aryan" family by the racial analysis fought back in a variety of ways. The Dravidian Movement, which has dominated the politics of Tamilnadu for a century, simply took over the racialized term "Dravidian" and used it to imply that there was indeed a community with a primordial racial identity in South India, and that meant it could handle its own cultural and political concerns. In Sri Lanka, the territorial boundaries between Sinhala-speakers and Tamil-speakers were too tangled to allow for a cultural or a political divide, and bitter recrimination continues, and the racialized language is still used to (mis-)define the question. In Guyana, the imagination of the community of South Indians went in a very different direction.

"Madrasi" Religion

The story of "Madrasi" identity in Guyana told so far might appear to be the story of a victim group. The planters and government officials did not like them, they became a minority even among Indians when new immigrants were not added between 1860 and 1900, and they had little opportunity to live near one another or continue with their language. The North Indians played up the racial divisions of the 19th century and used the term "Hindu" exclusively to describe the Protestant-style worship of their *mandirs*, led by their "Brahman" *pundits.*[11] What the "Madrasis" did in this situation was to develop their own distinctive religious tradition, which is now widely recognized as the much-studied Kali-Mai tradition.[12] In describing the role "Madrasi religion" played in helping define the South Indian identity of Guyana, we must try to keep in mind both the strong role memory played in the preservation of their rich tradition and the role selectivity played in forgetting other parts of that tradition.[13] No doubt the local "representatives" of that tradition, who were faced with the complex racist arguments of their day, were focussed on the question of how to build a strong community within that complex social environment.

The *pujaris* who lead the "Madrasi" religious tradition do not come from a specific caste tradition and claim to have learned the elaborate ritual practices and developed the ability to become possessed by the Goddess "from their elders".[14] To an outside observer the ritual practices of these *pujaris* look intense and personal, and I have heard two different anthropologists ask if they were recently developed or even if they were improvised during the performance. In fact, the ritual detail is very old. Comparisons between Guyanese ritual practice and similar practices found among French-speaking *pujaris* in Guadaloupe[15] and Reunion[16] in the Indian Ocean, or between Guyanese *pujaris* and Tamil-speaking *pujaris* in the Up-Country region of Sri Lanka[17], reveal a detailed similarity. In each of these settings where immigrants went in the mid-19th century, Māriyamman is the central object of reverence, and she is surrounded by male deities who assist the worshippers in various ways. In each setting, detailed ritual performances lead to possession states that enable the *pujaris* to offer relief to those who are ill or troubled by evil spirits. The memory of this complex 19th century ritual tradition is carefully preserved in Guyana in a form that one can no longer see in the Māriyamman temples of South India.

What is most interesting, however, in the way this religious tradition was developed to give expression to the "Madrasi" identity of Guyana is what is forgotten from the religious scene of South India from where it originated. In addition to Māriyammaṉ worship the religious scene of South India would include Brahmanical temples of Vishnu and Śivaṉ, *kavati* dance and military traditions associated with Murukaṉ, fire-walking associated with the goddess Draupadī, and rituals for a variety of other goddesses and protector deities. While memories from these traditions were certainly brought with the immigrants at the beginning (and a different subset of those memories were used to constitute the South Indian tradition in other indenture-based societies such as Mauritius or South Africa),[18] the imagining of the community in Guyana involved an important role for "forgetting" as well as for "remembering". The local setting in Guyana involved the Madrasi community in close interaction with fellow workers with both Afro-Guyanese and North Indian-Guyanese backgrounds, and they unconsciously decided on the development of a very simple and uniform pattern of worship that was replicated in a hundred or so settlements up and down the coast. The protector deities are still involved, but they are set in a uniform way around Mariyamman within a single compound in Guyana, and they serve the healing and exorcism activity she enables in this context.

Conclusion

Identity formation in the South Indian community of Guyana is a surprising story. One might have expected the South Indians to be totally assimilated into some local cultural system, either when the initial workers were crowded into slave quarters with their North Indian counterparts, or later when they were asked to live in the crowded settlements that had much earlier been established by the Creole-speaking Afro-Guyanese. Then, when they were openly disparaged in the racial style of the day by both the colonial managers of the society and their North Indian fellow workers, things must have seemed difficult. And then, when immigration stopped for four decades and they became a small minority, one might have expected that they would give up the effort to establish a separate identity altogether.

The religious identity they imagined for themselves in this situation needs to be analyzed carefully. First of all, it was realistic in acknowledging the social reality of the situation, and did not make any attempt to modify its religious ideas in order to fit into the racially defined style used by the missionaries and the North Indians.[19] On the other hand, it did not take a militant posture and develop its temple compounds behind a defensive ethnic boundary. We know that from very early on that the Afro-Guyanese, the North Indians and even, to a limited extent, the colonial whites and Amerindians, were fascinated by the possession states of the *pujaris.*[20] Gradually the Māriyammaṉ temple compounds became popular with anyone in Guyana society seeking healing or help with evil spirits. Now the person entering the temple compound is told that the deities to the North of the compound are vegetarian deities such as Krishna and Śiva and are meant for North Indians; that the black deity to Māriyammaṉ's left is Cankani Karrupaṉ and he can be of assistance to Afro-Guyanese and likes rum and cigars as offerings and worshippers who undergo a ritual whipping with a traditional twelve foot rope; that the white deity opposite Cankani Karrupaṉ is Munnesvaraṉ and can assist Europeans; and that the altar without any image at the far end of the compound is where Muslims pray. On the second day of the three-day festival, an image of the Goddess accompanies the entranced *pujaris* to every house in the settlement to offer healing and exorcism, and on the final day of the festival, all residents of the settlement are expected back in the temple compound for the picnic-like thanksgiving to the Goddess.

Clearly the "Madrasis" of Guyana found a way of defining their religious tradition in a way that allowed them to fit into the very integrated society that Guyana has become without losing their sense of identity. In his influential book on Tamil culture called *Fluid Signs* V Daniel[21] argues that a Tamil's identity was not defined by a line or boundary such as those that mark one *kiramam* or village off from others, but it was defined by a welcoming *ur* or undefined center that people feel they can call "home". The Guyanese defined such a center for themselves around an all-accepting Goddess. They were at once stubbornly remembering their tradition and forgetting other things that would make it difficult for them to open that tradition to others. As Jamsie Naidu, the *pujari* to whom thousands go from all over the Caribbean and even North America, and who has trained women, Afro-Guyanese and North Indians to be *pujaris,* says: "we will always pray to the Goddess as Māriyammaṉ because that is the way we were taught, but others can call her 'Kālī – Mai' if that makes them feel better."[22]

NOTES

1. Anderson, Benedict. 1983. *Imagined Communities.* New York: Verso.

2. Kaplan, Martha and John Kelly. 2001. *Represented Communities.* Chicago: The University of Chicago Press.

3. There had at one time been over 100,000 slaves, but the census of 1829 lists only 82,000. The 230 plantation owners had relied on the steady import of labor for what they considered an industrialized form of agriculture, and they had not encouraged the importation of female slaves, marriage or the settlement of the workers in community. RT Smith. 1962. *British Guiana.* New York: Oxford University Press.

4. When the author was doing field research in 1995, the sugar plantations were being managed by a nationalized company which had bought out Booker Inc. and a few others, who had over the years bought up what were originally 230 separately owned and operated plantations. Sociologically speaking, however, the 230 plantations were still easily identifiable in that the settlements at the end of each was still a vital community, and people were happy to show me the plantation housing in which their ancestors lived and the local sluices and ditches they still had to maintain.

5. The Indians made up 342,187 of the 654,716 living in Guyana in 1966 or 50.71 percent. (Dwarka Nath, *A History of Indians in Guyana, 1970* p. 232 quoting an estimate of the Registrar General)

6. The author has worked on the ship records that are housed by the government in Georgetown and list every single indentured worker. Dwarka Nath (1950, 1970) was an officer in the immigration department and his book provides a number of helpful appendices. See note 5 above.

7. An interesting insight into the continuing differences between North Indians and South Indians 50 years after the beginning of indenture is contained in letters sent to the newspapers in the 1890s by the mischievous gadfly, Bechu, who was at the time addressing a host of issues that concerned the Indian communities just by writing regularly to the newspapers.

One issue concerns the presence of "Madras' interpreters of the Immigration Department in the magisterial offices. Joshua Ramphul, a North Indian businessman from New Amsterdam (the second largest city and the area where the plantations were most heavily populated) writes and suggests that the Madras interpreter in New Amsterdam is a waste of government funds. "Perseus" then writes that the Georgetown office is staffed primarily with "Madras" interpreters, even though immigration from Madras had stopped for the time being "fifteen years earlier". And, finally, Bechu writes that he has long been puzzled at the "Madras" domination of that office, and argues that employees of the Immigration office should be obliged to learn Hindustani within 12 months of employment. (Seecharan C. 1999. *Bechu: 'Bound Coolie' Radical in British Guiana, 1894-1901.* Trinidad: University of the West Indies.What these letter writers did not seem to know is that Mr. Veerasawmy Mudaliar, a high caste South Indian, was the first Chief Interpreter of the Immigration Department and "wielded considerable influence among the Indians in the colony. He was allowed great latitude by the head of the Department while he served as Chief Interpreter, and he was highly respected by those with whom he came into contact." (Nath p. 94; see note 5. He was also the father of Joseph Aloysius Veerasawmy, "the first Indian magistrate in British Guiana", and in 1881 had been made the "zamindar" of the abandoned Huist Dieren plantation where he headed up an effort to start cooperative rice farming. Apparently he also provided "Madrasis" with jobs in the immigration office when he could.

The second issue has to do with rice farming. Long recognized as a natural crop for the

Guyana climate, rice was introduced from Louisiana by the Dutch and grown by runaway slaves from time to time. The sugar planters fought its introduction, and Guyana imported rice for food up until 1917. In spite of the planters, rice cultivation did begin in the Mahaica area soon after indenture started, and the manager of the Anna Regina plantation encouraged his workers to grow it. By the 1890s, thousands of acres were being cultivated, and by 1917 there was enough to shift from importation to an export market. Bechu, writing in the 1890s, sees rice-growing as a way to entice workers to stay in Guyana and cut the monopoly power of the sugar planters. (Seecharan, p. 159.) Bechu does not comment on the fact that rice is predominately a South Indian crop, but during my research in the 1990s rice farmers were clear that it was the growth of the rice industry at the turn of the century that had restarted the importation of South Indian immigrants in the first decade of the 20th century, and that South Indians had never been liked by the sugar planters precisely because they were always trying to push for this agricultural alternative. By the 1990s, others were growing rice, but the South Indian rice farmers claimed their ancestors were behind this initiative all along.

8. In his history of 1855 Henry Dalton wrote: "Indolent, dirty and vagrant in their habits, the Madras Coolies were inapt at the work for which they were intended, irregular in their attendance, and migratory in their ways; numbers abandoned the estates to which they were appointed to crowd about the town begging and filling the most menial situations for a bare pittance." (History of British Guiana, Vol. 1, p.472; quoted in Nath, 1970, p.35)

9. HVP Bronkhurst, *The Colony of British Guiana and Its Labouring Inhabitants* (London, 1888), is the best know of these missionary accounts.

10. A masterful biography of Max Muller has been written by Nirad Chaudhuri. *Scholar Extraordinary: The Life of the Rt Hon Friedrich Max Muller.* London: Chatto & Windus, 1975.

Romila Thapar summarizes the nature of the "Aryan" controversies in *Interpreting Early India.* New York: Oxford University Press, 1982.

11. In describing the similar indentured Indian society of Fiji, Brij Lal, who was himself raised within the North Indian segment of that community, describes the racist division in the following way: "Within the Indian community itself, the South Indians were the victims of cultural and ethnic stereotypes of the North Indians who displayed the traditional Aryan prejudices towards the Dravidian South Indians. Their generally smaller physique and darker skin, their different customs and unfamiliar tongues, were all subjects for North Indians' disparaging cultural comment and patronizing humour." Brij Lal. 2000. *Chalo Jahaji,* Canberra: Australian National University, p. 232.

12. The author provides a fuller account of this tradition in Younger *Playing Host to Deity: Festival Religion in the South Indian Tradition.* New York: Oxford University Press, 2002; Tamil Religious Traditions in post-Indentured Societies delivered at the Tamil Studies Conference of 2007 at Toronto; and in the forthcoming *New Homelands: The Hindu Traditions of the post-Indentured Societies (Mauritius, Guyana, Trinidad, South Africa, Fiji and East Africa),* New York: Oxford University Press.

13. I am, of course, borrowing the language of "memory and forgetting" from the chapter Anderson added to later editions of his *Imagined Communities.*

14. The author has made repeat visits to over thirty temple compounds, bunked with the ritual specialists for a three-day festival, and been introduced to a number of the grandfathers of current *pujaris.* Jamsie Naidu, about whom anthropological films were made in the 1970s and 1990s (by Philip Singer and Stephanos Stephanides, respectively, and who has trained many of the currently active *pujaris,* insists that even the ritual innovations he has made are within a carefully passed down tradition. (Interview 1995)

15. Nagapin, Jocelyn, and Sulty Max. 1989. *La Migration de l'Hindouisme vers Les Antilles.* Paris: Chez les Auteurs.

16. Conversation with daughter of Reunion *pujari,* 1998.

17. Ann Kingsolver. UpCountry Tamils. Paper delivered at the Tamil Studies Conference at Toronto, 2007.

18. The author's accounts of those traditions can be found in the paper delivered at the 2007 Tamil Studies Conference and in a forthcoming publication. See note 12 above.

19. One might contrast this approach with that taken by a reformer such as Arumuka Navalar who at much the same time in Jaffna was frantically arguing that the Tamils needed to imitate the missionary style both in spreading their message but, more importantly, in keeping to Aryan styles of religion and getting rid of goddess worship and rituals of exorcism and healing.

20. The Overseer of Labour on the Albion plantation, Leslie Philips (1923). *A Kali-Mai Festival in Guyana,* wrote in a pamphlet a detailed account of the colony-wide picnic atmosphere that developed around the "Madrasi" temple festival on his plantation in 1923.

21. Daniel, V. 1984. *Fluid Signs: Being a Person the Tamil Way.* Berkeley: The University of California Press.

22. Interview 1995.

Being Tamil in Norway: Negotiations of Well-Being and Identity

ANN SIGFRID GRØNSETH

Introduction

This paper explores how continuity in identity and personhood is challenged and constituted among different generations of Tamil refugees in Norway. It is based on a study among Tamil refugees residing on the north coast of Norway, in a fishing village called Arctic Harbor. The informants for this investigation were first-generation migrants from Sri Lanka who had escaped the war and succeeded in establishing a safe place to live and a fairly good income from work in the fishing industry. As a group, the Tamils were economically well integrated but socially segregated. Rather than entering Norwegian social arenas, the Tamils engaged in Tamil activities and established networks that strengthened a Tamil sense of identity and cultural continuity. In spite of many successful features in their re-establishment, most of the Tamils frequently visited the local health centre with various diffuse pains and illnesses. The purpose of the investigation conducted between 1996 and 2000, was to explore these pains and aches from a perspective of "being-in-the-world" (Merleau-Ponty1962 [1945]) and as embodied social experiences in which I engaged with concepts of doxa, habitus (Bourdieu 1989), and "self as an active orienting capacity" (Csordas 1994). Methodologically, it emphasizes an approach of "attending to" (Ingold 1993), sharing experiences (Grønseth forthcoming a and b), and exploring senses of resonance (Wikan 1992) with the Tamils in everyday life, together with systematic in-depth interviews and construction of "ethnographic narratives." Further, I discuss how Tamils' experiences of pain can provide a gateway to a cosmopolitan subjectivity. This is not an instrumental cosmopolitanism that makes us all worldwide alike as consumers of similar foods, trademarks, symbols, and broadcasting from a global marked. Rather, it is a cosmopolitanism that refers to an embodied ethic and aesthetic relation based on face-to-face experiences and intersubjectivity. In the following, I first introduce a context of fieldwork and a brief history of Tamil migration to Norway. Then I turn to two illustrative cases before proposing an analysis addressing challenges in Tamil identity and social relations.

Context of Fieldwork: Tamil Refugees' Social and Existential Experiences in Arctic Harbor

The study is based on a one-year fieldword[1] among Tamils who have sought refuge from the civil war in Sri Lanka, and who have re-established themselves in the fishing village in Arctic Harbor.[2] The Tamil population in Arctic Harbor was offered safety, well-paid jobs and good housing. They were all employed in the local women's traditionally low-status job as "cutters" in the fishing industry. The cutters use a small sharp filet knife to form the fish filet into a delicate piece by cutting off small parts that contain fish bones, or otherwise not clean areas. The job requires skill, speed, and efficiency.

Arctic Harbor is inland in a small fjord near the Barents Ocean and the open sea to the North Pole. The buildings and houses of Arctic Harbor surround the interior of the fjord and are mainly stretched along one main road and several side streets. The village extends approximately three kilometers. The great flat windswept mountains rise along the shore behind the settlements leading to the *Finnmarksvidda* plateau.[3] There is not a tree in sight, only a few bushes firmly secured between cracks providing shelter from the storms, which sweep the area. On a lovely summer's day it is still below 20°C, and the air may be thick with swarms of mosquitoes. The sun shines both day and night, never dipping below the horizon from May until July. Then between November and February, the sun gradually descends, and disappears altogether. During the winter blizzards, the roads are closed and covered by snow and ice.

Finnmark and Arctic Harbor became a testing ground for a national strategy relating to refugees. Never before had a group of refugees been asked to settle in the far north of Norway. The community prepared itself for the arrival of the Tamils. They wanted to introduce them to Norwegian values and local traditions through six "friendship-families" who would take special care of and introduce their designated Tamil family to the ways of life that were considered essentials for establishing a sense of well-being by the residents of Arctic Harbor. The Tamils were invited to dinners of typical local foods, and were taken on drives to see the landscape. They were also introduced to the Norwegian custom of hiking and cross-country skiing. The Norwegians took pride in introducing the newcomers to the local "good life" and introduced them to local food customs and encouraged an appreciation of the area and its physical environment.

This initial hosting of the Tamil was meant to integrate them into Arctic Harbor social life. This did not succeed. The Tamils did not respond by incorporating Norwegian and Arctic Harbor traditions and values into their lives, nor did they forge ties of friendship and other kinds of social relationships with Norwegians. In general, they politely withdrew from contact with Norwegians and sought relations with other Tamils in Arctic Harbor. The Tamils established a well-functioning local Tamil Association that arranged a broad spectrum of activities including sports, religious ceremonies, Saturday Tamil School that offers culture and language for the children, as well as other social gatherings. Although the Tamil population was well integrated into the local (and national) economy, they were socially and culturally segregated.

In spite of many successful features of their refuge, the Tamils frequently visited the local health center for consultations about various diffuse aches and pains. Exploring the issue of Tamils' suffering, it appears how Tamils' pains express embodied social experiences. However, the study does not reject that many Tamils' troubles and pains may be symptoms of post-traumatic stress syndrome (PTSD) related to war actions and losses,[4] or of the very hard and monotonous work that Tamils employ at the fish plants.[5] Nevertheless, I argue that Tamils' experience of resettlement in Arctic Harbor challenge and confront Tamils' familiar and taken-for-granted social relations and identity in ways that are perceived and expressed by the body and the self, living in a new and unknown social world and physical surroundings (Grønseth 2001, 2006a, b). Furthermore, these expressions are seen to reveal a certain knowledge and meaning related to social practices and relations in everyday life of Arctic Harbor.

Illustrative and frequent pains reported to me during fieldwork among the Tamils in Arctic Harbor were referred to as headaches, fatigue, dizziness, nightmares, loss of appetite, "uncertainty," "aloneness," "loss of self," and "no peace of heart." The aches presented during consultations at the local health centre were commonly focused on physical pains and also included painful breathing, hair loss, stomachache and various bodily pains (muscular) in shoulders, back, legs and arms. Considering that health personnel found it difficult to diagnose and treat the presented symptoms, I suggest an understanding that sees Tamils' aches and pains as related to a wider social and existential world. I propose an analysis where Tamils are seen as forced to reorient themselves and negotiate in a radically new social and cultural (and climatic) world, which enforces a deep insecurity in personal as well as group identity. Thus, I explore an approach that collapses the Cartesian dichotomy of body and soul and argue that Tamils embody ongoing social processes, which tend to produce diffuse enduring pains and fatigue.

Living without the familiar social and religious context, which gave form and meaning to their common social activities and relations, many Tamils perceived life in exile as fragmented and threatening to their existence as social persons and human beings. Most Tamils experienced a loss of what I refer to as a "Tamil wholeness" (see also Grønseth 2006c). Tamils did not only experience an extensive bereavement, but also experienced being pushed and pulled into new bits and pieces of what, by comparison, appeared as a "Norwegian wholeness." In this situation of being deprived of the familiar Tamil wholeness and confronted with parts of a Norwegian wholeness, Tamils experienced great social and emotional challenges. To handle such challenges and confrontations, Tamils found themselves forced to create practices and meanings in their radical new everyday life.

Taking the perspectives of embodiment and a phenomenology of "being-in-the-world" (Merleau-Ponty 1962 [1945]) highlights social and cultural processes as part of perception, existential experiences, and human capacities. By attending to these frames and concepts a revisiting of the empirical material on Tamils in Arctic Harbor demonstrates not only characteristics of segregation, stigma, and exclusion (see Grønseth 2006c), but also relations and moments of emotional compassion, empathy, and solidarity. Before I turn to the analysis, I first present a brief history of Tamil migration to Norway. Then, I introduce two case studies that illustrate how Tamils, under certain circumstances, can experience a bridging empathy and mutuality that widens the otherwise-present gaps between selves and others.

Tamil Migration to Norway

During the 1980s and 1990s there was, and there still is a steady though decreased flow of Tamil refugees seeking asylum in Norway. Since Norway banned immigration in 1975, the main passage into Norway in the early 1980s was through the Norwegian system of Folk Colleges or *Folkehøyskoler.* Folkehøyskole is a type of private boarding school that offer a variety of subjects and attract mostly youth, but also adult persons, to their one-year studies. Third World students had admission to these schools and this served as a loophole in the immigration ban of 1975. Many Tamils found it less expensive and safer to raise the economic guarantee required for living costs than to pay an agent to arrange a "refugee travel." The Folkehøyskole students commonly used the opportunity to seek further admission to the regular school system and thus remained in Norway on temporary visa until they had completed their studies. After 1983 and the outbreak of the civil war in Sri Lanka, many Tamils found that if they dropped out of school, it was difficult for the Norwegian immigration authorities to force their return to Sri Lanka. According to official statistics, the total Tamil population in Norway in 1987 was 1881, and a substantial percentage of this population had immigrated through the Folkehøyskole system (Fuglerud 1999). Obtaining a visa as a Folkehøyskole student was an open possibility until 1989. From then on, the immigration authorities stopped this immigration practice by applying the "criteria for possible return," which they also used for ordinary visitors from the Third World. This implies that a visa was not granted if there was reason to believe that the applicant could and would not return after completing an educational program. Considering the war in Sri Lanka, this criterion excluded young Tamils from further student visas.

Legally, the Tamils have two options when seeking refuge. They may apply directly to embassies for a visa that is rarely granted, or they may withdraw to one of the sordid camps on the outskirts of the combat zone. The third possibility, that many thousands have chosen over the last ten or fifteen years, is the illegal path across bordered spaces, the journey that breaks international regulations. In this type of travel, the outcome of the escape-journey depends on the individual and the guide who has been entrusted with both money and confidence. As Fuglerud (1999) and Farmanfarmaian (1992) point out, by choosing this path, the refugees become active agents rather than passive subjects. This means that they "maintained a sub-systemic freedom and mobility that facilitated the exercise of their subjectivity, constantly challenging, negotiating and rupturing the systemic inscriptions that were aimed at containing them" (Framanfarmaian 1992:92).

Another consequence of the refugee policy is that when the migrant finally arrives at the destination of refuge, many of them would have violated the condition of their stay. They would have already broken the rule of "first-country" regulation on their way. To remain in Norway they must invent a story and hold on to it. With Norway's increased emphasis on immigration control, in principle, there is no time limit regarding a re-evaluation of a legal status if it is found that false information has been given (Fuglerud 1999). Accordingly, there is no possibility for the refugee to leave behind the strains and difficulties of the flight. Knudsen (1988, 1990) has stressed how Vietnamese refugees were forced to construct and present life stories to secure their rights in the host country. Given this practice, self-presentation and control over biographical data become critical problems.

There is reason to believe that the situation of constructing untruthful life stories has an impact on the refugees' self-identity. As Giddens (1991) points out, self-identity is about gaining a sense of oneself through a shared and intersubjective story of how one has become and where one is going. When Tamil refugees are not able to communicate a sustained biographical narrative that makes a continuous and reflexive self-identity possible, many end up with feelings of self-alienation. Not going further into the problem of self-presentation, this paper will focus on the local context of resettlement, in which Tamils are seen to struggle with similar but different issues related to well-being, identity and community. The following section presents two cases mentioned earlier. I then propose an analysis addressing challenges in Tamil identity and social relations.

Case: Lakshimi: "I need to find power so I can act and be strong"

I met Lakshimi several times in different settings over a period of some two years (1998–2000). I met her, for instance, together with other Tamil families having tea, at Tamil birthday parties, in her home for visit, and out in the shops. When we met she always offered small new bits of her experiences in Arctic Harbor. Here I present a short version of her story teasing out information of value for this paper. Lakshimi, as most of the other Tamil women, came to live with her husband whom she had married some time ago and thereafter waited for the Norwegian government to make a grant for her to re-unite with her husband in Norway. Lakshimi and her husband Sivarajah had met several years ago at some of the larger family gatherings when they still lived in Sri Lanka. At some later point, their parents agreed that they would be a good match for marriage. From exchanging letters on the subject, Sivarajah had expressed a positive interest in Lakshimi. When his family approached her, she knew that Sivarajah was doing well in Norway and was eager to take the opportunity of leaving for what she thought would be a better turn in her life. Upon arrival in Arctic Harbor, she quickly started her work at the fish plant along with the other Tamils. At that time she was 28 years old. Only half a year later she became pregnant and was on sick leave the last two months before she gave birth to her baby boy. Lakshimi told me how she had worried throughout her pregnancy and experienced the delivery as a very distressing experience. Not because the nurses were not helpful and comforting, but because she felt so immensely alone, insecure, and afraid.

Lakshimi was very concerned about not being able to take proper care of herself during pregnancy and that her child might be of bad health. She had taken care to purify herself by a diet of vegetables and cleanliness, pray at her household shrine, offer ritual foods and sweets, and give the Gods her sincere vows. Lakshimi told me that she was not sure that doing her household *puja* would be enough to ensure the Gods' mercy and good fortune for her baby and family. She felt a strong urge to visit the temples back home. Not being able to do so, she had sent money to her sister who lived in their home area and asked her to offer food, and have the priest bless her family. In return, Lakshimi received blessed strings that she knit around her stomach to protect her baby from evil forces. She also got an amulet for good fortune that she kept around her neck or in her pocket. She gave birth at the hospital that was a five-hour drive from Arctic Harbor. Her husband went with her, but she felt helpless and left alone in what to her was an unknown and frightening place. When driving the car to the hospital they crossed the windswept mountains all covered in snow and ice. Lakshimi held her amulet firmly in her hand and prayed that this empty and cold landscape would not harm her family.

About a month after birth, Lakshimi and her husband arranged for the crucial shaving ceremony of their baby. Lakshimi felt a deep worry about not being able to bring their baby to the Tamil Hindu temple to take part in the religious ceremony conducted by a Tamil Hindu priest, as well as the social gathering at the temple with fellow Tamils. Lakshimi and Sivarajah did a self-composed version of the rituals related to the shaving ceremony at their household shrine and invited only a few friends in Arctic Harbor to share ritual foods. Lakshimi was happy about the gathering, but felt very lonely and insecure. In the following months, Lakshimi continued her ritual cleansing and puja at the household shrine. She constantly felt the sadness and insecurity of not being able to visit the temples.

During her time in Arctic Harbor Lakshimi came to develop bonds with people that she would not usually relate to. There were three young Tamil women who had come to Arctic Harbor within the same autumn. They all arranged for Hindu wedding celebrations during the same winter and started their work as cutters at the fish plant. Lakshimi was the first one to carry a child, but the others soon followed. These women had no history together other than seeking escape from Sri Lanka and marrying young men who offered them security and safety in this radical new climatic and social surroundings of Arctic Harbor. Lakshimi said:

> These women are my friends, but I do not find confidence in them. They are the ones that we invited for the one-month ritual of our baby, and they are the ones I turn to for any favors I need. There are also two other families that we have relations with. My husband shared time with them in the asylum-seeking centre. It is difficult to make friends here [in Arctic Harbor], but we need each other. There are many things I do not want to know or speak about with my new friends. It is better that way. If we speak of everything, it might be difficult to remain in our friendship. Living in Arctic Harbor I have no kin or family near me. I need to look [at] who is here, who does well, and who I can trust to help me. It is difficult. Not having my family here, not having a temple to visit makes me feel very lonely. I am troubled with headaches. Sometimes I feel dizzy and very weak. I do not always recognize myself. Who am I? I need to find power so I can act and be strong. Some day in the future I want to [be] educated and have a good job. I want to help my family and make them proud.

Case: Bavishan: "I need to gain power and make friends."

When I met Bavishan he was seventeen. He told me that he had great difficulties at school. Not only did he struggle with Norwegian, but he emphasized how he had lost years of education because of the war. Before his father's escape and re-union in Arctic Harbor, the family's house was burnt down and his family had constantly moved around. Bavishan had gone to five different schools. He told me how his younger siblings and himself had been hit by the young teachers, often with a stick, when they had failed to come to school or not done their homework. Since Bavishan's family had moved several times they had not been able to maintain many friendships. In his young life featured by rupture and loneliness he said that one of the few places that made him feel peace at heart was when he visited the local Tamil-Hindu temple. "Being with the gods," Bavishan felt "protection and a sense of togetherness." Today, in Arctic Harbor, he keeps a picture of his favorite God, Pillear, under his pillow. At night, he used to slip his hand under the pillow and touch the picture to help him fall asleep. In Arctic Harbor Bavishan and his siblings used to stay together and made few friends. Bavishan told me that at home in Sri Lanka, their father had used to hit and bash him and his siblings for wrongs they did. Today there was no one who hit them, but it was cold and very lonely. Reflecting on his life Bavishan said he was not sure about what was the worst or best:

> "What is the best? To live in Sri Lanka with warm climate, good food, temples, but also the bombing, changes of school and hitting? Or, to live here where it is cold and no friends, but where it is safe and no one hits me? What can I say? Every morning, when I wake up, I think of home [Sri Lanka]. It is often difficult to fall asleep and I wake up again. I am troubled with headaches and I do not feel hungry. Sometimes I stay home and make drawings. My mother gives me blessed strings to wear around the wrists and ankles for protection and strength. I feel very alone. I need to gain power and make friends. I play soccer and learn data with the Tamils. It is not easy for us [the Tamils] to be together. I practice scoring goals with one of the boys. Our families are not together, but my mother approves. It gives me strength and reputation as a good soccer player.

Once Bavishan showed me a picture of his class in Arctic Harbor. I asked him to point out the ones he would like to be friends with or a girl he fancied. He pointed toward a smiling sweet girl with long dark brown hair. I asked if they had spoken. He said that he seldom spoke with anyone in his class, but that he liked to secretly look at her and sometimes they exchanged glances. Also, there was one boy he used to meet at the library. They used the computer together and shared comics. Together they explored possibilities for future life and searched for avenues to fulfil dreams and hopes. Bavishan said he wanted a Norwegian education. The family was planning to move to Oslo next summer where he could continue higher level education. I asked if he wanted to return to Sri Lanka. He replied:

> When peace comes I will return to rebuild the country. But now, I want to stay here. I want to be educated. Who knows the future? Maybe I will marry a Norwegian girl? In Sri Lanka the women stay home. I think it is good that the girls make decisions about education and work. I like Norwegian girls. My parents would like me to marry a cousin. They have not arranged for it, but I know. If I find a Norwegian girl I will make them see that it is good. I will not stop being Tamil, but I need to make my own relations. When they see that I do well, my parents will learn that Norwegian ways are fine too. They will see that I am strong. I admire my father and I will always fight for Tamil Eelam. I will support my family and siblings. But, I must do it my way.

In the following section I suggest that the creation of the individualized ritual practices and social relations can become meaningful when understood within frames of *shakti*-power. The next section discusses how the challenges to Tamil identity open up a turn toward cosmopolitanism.

Shakti *as a Bridge to Individuation?*

Within the Hindu philosophy of life the concept of *shakti* (Wadley 1977) draws attention to a force or power that one can attain as individual person. It is a term that addresses how individuals by conduct, action, consumption, and engagement can acquire moral qualities and power that are not given by birth. When Tamils in Arctic

Harbor were faced with social fragmentation and loss of collective ritual practices they not only suffered, but were also forced toward reorientation and inventive creation of "being-in-the-new-world." In search for well-being and continuity in identity and personhood the cases of Lakshimi and Bavishan illustrate how many Tamils in Arctic Harbor turn toward relations that are featured by individually created practices and experiences, more than collective principles of kin, caste, and temple practices. Not being able to attend the Tamil-Hindu temple to take part in religious and social life, Lakshimi increased individual rituals of purification and prayers at her household altar. Such an individualistic turn toward religious practice was experienced as highly ambiguous and not fulfilling. This, I suggest, relates to how being Hindu is a matter of taking part in social ritual life and doing specific activities, more than practicing an individual and intellectual devotion to a metaphysic whole. For the Hindu practitioner it is by taking part in social and religious activities that one demonstrates devotion and earns their mercy.

Lacking temples, statues of Gods, priests, and social practices leave Bavishan and Lakshimi with a sense of great vulnerability and insecurity. In response, Bavishan needed Pillear's picture to fall asleep and Lakshimi increased her individual practice of purification, prayers and vows. However, they did not feel satisfaction or "peace at heart" by this. The cases of Bavishan and Lakshimi illustrate how Tamil Hindus experience religious practice not as a question of seeking personal metaphysical knowledge and understanding, but as a quest for taking part in social life and experiencing some of the wonders in the world of Gods. As Fuller notes (1992:5): "ordinary [Hindu] people see relationships with the deities as fundamental in their lives." When not fulfilling the requirements of this relation, Bavishan and Lakshimi are left with a sense of weakness and exposure they must combat. The combat, I suggest, is played out by means of individual creativity and agency. The cases of Bavishan and Lakshimi show how they turn to an individual ritual practice and create friendships based on sharing experiences in their new environment rather than pre-established kin and caste relations.

The power of *shakti* in the context of Arctic Harbor and Norway, a westernized cultural context, is that it emphasizes individualistic aspects rather than the more social dimensions such as *dharma*. Thus, I propose that dimensions of *shakti* can provide Tamils with the ability to gain and increase individual and personal spiritual, moral, and social power. As such, *shakti* can create a juncture between Tamils' (by degrees) relationally—and Norwegians' individually—defined constitutions of person and self.

As the birth-given rank of caste and kin does not serve as adequate organizing principles for social relations, the more fluid and flexible qualities of *shakti*-power provide a structural dimension for constructing social relations. Let me briefly expand on this concept. The religious term *shakti* holds qualities of strength, energy, and vigor, and its strength is based on a spiritual embodied force (Wadley 1977).

This may correspond with how Marriot and Inden (1977)[6] refer to a non-duality between action and substance. *Shakti* is neither just a physical nor simply a moral power, but both. "*Shakti* is a result of morality or right action, which is transformed into an embodied *shakti*, which results in a transformed physical state (bodily substance)" (Wadley 1977:139, parentheses in original). From such ideas, one may see that religion has no separate realm, but it is part of everyday life.

Acknowledging that *shakti*-power is a fundamental idea in Hindu religion, one can also argue that *shakti* is an ordering principle both in the "god–human" and "human–human" relationships. In regard to such a view, some of the apparent inconsistencies in caste ranking may be enlightened. Within the caste ranking system, individuals and castes can negotiate a higher rank by increasing material prosperity and political influence. This is commonly symbolized by food transactions that mark an increased purity (Marriott 1969:114–115). When adding the dimension of *shakti*, it appears how material prosperity is closely linked to people's perceptions of someone's powers. Wealth tends to be interpreted as an indication of a family or a person's correct actions, and as such, their embodied powers seem to increase.

Increased power and the ability to control and command the lives of others follow higher status. Stressing the importance of a *shakti*-power in social relationships, Wadley (1977) disputes Dumont's notion that pure and impure dominates Hindu society. Wadley argues that power and purity are inseparable elements in the Hindu ideas of being and action. Power is embodied and a characteristic of the state of any being. Additionally, all beings are in some kind of state of purity. A person's quantum of power and purity in life is related to his or her actions. His or her fate is derived from correct and incorrect actions in previous lives. Thus, in this life, an individual's bodily substance changes through various transformations and transactions; likewise one's power and purity changes along with the shifting substances and actions. People know which gods are powerful, or have *shakti*, by what and how many requests and favors they can grant. Similarly, people know which persons are forceful and have *shakti* by noting what they can do for other people on earth.

The connections that Lakshimi and Sivarajah made with young Tamil families, and whom they involved in their lives, may well be seen as connected to a search for qualities of *shakti*-strength and power. By including them in their life despite not being of kin or caste, they demonstrated their own prosperity and an ability to support and facilitate for others. Moreover, Lakshimi and Sivarajah experienced these families' success and ability to grant favors to others. While living in hardship compounded with loss and unfamiliar surroundings, Lakshimi and Sivarajah demonstrated power by being able to conduct vital religious rituals and celebrate their baby's 30th day after birth. To celebrate, they invited other Tamils that I suggest are "right to be with" in terms of holding spiritual force and purity. The case of Bavishan is a good example of one striving to build relations and gain power, not by conceding to traditional regulations of social relations, but by building personal relations with others who shared mutual recognition and practices meant to fulfill hopes and goals for the future.

Sharing experiences in the new and unknown context of Arctic Harbor, Tamils such as Lakshimi and Bavishan established bonds between them which challenge and conquer the traditional ties of kin and caste. I suggest that the new bonds are an expression of how Tamils figure new ways of "being-in-the-world" in which the body, as a perceptive capacity, reorients and creates new relations that provides the individual with a minimum of a sense of meaning, self, and personhood.

By similar, yet different ways, Tamils gradually reinforce more individual and flexible criteria for "who are the proper ones to be with." Living in Arctic Harbor they are forced to be with people who they usually would not be with, but simultaneously they learn to appreciate and value new ways of establishing social relations and friendships. I propose to see this process in light of Tamils' embodied appreciation of *shakti*-power as a venue for transformation and a principle for interacting in social relations. I argue this by acknowledging that *shakti*-power implies a deep interconnection between religious and social life and results from individual moral or right action. In the following I discuss how an individuating turn of identity can be seen to open the door to a cosmopolitan interconnection between all human beings.

Challenging Identity: A Turn Toward Cosmopolitanism

The cases of Bavishan and Lakshimi are powerful examples that refer to how they suffered from a sense of aloneness, challenges in self-identity, and a need for "gaining power and friends." On an interpretive level, statements of needing to "gain power and friends," can fruitfully be understood to express a bridging between traditional and indigenous values with a realization of the need to connect to new others, here being Norwegians and unfamiliar Tamils (not kin or caste related). Tamils' indigenous social relations are governed by principles of kin and caste as a hierarchy of distinct categories and groups into which one is born (see Pfaffenberger 1982, Dumont 1980 [1966], Barnett 1975, Bayly 1999, Fuller 1996, Searle-Chatterjee and Sharma 1994, *Deepa 2005 and others).* When the hierarchy of kinship and caste groups was fragmented and incomplete as in Arctic Harbor, Tamils' social relations and self-identity became vulnerable and insecure. In exile the Tamils were left without familiar and habituated patterns for how to be a person and how to be together. In this context, I suggest that achieved individual and personal attributes and qualities became pivotal when negotiating and establishing identity and social relations.

In the challenges of life, Lakshimi and Bavishan confronted—as we all do—moments and situations that were experienced as uncertain and painful. This was not the pain from a physical injury or pathology, but from an existential challenge to expand their lives into something or someone unfamiliar and new. In this endeavor, I suggest, lies an opportunity for cosmopolitism. It is based on an understanding that our being as humans and persons is not a fixed and closed entity, but rather an open and flexible cluster that is ready to connect with its environment and other people (see Daniel 1984, Csordas 1994, Peirce 1932, Merleau-Ponty 1962 [1945]). Such a view implies a certain agency derived from the realm of intersubjectivity understood as shared experiences that take place within and between self and other (see also Grønseth 2007 and Forthcoming a and b).

Sharing experiences and engaging with unfamiliar and new "others", like the cases of Lakshimi and Bavishan illustrate, challenges already established identity, values, practices, and social relationships. In moments of rupture and "out of the ordinary," I suggest that Lakshimi and Bavishan experienced an empathetic connection and recognized a common humanity despite the unfamiliarity of cultural and social differences. One should here note that to experience empathy and mutuality across individual, social, and cultural distinctions, does not necessarily imply harmony and complete wholeness, but often include friction and fractions. Furthermore, in moments of engaging and connecting to unfamiliar others, doxic[7] (Bourdieu 1989), habituated, and familiar values are contested. Considering the embodied level which is disturbed, it can generate an experience of bodily pain, such as Lakshimi and Bavishan's dizzinesess, headaches, loss of appetite, and sleeplessness.

Such moments of "painful dispute" can trigger a transgression of established perspectives, and thus pave the way for new perceptions and actions. Bavishan's future plans incorporated new practices such as to marry a Norwegian girl of his own choice and already he was involved in social relations based on individual qualities and capacities, rather than birth-defined relations of kin and caste. In response to experiencing great challenges to his self-identity, he stated that he will stay Tamil, but in his own and new ways. Lakshimi's hopes for the future included a Norwegian education and job which makes her a woman who transgresses the expected and traditional paths of a Tamil woman. In the loss of kin, temple, and family, Lakshimi experienced a feeling of loss of identity and acknowledged a need to gain power to act. Experiencing the pain of being "alone," "uncertain," and bound to indigenous practices and meanings, Bavishan and Lakshimi stretched themselves out and into a new world seeking new identities, meanings, values, and practices. These agentive and creative moments give a potential for cosmopolitanism as it here refers to a response to the recognition of the other as a mutual and relational part of oneself.

Calling upon an embodied cosmopolitanism of esthetics, ethics, and empathy generated from the realms of face-to-face relations and intersubjectivity can run the risk of a naivety that avoids dealing with structural power and systemically asymmetric relations. Rather, I propose that studying experiences of physical aches and pains as part of the embodied social experiences and "being-in-everyday-life" can give access to often unspoken knowledge about identity and social life. Relations of power, stigma, and degradation are thus addressed on a level that does not dismiss, but which goes beyond structures of indifference so as to capture the ways in which groups and individuals experience, express, and negotiate their pain and agony within a life-project of seeking identity, community, recognition, and well-being.

It is by the difference of the other that the self negates and asserts itself. It is by relating to the other Tamils and Norwegians that Bavishan and Lakshimi constituted themselves as human beings and persons within their new social and cultural environment. In Bavishan's drive and capacity to connect to others in new ways and with strength, his mother (and father) recognized a power in her (their) son that resonated with familiar aspects of habituated values his mother could approve of (see below). By Lakshimi's persistent individual religious practice and relations she sought power and strength to enter into Norwegian arenas for education and thus be able to help her family. Both cases demonstrate how identities and relations that are out of the ordinary are allowed by showing a kind of power and respectability that transfer social rules for interaction. It is in this transferring juncture that I suggest that *shakti* allows a Tamil a process of individuation and opens the way for a cosmopolitanism which appreciates a sense of esthetic and ethic human mutuality across differences.

Concluding Remarks

In this paper I have presented how Tamils experienced aches and pains which are understood by perspectives of embodiment that collapse the dichotomy of body and mind. By such an approach it is revealed how pain can express a kind of knowledge about identity and social relations and exert a complex agency derived from the realm of intersubjectivity. From these shared experiences is addressed how one can experience empathy and mutuality across individual, social, and cultural differences. It should again be noted that such mutuality often includes frictions and are not necessarily smooth and harmonious. Rather, it is a kind of common equality that is recognized by and through differences.

Further, this paper has emphasized how Tamil refugees, here represented by Lakshimi and Bavishan, break through traditional and indigenous patterns of social relations that limit (and sometimes stigmatize) Tamil relations. Bavishan did not want to become a Norwegian; rather he said he will stay a Tamil, but in his own and new way. In Lakshimi's insecure self-identity, she turns to a more individuated relation to her Gods and other Tamils, together with the possibility of taking Norwegian education and challenging established Tamil views of womanhood. By Lakshimi and Bavishan's individual search, conduct, and engagement in creating self-identity and relations with unfamiliar others, I propose that these cases demonstrate an individual power that can be interpreted within Hindu concepts such as *shakti*. Thus, Tamil self-identity and community can incorporate new practices and meanings that bridge between the former, indigenous aspects of social life that the asylum seeker brings as well as a cosmopolitanism. As such, new Tamil identities can embrace an appreciation of individuation and distinctions as part of a common humanity.

NOTES

1. After a few years of shorter field-visits, I was in September 1999 enabled to set out for a one-year fieldwork among the Tamil refugees in one of the small fishing villages. I employed participant observations and conducted interviews among the Tamil population and health staff.

2. Arctic Harbor is one of several fishing communities along the northern coast of Norway where there is a substantial settlement of Tamils; there were about two hundred Tamils in a population of approximately 2500 inhabitants in the period of 1999–2000. The numbers vary as the population as a whole is shifting, mostly according to fluctuations in the need of labour in the fishing industry.

3. The inhabitants of *Finnmarksvidda* are mostly the indigenous Sami populations that traditionally make a living as reindeer (caribou) herdsmen. Along the coast there is a more mixed population consisting of Sami peoples combining fishing and reindeer keeping and non-Sami Norwegian inhabitants.

4. Core symptoms of PTSD include persistent reexperiencing of the traumatic event, numbness and avoidance of stimuli associated with the trauma, and autonomic hyperarousal (DSM-IV; American Psychiatric association, 1994). Dissociative disorders, somatization disorders and affective disorders are among other possible consequences of exposure to traumatizing events (van der Kolk *et al.* 1996).

5. Typical work-related symptoms are muscular aches, tensions and inflammations in arms, shoulder and back, sometimes also legs and feet.

6. South Asian's moral qualities are altered by changes in his or her body. This may result from eating certain foods, engaging in specific kinds of sexuality, taking part in certain ceremonies or when the body is under other certain influences. Hence, bodily substance and code for conduct are not fixed but fluent and not distinct but immanent features. Actions are seen as hooked onto codes that transform the substances and as such, action, codes, and substances can all be seen as embodied (Marriott and Inden 1977). One should also note that the term "substance" in South Asia refers not only to the natural substance contained within the body, but also to that which passes between bodies, such as the contents or media of transactions. Similarly, codes of conduct refer not only to norms of interactions, but to ways of being, to inner qualities or values of substances attained through actions by persons. Hence, one may see norms of actions as being embodied or transactions as substantiating a code. Taking into account how Hindus perceive substance and action as part of the same whole, one can admit to an understanding of Tamils in Arctic Harbor who experience the immense changes not only in their actions and minds, but also in their bodies.

7. "Doxa," refer to issues that are not part of discourse, not questioned or reflected upon, but rather seen as "natural" (Bourdieu 1989).

WORKS CITED

Bourdieu, P. 1989. *Outline of a Theory of Practice.* Cambridge: Cambridge University Press.

Bauman, Z. 1995. *Modernity and Ambivalence.* Cambridge: Polity Press.

Barnett, SA. 1975. Approaches to Changes in Caste Ideology in South India. In *Essays on*

South Asia, edited by Burton Stein. Hawaii: University Press of Hawaii.

Bayly, S. 1999. *The New Cambridge History of India IV. 3: Caste Society and Politics in India from the Eighteenth Century to the Modern Age.* Cambridge: Cambridge University Press.

Csordas, T, ed. 1994. *Embodiment and Experience. The Existential Ground of Culture and Self.* Cambridge: Cambridge University Press.

Daniel, V. 1984. *Fluid Signs. Being a Person the Tamil Way.* California: California University Press.

Deepa, SR. 2005. The Ethnicity of Caste. *Anthropological Quarterly* 78, 3: 543–584.

Dumont, L. 1980 [1966]. *Homo Hierarchicus: The Caste System and its Implications,* Complete Revised English Edition. Chicago and London: John Hopkins University of Chicago Press.

Fuller, CJ, ed. 1996. *Cast Today. SOAS. Studies on South Asia: Understandings and Perspectives.* Delhi/New York: Oxford University Press.

Grønseth, AS. 2001. In Search of Community: A Quest For Well-Being Among Tamil Refugees In Northern Norway. *Medical Anthropology Quarterly* 15, 4: 493–514.

Grønseth, AS. 2006a. Experiences of Illness: Tamil Refugees in Norway Seeking Medical Advise. In *Multiple Medical Realities. Patients and Healers in Biomedical, Alternative and Traditional Medicine,* edited by Helle Johannessen and Imre Làzàr. London: Berghahn Press. 148–162.

Grønseth, AS. 2006b. Experiences of Tensions In Re-Orienting Selves: Tamil Refugees In Northern Norway Seeking Medical Advice. *Anthropology and Medicine* Vol. 13, No. 1 (April 2006).

Grønseth, AS. 2006c. *Lost Selves and Lonely Persons. Experiences of Illness and Well-Being among Tamil Refugees in Norway.* Trondheim, Norway: Norwegian University of Technology and Science.

Grønseth, AS (Forthcoming a). Sharing Experiences with Tamil Refugees in Northern Norway: Body and Emotion as Methodological Tools. In *Mutuality and Empathy. Self and Other in the Ethnographic Encounter,* edited by Anne Sigfrid Grønseth and Dona Lee Davis. For review with Kingston Publisher, UK.

Grønseth, AS (Forthcoming b). Introduction: Mutuality and Empathy. Self and Other in the Ethnographic Encounter. In *Mutuality and Empathy. Self and Other in the Ethnographic Encounter,* edited by Anne Sigfrid Grønseth and Dona Lee Davis. For review with Kingston Publisher, UK.

Ingold, T. 1993. The Art of Translation in a Continuous World. In *Beyond Boundaries: Understanding, Translation and Anthropological Discourse,* edited by Gisli Pàlsson. Oxford: Berg Publisher.

Jackson, M. 1989. *Paths Toward a Clearing. Radical Empiricism and Ethnographic Inquiry.* Bloomington: Indiana University Press.

Kleinman, A, Veena Das, and Margaret Lock, eds. 1997. *Social Suffering.* California: University of California Press.

Kleinman, A, and Joan Kleinman. 1995. Suffering and Its Professional Transformation: Toward and Ethnography of Interpersonal Experience. In *Writing at the Margin: Discourse Between Anthropology and Medicine,* edited by Arthur Kleinman. Berkeley and London: University of California Press.

Levì-Strauss, C. 1966. *The Savage Mind.* Chicago: Chicago University Press.

Merleau-Ponty, M. 1962 [1945]. *Phenomenology of Perception.* London: Routledge and Kegan Paul.

Nussbaum, M. 1986. *The Fragility of Goodness: Luck and Ethics in Greek Tragedy and Philosophy.* London: Cambridge University Press.

Peirce, CS. 1932. *Collected Papers*. Vols. 1–6, edited by C Hartshorne and P Weiss. Cambridge: Harvard University Press.

Pfaffenberger, B. 1982. *Caste in Tamil Culture. The Religious Foundations of Sudra Domination in Tamil Sri Lanka*. Syracuse, New York: Maxwell School and Foreign and Comparative Studies.

Scheper-Hughes, N, and Margareth Lock. 1987. The Mindful Body: A Prolegomenon To Future Work in Medical Anthropology. *Medical Anthropology Quarterly* 1: 1–36.

Searle-Chatterjee, Mary, and Ursula Sharma, eds. 1994. *Contextualising Caste: Post-Dumontian Approaches*. Oxford: Blackwell.

Wadley, S. 1977. Power in Hindu Ideology and Practice. In *The New Wind: Changing Identities in South Asia*, edited by Kenneth Davis. Hague and Paris: Mouton Publishers.

Wikan, U. 1992. Beyond the Words: The Power of Resonance. *American Ethnologist* 3: 460-482.

Being Dalit, Being Human: Celebrating a World Without Walls

BAMA

Generally when a child is born we don't welcome it merely as a human being. We see whether it is male or female. And our welcome often depends upon the gender of the child. When a child is born, its language, religion and caste are determined. Starting with its gender bestowed by nature, it is the other social factors like caste, religion, language, class, etc. that nurture and help the child to grow into human being. Among these social factors, the one that cannot be changed is caste. In Indian society you can change every social situation except caste. It is not an exaggeration to say that one's caste follows one even to one's grave. It is in such a caste-ridden, caste-minded and caste-oriented society that I was born and grew up as a dalit woman. I am very happy to share with you certain dimensions of such an existence and am grateful to you for this opportunity.

The Pain and the Joy

I was born in a small village in the foothills of the western mountain ranges in Tamil Nadu. Hills dense with trees, scenic and beautiful forests in the foothills with wild animals, different kind of plants, creepers, grasses and insects—all these diverse forms of life's journey began in the midst of my dalit brothers and sisters. My dalit brothers and sisters, they were segregated on account of their caste, were caught in the iron grip of poverty and tossed about in a hostile world of oppression and violence by their own ignorance and the hatred and non-acceptance of their human dignity by the rest of society; their only assets were their bodies and their life breath was back-breaking hard labour. The lullabies of a cradle song announce our birth and when we die there is always a dirge. In between this birth and death, ours is an existence that can stand the scorching heat of the sun and enjoy the cool breeze from the woods, and the summer showers of joy. It is an existence that preserves in itself a humanity that is ever fertile and immortal. All this added to the vigour of my childhood. On the one hand, in the relaxed village ambience there was the freedom to move around anywhere without any inhibition and the certainty to meet with genuine affection and kindness, transparency of mind and heart, a caring that was real and a love that was authentic and unadulterated. And together with this was the incomparable capacity for hard physical labour!

On the other hand, there was the curse of caste and untouchability, poverty and violence, impoverishment and illiteracy, oppression and segregation, blame and humiliation, ridicule and exclusion, threats and intimidations and inabilities and an utter lack of opportunities and freedoms. Theirs was a life often destined to destruction and ruination. In spite of all this, and more importantly in the midst of all this, that dalits had the ability to keep alive the flame of human love and hope is truly the triumph of humanity. And this blossoming and fruition of humanity in the face of heavy odds is the very heart of dalit existence and culture. We are able to laugh forgetting the pain of life even when we meet with obstacles and sorrow. When we are shunned as untouchables, unseeables and unapproachables and excluded from human discourse and fellowship by our so-called fellow humans we are able to bond with nature and our lives become part of the symphony of the earth and the sky, hills and clouds, animals and birds, flowers and dew drops, water and fire. With its inbuilt qualities of resistance, defiance and resilience, our culture enables us to live in this dehumanizing situation with dignity and without losing our humanity.

The Impact of the Dominant Caste Ideology and Culture

When we speak about dalit existence we have to speak also about the impact the dominant brahminic caste culture had and has on it. The caste people not only segregated dalits through sheer physical violence, heaped contempt and ridicule on them and imposed caste rules of purity and pollution on them and demanded hard physical labour from them, they succeeded also in injecting a servile consciousness into their psyche through their caste ideology, making dalits accept their inferior status. So the oppressors not only dehumanized and degraded the dalit existence they also degraded and demonized their consciousness.

The dominant caste perceives dalit culture as inferior, dirty, immoral, impure, cunning, good for nothing, dishonest, collective, quarrelsome, ungrateful and ugly, while the dominant culture perceives itself to be pure, superior, individualistic, authoritarian and acceptable. To give you an idea of the brahminic ideology, let me quote Annie Besant, the founder of the Theosophical society who was a champion and an outspoken spokesperson of that foul ideology. Arguing against schooling of dalit children along with the children of the so-called high caste people she says:

The children of the depressed classes (dalits) need, first of all, to be taught cleanliness, decency of behaviour, and the earliest rudiments of education, religion and morality. Their bodies, at present, are ill-odorous and foul with the liquor and strong smelling foods out of which for generation they have been built up; it will need some generations for purer food and living to make their bodies fit to sit in the close neighbourhood of a school room with children who have received bodies from an ancestry trained in habits of exquisite personal cleanliness, and fed on pure food-stuff.

Through rigorous religious indoctrination and strictly enforced social mores emanating from the notions of purity and pollution, authority and social status, dalits are thoroughly brainwashed and made to believe that their culture is inferior and that the caste culture is superior. Their daily struggle for survival did not offer them any possibility of escaping the caste tentacles; and so, they were forced to create what seemed to be a subservient cultural space for themselves within the parameters of the dominant culture. Within the brahminical Hindu caste system they are condemned as polluted creatures. They are repeatedly reminded through various cultural codes that their culture is to be servants of others. The repressive hierarchical caste system dehumanizes the dalits, and implants slavery deep down in their unconscious minds. Through the menial occupations they are forced to engage in as a symbolic expression of their inferior status, and through verbal abuse, and often through physical violence, they have been told again and again of their degradation. They gradually come to believe that they are degraded persons and reach a stage where they themselves voluntarily hold themselves apart and submit to the brahminic cultural hegemony. It is a classic case of one culture being ruled or dominated by another group or class whose everyday practices and shared beliefs provide the foundation for complex systems of domination. In the Brahminic system of domination, the untouchable is the necessary "other" who ensures the religious purity and material well being of the Brahmin and the other upper castes. The untouchable does not live for them self; they exist so that they may live for others.

The Empowering Dalit Culture

However, to think that the dominant culture holds complete sway over the lives of dalits and that it erases out any identity of their own smacks of a too simplistic understanding of dalit life. Dalits with their deep sense of the impermanence of life in this world accept birth and death as the inevitable realities of life. They cherish the deeply humane values of life.

The fundamental principle of their life could be articulated as, "All should enjoy all the good things of life; for this to happen we should create a situation where there is no lack of good things." In my writings I have attempted to record a culture that is vibrant, resilient, argumentative, and subversive with its rustic humour, with its raw energy and vitality manifested in hard physical labour without which Annie Besant and her Brahmins and higher castes would not have had their 'pure food' and other necessities of life! In the dalit culture we find equality within their own social grouping and utter informality in relationships that facilitates a greater equality between the sexes, more flexible relationships such as informal and intimate personal relationship between husband and wife, romantic love and adventures and relaxed pollution rules. Unpuritanical to its core, it allows for frank indulgence in pleasure, enjoyment of food, drink and leisure and a love for music and dancing. Often it could surrender to irrational impulses, emphasizing union and undifferentiation, and transgressing taboos. I remember asking my students in the fourth standard about the uses of teeth. One sprightly lad stood up and told me with obvious pleasure how he used his teeth to bite bones and chew and eat beef., While other dalit students agreed cheerfully, the non-dalit children sniggered snobbishly. Dalit culture glorifies the collective and communal life, nurturing and celebrating their corporate identity. This corporate identity extends not only to the realm of the human, but it can extend in a very natural manner to the animal and plant life too. While taking pride in and celebrating this culture, dalits are engaged in unmasking the inhumanity and everyday violence embedded in the casteist social order with a view to destroying it and building an alternate humanistic culture. This starts with protest and revolt.

Dalit Existence in My Writings

In my writings I have tried to delve deep in to the dalit psyche as it struggles to liberate itself from victimhood and become militant in order to assert its humanity and to celebrate the deeply humane, vibrant and down-to-earth dalit culture. I show how dalit men and women react against and resist the inhumanity of caste oppression. I agree with the critic who described the characters in my stories in the following manner, "They possess a rare spirit which allows them to grasp life by the scruff of it neck and cope with whatever it throws in the face. Resilient and rebellious, they refuse to be cowed down and no matter how many blows fall on their heads, they seem cheekily [to] thumb their nose at adversity. And they laugh, sing and celebrate with vigour." It was an experience of sheer delight for me to describe people who affirmed and celebrated their right to be human like everybody else, belittling the caste laws and traditions fearlessly and with gay abandon. These were some of the people with whom I rubbed shoulders and whom I knew so well.

Conclusion: The Need to Reinvent Tamil Culture

I shall conclude with a few reflections on the theme of this seminar: Being Tamil, Being Human from a dalit perspective. Even today Tamil society and culture are deeply infected with virus of caste, and the violence and inhumanity it brings with it. Every now and then we read in the newspapers about caste discriminations and violence. No religion, no political party, no institution is free from it. Two months ago in a Christian village where the dalit Christians are in a minority, the dominant caste Christians washed the church and the main street with phenol and destroyed and burned the hearse after the funeral of a dalit Christian because, according to them, the church, the hearse and the streets had been polluted by the dead body of the dalit Christian. Barely a month ago, on April 17, 2008 the national newspaper, *The Hindu,* came out with the headline, "Electrified Wall Divides People on Caste lines" with a colour picture of the offending wall. The report said: With a long history of caste animosity against Dalits behind them, the case Hindus of the village (Uthapuram, near Madurai) have electrified a 600-metre long wall which passed through pockets that were meant to be for common use by people of all castes. The wall is intended to block common entry points, thereby preventing the castes from intermingling. It has there been since 1990, but electricity is being passed in the nights using iron rods for the past ten days." The Berlin Wall has fallen, but the caste walls dividing the Tamils from their fellow Tamils, fragmenting the Tamil consciousness and unity are being strengthened. I am happy to report that on account of political pressure, a section of this wall of shame, which is a symbol of caste oppression, has been demolished by the government to create access for Dalits to the other parts of the village. We know that caste and untouchability were not our Tamil society and culture. It knew only of geographic divisions based on ecological considerations: Palai, Neithal, Mullai, Marutham and Kurunji. I believe what Baba Saheb Ambedkar said about division of labour is applicable to ancient Tamil society.

If division of labour is a necessary feature of every civilized society, then it is argued that there is nothing wrong in the caste system. Now the first thing that is to be urged against this view is that the caste system is not merely a division of labour. It is also a division of labourers.

In the early Tamil society there was only a division of labour and not a division of labourers based on the rules of purity and pollution with its ideological justifications. Ancient Tamil society was based on deeply human values which encouraged social mingling and mobility.

Today, the alien and imported ideology of caste which is divisive and inhuman rules our thinking and guides our social relations. As all of us know, caste has been a great survivor. Though it is basically feudal in its values it has survived through colonialism, capitalism and even communism and Periyar's rationalism. In the post-modern globalized world we need to return to our original Tamil cultural roots if we want make our contribution in creating a global civil society which will usher us into a future that is humane and inclusive, and open to the values of greater equity, equality and freedom. I believe that dalit culture has preserved for us the original values of the daughters and the sons of the Tamil soil and that these values can point to us the way of humanizing the emerging global culture. It is up to us to shape our present, learning from the past, and intuiting future challenges and the possibilities of building a more humane world, a world without walls!

Contributors

BAMA is a pioneering Dalit novelist from Tamil Nadu, India. Her first novel *Karukku* (1992), is not only the first autobiographical work of its kind but written in the Dalit dialect of her community it broke new ground in both fiction writing as well as in the use of the spoken language in fiction. *Karukku* has won several awards and has been translated into many languages. Bama has subsequently written two more novels, *Sangathi* (1994) and *Vanmam* (2002) and two collections of short stories, *Kusumbukkaran* (1996) and *Oru Tattavum Erumaiyum* (2003).

GIL BEN-HERUT for his Master's thesis at Tel-Aviv University, submitted a paper titled "The Descent of Goddess Ganga on Shiva's Head". The thesis includes a translation from Sanskrit to Hebrew of a courtly poem composed by Nīlakaṇṭha Dīkṣita. The thesis' research focuses on human identity formations in the genre of courtly prose and on reconstructions of the God-Human relationship in the late medieval South Indian region. He has recently begun his Ph.D. studies through which he is interested in further exploring the complex relationship during the late medieval time between extreme religious practices and mainstream religion, as it is manifested mostly through diverse literary spheres.

DAVID BUCK's principal research interest is in the academic and literary translation of Tamil literature into English. Currently he is working as a co-translator, with M. Kannan of the French Institute, Pondicherry, on a translation of *Dalit Literature: My Experiences,* edited by Kannan M, which includes essays by Dalit writers as well as previously unpublished works by them. Recently, he has translated *Kutrala Kuravanji* (2005). He was a co-translator, with the late K Paramasivan, of *The Study of Stolen Love* (1997), and also translated *The Song of Pampatticcittar* (1976).

R CHERAN is an Associate Professor in the Department of Sociology and Anthropology at the University of Windsor. He has published seven anthologies of poetry in Tamil. His poems have been translated into English, German, Sinhala, Kannada and Malayalam. His co-edited publications include: *History and Imagination: Tamil Culture in the Global Context,* Toronto:TSAR, 2007; *New Demarcations: Essays in Tamil Studies,* Toronto: Canadian Scholars' Press, 2009. His recent publications are: *Pathways of Dissent: Tamil nationalism in Sri Lanka,* New Delhi: Sage, 2010 and *Empowering Diasporas: Dynamics of Post War Tamil Transnational Politics,* Berlin: Berghof Foundation, 2011.

SUDHARSHAN DURAYAPPAH teaches at the University of Toronto, Scarborough and the Royal Ontario Museum. His research interests include Hinduism in the

Diaspora, Trans-Asian Religious routes of the 7-9th century A.D., Iconography and Tamil devotional poetry. He is also on the organizing committee of the Tamil Studies Conference.

FRANCIS CODY is an Assistant Professor in the Department of Anthropology and the Asian Institute at the University of Toronto. His research concerns the cultural politics of written language in Tamil South India. He is currently working on a book manuscript on literacy activism and state formation in Tamilnadu, and beginning a new project on the social history of newspapers and reading publics in the same region.

GLYNIS GEORGE is Associate Professor in the department of Sociology, Anthropology and Criminology at the University of Windsor, and teaches in the areas of gender and culture, social justice and international perspectives on culture and crime. Her recent publications include "Interpreting Gender Mainstreaming by NGO's in India: a Comparative Ethnographic Approach", Gender, Place and Culture 14:6 (2007), *The Rock Where We Stand: An Ethnography of Women's Activism in Newfoundland* (2000); and *Violence and Poverty on the "Rock": Can Feminists Make a Difference?,* Canadian Woman Studies (2000).

ANN SIGFRID GRØNSETH is Associate Professor in the Faculty of Social Sciences at Lillehammer College, Norway, and teaches in fields of health, life-quality and social anthropology. For more than 10 years she was employed as a Special Consultant at Violence and Trauma Competence Center, University Hospital of Northern Norway where she engaged in research, teaching and clinical supervision. Her publications include, "In Search of Community: A Quest for Well Being among Tamil Refugees in Northern Norway," Medical Anthropology Quarterly 15(4) (2006); "Experiences of Illness: Tamil Refugees in Norway Seeking Medical Advise," in *Multiple Medical Realities: Patients and Healers in Biomedical, Alternative and Traditional Medicine* (2006).

CHELVA KANAGANAYAKAM is a Professor in the Department of English at the University of Toronto and is also the Director for the Centre for South Asian Studies at the University of Toronto. His research interests are in Southeast Asian literature, contemporary Indian and Sri Lankan writing, literature of exile and postcolonial theory. His major publications include: *Moveable Margins: The Shifting Spaces of Canadian Literature* (2005); *Counterrealism and Indo Anglian Fiction* (2002); *Lutesong and Lament: Tamil Writing from Sri Lanka* (2001); *Dark Antonyms and Paradise: The Poetry of Rienzi Crusz* (1997); *Configurations of Exile: South Asian Writers and Their World* (1995), and *Structures of Negation: The Writings of Zulfikar Ghose* (1993).

RAMASWAMI MAHALINGAM is Associate Professor in the Department of Psychology at the University of Michigan. His research primarily focuses on how the relationship between social marginality and intersecting social identities shape psychological well being. He is particularly interested in the relationship between gender and immigration. His recent publications include "Essentialism, culture and power: Representations of social class" in *Journal of Social Issues* 59:4 (2003), and *Cultural Psychology of Immigrants* (forthcoming).

CHRISTER NORSTRÖM is a researcher at the Department of Social Anthropology, Stockholm University. He wrote his thesis on the Paliyans, the hunter-gatherers of the Palni Hills. His current research in Tamil Nadu concerns food security and changing food patterns among farmers in the foothills of the Palni Hills. His publications include: *They Call for Us: Strategies for Securing Autonomy among the Paliyans, Hunter-Gatherers of the Palni Hills, South India* (2003); *Livelihood Strategies of Forest Dwelling Tribes in South India: Cases From Tamilnadu,* Christer Norström and Lawrence Surendra (eds) (2008).

JANET O'SHEA's main area of research is the South Indian dance form bharatanatyam. She is Reader, School of Arts and Education at the Middlesex University. She has trained in Balasaraswati's style of bharatanatyam, as a student of Nandini Ramani, of Chennai, India. She has published articles in a range of periodicals, including *The Drama Review*, *Dance Research Journal* and *Asian Theatre Journal* as well as in *Pulse and Confluences*. Her research activities have been supported by the American Institute of Indian Studies, the British Academy, and the Arts and Humanities Research Council.

VIJAYA RAMASWAMY is Professor, Centre for Historical Studies, Jawaharlal Nehru University, India. Her interests include such varied fields as south Indian folklore, religious studies, and gender studies. Her publications include, *The Historical Dictionary of the Tamils* (2007), *Walking Naked: Women, Society, Spirituality in South India* (1997), *Divinity and Deviance: Women in Virasaivism* (1996). She is currently engaged in writing *Crafts and Craftsmen in South Indian History* (forthcoming) and *Tamil Myths and Legends* (forthcoming).

SUSAN SCHOMBURG's research focuses on Islamic Tamil history and culture, incorporating historical, literary and ethnographic research methods. She is Assistant Professor, Department of Religious Studies, Bates College, USA. Special research topics of interest include Tamil Sufism, Hindu-Muslim "shared spiritualities" (the Tamil Muslim cittars), Tamil dargah culture and ritual practices, and Tamil women's religious experience. Her publications include, *'Reviving Religion': The Qadiri Sufi Order, Popular Devotion to Sufi Saint Muhyiuddin" Abdul Qadir al-Gilani and Processes of 'Islamization' in Tamil Nadu and Sri Lanka* (dissertation; 2003) and "Lovely Recalcitrant Women: Tay Tamil, Cultural Agency, and Islamic Histories" in *History and Imagination: Tamil Culture in the Global Context* (2007).

DALBIR SINGH is a PhD candidate at the Graduate Drama Centre as well as the Centre for South Asian Studies at the University of Toronto. His publications have appeared in such journals/anthologies as *Canadian Theatre Review*, *Critical Perspectives on Canadian Theatre*, *She Speaks*, and *Red Light: Superheroes, Saints and Sluts*. He also recently served as Artistic Director of 'The Festival of Original Theatre

2011: Post-Colonial Theatre' (GDC, UofT).

A VELUPILLAI's research interests are historical studies of Tamil language, literature, culture and people. He was formerly Professor of Tamil, University of Jathna and is currently a Faculty Associate in the Department of Religious Studies at Arizona State University, USA. His publications include *Tamil Ilakkiyattil Kalamum Karuttum* (1969), *Study of the Dialects in Inscriptional Tamil* (1976) and co-editor (with Peter Schalk) of *Buddhism among Tamils in Pre-colonial Tamilakam and Ilam* (2002).

JENNIFER YIM's doctoral dissertation research focuses on Asian American men, masculinity, coping, and well-being. A recent publication, "Culture, masculinity, and psychological well-being in Punjab, India", was issued in the 2006 *Sex Roles* special issue on masculinities with Ram Mahalingam.

PAUL YOUNGER is Emeritus Professor Religion at McMaster University. He studied at Banaras Hindu University and Princeton University. Since 1964, he has taught at McMaster University in Hamilton, Ontario, and he and his family have raised sheep on their farm nearby. His most recent books are *The Home of Dancing Sivan: The Traditions of the Hindu Temple in Citamparam*, 1995; *Playing Host to Deity: Festival Religion in the South Indian Tradition*, 2002; and *New Homelands: Hindu Communities in post-Indenture Societies* (Mauritius, Guyana, Trinidad, South Africa, Fiji and East Africa), forthcoming, Oxford University Press.